Educational and Psychological Testing

A Study of the Industry and Its Practices

Educational and Psychological Testing

A Study of the Industry and Its Practices

Milton G. Holmen
and
Richard Docter

RUSSELL SAGE FOUNDATION
NEW YORK

PUBLICATIONS OF RUSSELL SAGE FOUNDATION

Russell Sage Foundation was established in 1907 by Mrs. Russell Sage for the improvement of social and living conditions in the United States. In carrying out its purpose the Foundation conducts research under the direction of members of the staff or in close collaboration with other institutions, and supports programs designed to develop and demonstrate productive working relations between social scientists and other professional groups. As an integral part of its operation, the Foundation from time to time publishes books or pamphlets resulting from these activities. Publication under the imprint of the Foundation does not necessarily imply agreement by the Foundation, its Trustees, or its staff with the interpretations or conclusions of the authors.

Russell Sage Foundation
230 Park Avenue, New York, N.Y. 10017

Contents

Preface

During the summer of 1965, pickets were marching in front of the national headquarters of the American Psychological Association in Washington to protest educational testing. Less than a mile away, on Capitol Hill, staff members of several Congressmen and Senators were independently preparing for hearings in which serious charges against certain testing practices would be heard. Distinguished psychologists would add fuel to the fire by applauding some of these charges, while others would testify that isolated examples of poor practice were being overgeneralized. Meanwhile, important concerns about testing were being reviewed in the headquarters of the Equal Employment Opportunity Commission (EEOC). In addition to policy questions, the EEOC was trying to evaluate hundreds of written complaints which involved testing in employment selection and promotion cases.

As far as educational and psychological testing was concerned, the climate in Washington, D.C., didn't change much with the coming of Fall. However, a committee of psychologists, including several highly experienced testing experts, did hold a planning session at the request of the Board of Professional Affairs of the American Psychological Association. One of the things which emerged from these discussions was recognition of the need for better information about the industry which generates tests and test-related services. It was apparent, for example, that part of the criticism about testing did not actually pertain to what most psychologists would call tests, but rather to questionnaire forms, interviews, and other such procedures. What was needed, they believed, was a more thorough analysis of the testing scene, with particular focus upon the producers and distributors of tests. The present report grew out of the need for such an investigation.

With the support of Russell Sage Foundation, in the summer of 1966, we began a study of the organizations which comprise the testing industry, the structure and organization of the industry, the personnel involved, and the manner in which the professional associations tie into the problem of technical standards and ethical practices. We were interested in finding out what capabilities different kinds of companies had for meeting established standards for test development, and in learning how these organizations actually function. Our basic strategy was more like the work of investigative reporters than that of experimental psychologists.

Our first step was to review the criticisms of testing which had been made in congressional hearings, EEOC and Federal Employment Practices Commission charges, technical literature, professional meetings, and in the popular press and books. We next asked persons within the testing industry to tell us their ideas about the problems and issues which they felt were of greatest importance. The concepts derived from these discussions were then translated into a structured interview format which we used as a basis for talks with scores of persons, not only within the testing industry, but with the critics of testing as well. These interviews were supplemented by use of brief questionnaires which were sent to the various state departments of education, by participation in testing conferences held at several professional meetings, and by meetings with government agencies concerned with testing.

This has not been a nose-counting type of research project in any sense of the word. Our mission was to try to piece together a peculiar kind of jigsaw puzzle and to make its design a bit more comprehensible. We have also been highly evaluative and have commented critically where we believed this to be justified.

In addition to examining the testing industry, we have related this study to the public policy issues which underlie many of the criticisms of testing. For example, the question of who uses tests and what kinds of preparation such individuals should have is a crucial issue. When we attempted to evaluate the quality of testing practices in various settings, even in a tentative way, we realized that the entire assessment system had to be considered, not merely the tests themselves. This certainly is not a new discovery. However, we developed a set of criteria for assessing the competence of six testing subsystems; we think these criteria are key dimensions of any assessment system.

In the latter chapters of the text, we review problems relating to the development of testing standards and the ethical and other problems involved in their application. We discuss several aspects of discrimination in employment and the theory problem of invasion of privacy. Finally, we make recommendations for action by persons and organizations who influence the gatekeepers in our society.

We owe a tremendous expression of thanks to all who have contributed to this study, whether through personal interviews or by writing to us in response to our various inquiries. An openness and willingness to be self-critical is one of the strengths of the testing industry. We did not accept uncritically the information given us, and, when we needed it, we were given access to records, reports, and people which made it possible to verify facts from original sources. We sincerely appreciate the fine cooperation which was given where we went. A special vote of thanks goes to David A. Goslin of Russell Sage Foundation, one of the most knowledgable people we know concerning educational and psychological testing; he was a helpful critic and guide throughout the course of the study. We are also most appreciative of the considerable assistance given by Orville G. Brim, Jr., in all phases of the project; to Launor Carter for assistance in its planning, and to Samuel Messick and William B. Michael for suggestions and criticisms in the study's closing phases. To Mary A. Harrison we express our appreciation for her very helpful editorial guidance. We also wish to express our appreciation to the Research Institute for Business and Economics, University of Southern California, Graduate School of Business Administration (USCRIBE) and its director Dr. Joseph Ehrenreich for assistance in planning and administration of the project. We take full responsibility, of course, for the scope and accuracy of our observations, the adequacy of our analyses, and the relevance and practicality of our recommendations.

Milton G. Holmen
University of Southern California

Richard Docter
San Fernando Valley State College

1

The Uses of Tests: A Critical Survey

A black parent angrily questions his school board about the value of an IQ test: "What good does it do my child to have these low scores following him into every class?" Other parents denounce the tests and argue that the scores do not accurately reflect the intelligence of their children. A considerable time later, following numerous confrontations on the testing issue, the school board votes to stop all intelligence testing in the first three grades. But parents continue to ask: "Why not stop intelligence testing altogether?" They are joined by some teachers who say that intelligence test scores actually do more harm than good. Does a school really need IQ data on each child? Of what value is this information? What harm might this data cause?

Carlos is out of work. He follows up a lead for openings in a small electronics assembly plant. He has had experience as both a wireman and a solderman, and he thinks his chances for employment are excellent. The personnel office asks him to take a five-minute paper-and-pencil test which asks him the meanings of many words he does not recognize and such questions as "What is the meaning of R.S.V.P.?" The personnel manager is polite, but the decision is "Don't call us, we'll call you." Carlos files a complaint with the Fair Employment Practices Commission and with the Federal Equal Employment Opportunity Commission. He is convinced that tests are unfair. Is Carlos right? Are there examples of job-testing programs that actually work to the benefit of minority groups by being more "color blind" than interviewers? How can we distinguish between good and bad testing programs? Are the tests at fault, or does the problem result from the way tests are used?

1

Testing practices such as these not only offend many people, but they also raise issues of public policy. Critics have voiced indignation about discrimination which may result from inappropriate use of test results, the emphasis on testing in schools, and testing as an invasion of privacy. Congressional hearings have investigated testing in and out of government. As a result of public criticisms, the military services have reviewed their testing programs, as have many businesses. Lawsuits concerned with testing have been tried in municipal, state, and federal courts. Some state legislatures have enacted laws that not only designate the general conditions of test use, but also specify how certain test scores will be used.

The basic reason for all the concern and complaints is that test results lead to classification and labeling procedures that often directly influence people's lives. This function of tests makes them both potentially valuable and highly controversial. If one is totally committed to the premise that every man deserves a chance to prove himself through assignment to a job, then one may perceive tests as nonfunctional job barriers. On the other hand, if a person is committed to the premise that jobs should be assigned on the basis of some form of "merit" examination, it does not take him long to conclude that objective testing may be superior to purely subjective evaluations.

But what kind of objective measures should be used? Have tests been oversold? Who are the authors and publishers of tests in America; and are tests used in the way these authors and publishers intended? What professional standards have been developed to try to improve the science of human measurement? This report is concerned with these questions and many others. But before attempting to consider any of them more extensively, let us review, first, the major uses of standardized psychological and educational tests, and second, the most frequent criticisms of these materials.

The Three Major Uses of Tests

Just as there are many different kinds of tests, so are there many different reasons for testing. We can, however, cite three main objectives of testing programs: (1) testing in counseling, guidance, and clinical work; (2) educational achievement testing; and (3) testing for selection and placement. These objectives are by no means completely independent of each other. They may, however, differ in terms of the purposes of testing, in the kinds of tests used to meet each objective, and in the qualifications of the personnel responsible for carrying out testing activities. Equally important, there seem to be great differences in the amount of testing that goes on in each area and the amount of criticism that this testing has generated.

Testing in Counseling, Guidance, and Clinical Work

The major distinguishing characteristic of testing for the purpose of counseling, guidance, and clinical work is that an individual service is offered; often the client can accept or reject any or all recommendations. Since test applications in counseling, guidance, or clinical work require extensive individual consultation, such testing is highly expensive. This is one of the reasons why tests used for these purposes represent only a very small portion of the market for tests in this country. About 5 percent of the tests sold annually are used in counseling, guidance, and clinical work.

In the typical school district, some kind of counseling and guidance program is usually operated at the high school level. The goals are to acquire information believed useful in assisting students who are making educational and career decisions and to organize testing data so that students may make better goal selections. A strong guidance program generally includes group testing designed to reveal educational achievement, vocational interests, and verbal and quantitative aptitude. The results of testing are usually interpreted to each student in brief individual interviews. These guidance services may blend into counseling responsibilities in a number of ways; for example, the potential high school dropout who has the aptitude for success in college obviously is in need of more than career-guidance information.

Clinical psychologists also use tests in their efforts to understand and predict behavior. Not long ago, testing was one of the major activities of clinical psychologists working in outpatient clinics and hospitals. As the importance of labeling and diagnosis has given way to more direct concern for psychotherapeutic intervention, however, the role of testing has declined. At present, the administration and interpretation of tests is a small part of most clinical psychologists' assignments.

The school psychologist faces a different situation; one of his unique capabilities is the assessment of intellectual and psychoeducational development. Testing continues to be an important part of this work. When decisions must be made regarding assignment of a child to a regular classroom or to some special educational program, such as one for mentally retarded youngsters, formal testing is considered mandatory. In fact, making individual assessments and predictions of the educational progress of children of low intelligence is one of the oldest problems that clinical and school psychologists have faced.

Educational and Intelligence Testing

The overwhelming majority of school districts carry out some form of educational-achievement testing program; in many states these programs are coordinated on a state-wide level. The intent of all programs is to measure student progress relative to educational goals. Nonetheless, the amount of achievement testing, the quality of this assessment, and the manner in which the results are used vary greatly among school districts across the nation. We estimate that at least 200 million achievement-test forms and answer sheets are used annually in the United States; this represents roughly 65 percent of all the educational and psychological testing that is carried out.

Teachers are interested in these test results, for they provide one criterion of the success of their instructional efforts. The scores earned in any class may be readily compared to other classes in the same district or state, or they may be compared with national norms. School administrators are highly sensitive to the social and political implications of evaluation testing; in some areas, achievement-test scores are not made available for public scrutiny. Where scores are made public, there seems to be no end to the imaginative interpretation of the results, in accordance with the motives or biases of the person offering his interpretation. For example, the Superintendent of Public Instruction in a large state recently interpreted the state-wide reading averages as deplorable; the next year, while running for re-election, he interpreted virtually identical results as showing marked improvement.

Minority-group leaders have occasionally played the same game, as have school board members and elected public officials. The basic idea seems to be to use achievement-test scores to prove whatever point one may wish to make. When test results are of major significance in the evaluation of educational programs, intense pressures are exerted to make a favorable showing on achievement tests. To show improved scores, it is not necessary to pilfer a test or to coach students on specific test items; this probably would not be helpful because most school districts use multiple forms of the same achievement tests. A more familiar way to prepare students to take achievement tests is to prepare work sheets and other class exercises in the same format as that used on achievement tests. In this way the student gains practice in responding to the kinds of problems posed by the tests. Although no dishonesty attaches to such practices, students with this training in test taking may be expected to earn better scores than comparable students without such preparation.

The greatest impact of achievement testing is undoubtedly related to the way in which school administrators use test results. For example, schools with low achievement scores which reflect a need for remedial programs may receive supplemental funding for special projects. Test results are also important in shaping and modifying the school curriculum. One of the criticisms of educational achievement testing is that the curriculum becomes rigid; however, considerable opportunity also exists for tests to contribute to the renovation of both the curriculum and instructional practices.

Intelligence testing is also carried out in schools. Historically, the research and development of intelligence tests has been of high quality, although the tests themselves have not always been used properly. For example, Mexican-American parents have severely criticized testing procedures; as a result of some tests, a highly disproportionate percentage of minority children are placed in classes for the mentally retarded. Indeed, the assessment of bilingual children, especially Mexican-American and Puerto Rican youngsters, has presented a special problem. Since most testing procedures available for the assessment of intelligence have been standardized on Caucasian children raised in the United States, such procedures are of no value when applied indiscriminately to children who have grown up under different cultural conditions.

How much faith do teachers place in the results of intelligence tests? Quite a bit. Using survey questionnaire techniques, Goslin (1967a; p. 131) found that most teachers in his sample believed that achievement and intelligence test results were accurate reflections of a student's academic and intellectual development. Many teachers felt that, when decisions are made about pupils, "considerable weight" should be given to test scores. Even more disturbing, Goslin found that the more psychometric training teachers reported having, the more they were inclined (1) to accept the idea that intelligence differences are innate and (2) to rely heavily on test scores as factors in counseling and placement recommendations. We should take little comfort in the fact that a substantial percentage of teachers using tests indicated that they had not received even minimal training in testing theory and practice.

A few states have well-developed professional standards designed to ensure that persons using tests in schools have certain minimum qualifications and experience. Too often, however, the individual assessment of children has been left to partially trained psychologists or teachers who received little or no supervision as they learned to administer tests. It is not surprising, therefore, that we continue to see examples of poor professional practice.

Testing for Selection and Placement

People differ greatly in interests, aptitudes, and potential for success in various jobs or training programs. The assessment of these individual differences and the problem of understanding how such differences relate to the prediction of behavior is one of the historic concerns of psychology. Shortly after the turn of the century, tests that could be scored objectively were developed for the purpose of evaluating intellectual development in school children. Test results thereby became one of the sources of information to be considered in the educational selection-and-placement process.

Personnel testing in industry and government was accelerated with the start of World War I, when a group of psychologists extended the pioneering work of Arthur Otis and produced several test batteries designed to facilitate selection and placement for the Army. Since that time, despite a remarkable growth in the science of psychometrics, the basic problem of selection and placement has remained the same: How should those human attributes which are uniquely essential to successful performance in a training program or a job assignment be measured? The prediction of behavior is at the core of selection-and-placement testing. We estimate that approximately 30 percent of the total market for tests is devoted to this type of testing.

SELECTION AND PLACEMENT IN EDUCATION. Data from academic achievement tests often contribute to educational selection-and-placement decisions regarding differential assignment to classes. While great differences exist among schools and school districts, it is very common to organize classes so that children tend to be grouped together on the basis of ability. We shall not attempt to evaluate here the merits of this arrangement; we shall simply note that ability grouping is an educational strategy that has been increasingly questioned by both educational leaders and the critics of education. To the extent that tests have been seen as one of the central tools for the perpetuation of ability grouping, testing has been indicted as one cause of an educational format that some see as undesirable.

By the time a student reaches high school, he must begin to make some choices that have career implications; if he does not complete college preparatory educational requirements, his chances of gaining admission to college are obviously reduced. Standardized tests are typically not used to control admission to different types of high school educational programs. Nevertheless, various kinds of tests often used in the counseling and guidance process can provide data which may influence a student's selection of an academic pathway and thus of career possibilities. It is certainly possible to misuse tests in a guidance situation. But, despite one searing attack on the counseling and guidance professionals and the tests they use (Black, 1963), school testing specialists usually have far stronger qualifications for working with tests than do their counterparts in industry and government.

Another example of test utilization in education is that of college-selection testing. Except for the two-year community college, colleges commonly require some kind of admissions testing as part of the over-all application process. Preparation for admissions testing often begins in high school with a preliminary test battery which serves two purposes: (1) the student gains experience in taking a college admissions-type test, and (2) the student gains some appreciation of his ability to perform on this kind of test. Most college-aptitude tests give considerable weight to the assessment of verbal abilities (word knowledge, reading comprehension, the structure of language, etc.), and quantitative abilities (algebraic problem solving, basic arithmetic competences, etc.).

Colleges vary widely in their uses of test scores; indeed, they continue to debate not only how scores should be used but whether scores should be used at all. Critics of college-selection testing have consistently pointed out that even the most refined college-aptitude testing programs yield very modest short-term predictions of college performance, for aptitude is only one of many factors that determine college success. The case in favor of including aptitude-test data as part of the selection criteria reduces to the argument that aptitude tests and high school grades predict college performance as well as any indicators can. At the graduate level, many schools require applicants to take a specialized examination designed to assess their competence in a certain academic area.

Testing to predict success in training is by no means restricted to college-admissions testing. For example, tests have long been used to help select individuals who seek training in scores of technical and professional areas, among them positions as air controllers, physicians, and electronic technicians.

SELECTION AND PLACEMENT TESTING IN INDUSTRY. Some large corporations have developed highly sophisticated personnel testing programs which have been carefully designed and constructed by personnel psychologists. The continuing evaluation of the predictive effectiveness of such testing is a critical requirement that has long been recognized. Unfortunately, this requirement has often not been met, especially in small companies. Since personnel tests are quite easy to obtain, personnel workers with little or no training in test theory or practice can order a set of materials and institute a testing program. The naive use of test scores as a basis for selecting employees is a common outcome. Some of the most frequently used personnel tests are very brief paper-and-pencil procedures which principally measure verbal abilities and academic achievement. The fact that these scores are used as the primary basis for awarding jobs, although there is little or no evidence that such scores actually predict job success, has been the root of extensive criticism of testing in industry. Such practices are considered unprofessional by testing specialists; they are now prohibited by regulations of both the Equal Employment Opportunity Commission and the Office of Federal Contract Compliance.

Whether the testing program is based on a carefully validated battery of measures or on the "quickie" testing just described, the objective is often the same: the prediction of success in training or on the job. There is evidence of the value of sound personnel testing programs. But since even the best tests fall short of perfect prediction, the trained testing specialist uses test scores cautiously, paying special attention to those differences in the testee's background which may be a hindrance to effective test performance. Since many tests have been designed and standardized for application to the "typical" job applicant, the individual from a foreign culture or from a minority background will be at a marked disadvantage. Testing professionals and minority-group critics of testing are in agreement that tests primarily designed or validated for one group must not be assumed to be equally applicable to a different group. Similarly, there is agreement that tests used for job selection must be shown to predict success.

SELECTION AND PLACEMENT TESTING IN GOVERNMENT. Millions of tests are used each year in schools and industry; it should be no surprise, therefore, to find that government agencies—municipal, state, and federal—also make extensive use of educational and psychological tests in personnel selection and placement. This testing is usually carried out either through contracting with a testing organization or, more frequently, under the control of the personnel department of a government unit.

Although tests developed for personnel selection in industry are usually validated against some kind of independent criterion of success in training or on the job, much civil service testing for job selection is based on assessment of job knowledge. Predictive validity studies of these tests are extremely scarce. One reason for this lack is that merit-system test materials must often be made public following each round of testing; therefore, a stable battery of assessment measures cannot be constructed. At the level of municipal government, this one-time test use remains the most typical pattern for testing programs. Far greater psychometric sophistication is seen in many state government personnel-selection programs.

There appears to be less public criticism of the armed forces testing programs than of any other assessment program of comparable size. Perhaps this is partly due to the military's half century of commitment to develop sound testing programs for the prediction of success in various military assignments. In any case, considerably greater investment has been made in production of high-quality tests for the military services than for most other personnel-selection testing. In many ways, military test-development programs offer a model of excellence and a format for the type of comprehensive assessment system which we consider essential.

Criticisms of Testing

Educational and psychological testing has come in for a great deal of criticism, especially during the past twenty years. Comment has included allegations that testing is linked to thought-control efforts; that there is manipulation and undue influence on school curricula, especially at the secondary level; and that tests promote an unwarranted invasion of privacy. Criticisms have come from civil rights spokesmen, from educators, from the critics of education in America, from sociologists, psychologists, philosophers, from politicians, journalists, and public administrators.

Criticisms about testing were especially bountiful in the years between 1955 and 1965. No single focal point of discontent was identified; criticisms, both major and minor, were hurled at testers in schools, in industry and government, and in clinical and research work. The best summary of this literature is a selected annotated bibliography prepared by Pasanella, Manning, and Findikyan (1967) for the Commission on Tests of the College Entrance Examination Board. In a report prepared for this Commission, Goslin (1967b) independently catalogued ten criticisms of tests. Some of these deal primarily with tests of ability or achievement, but most apply also to personality testing.

Five Criticisms Bearing on the Validity and Utilization of Tests

TESTS DISCRIMINATE AGAINST SOME INDIVIDUALS. It has been strongly argued that some testing programs have consistently failed to take into account differences in cultural background and in unique individual attributes. Such failure unquestionably influences test results and may, therefore, penalize the testees. A major concern is whether tests developed primarily for use with Caucasian subjects can be administered to minority-group members. Many of the latter may have educational and cultural backgrounds markedly different from those of the subjects used in the standardization of any particular test. Employment-selection tests have especially been denounced by minority-group representatives as too often containing built-in bias which favors the middle-class white person and discriminates against the minority applicant. While respected testing professionals may disagree on the interpretation of specific data purported to prove or disprove this point, they agree that tests lacking in job-related validity have no place in selection-and-placement testing programs.

TESTS PREDICT IMPERFECTLY. No standardized tests are perfect predictors of future behavior. Even the most enthusiastic proponent of objective assessment techniques would insist that his ability to foretell behavior is highly dependent on such factors as the individual(s) to be tested, the behavior to be predicted, the time over which prediction is to be attempted, and the criterion measures used to establish predictive effectiveness. But even with all these qualifications, critics of testing have come to the conclusion that many tests are weak and unsatisfactory devices which mislead naive test users and result in harm to those tested. Many critics have just about given up on tests, for they see them as falling far short of the ideal applications envisioned by their creators and their publishers.

One of the most frequently cited criticisms pertains to the continued use of poorly validated or unvalidated tests in employment selection (Cooper, 1968; Enneis, 1969). No defense can be made for such testing, for it is fundamental that all test results become meaningful only to the extent that appropriate validation data are available. Testing professionals have agreed upon and established a set of rules for defining the process of test validation. Despite these rules, poorly validated and unvalidated tests are used extensively in educational settings at all levels, in business and industry, and in civil service merit-selection programs.

As we develop a format for the evaluation of assessment systems, we shall see that the problem of test validation encompasses many issues which go beyond establishment of certain formal psychometric properties which may be present to some extent in any test. The proper use of tests must encompass a variety of responsibilities independent of the attributes of any particular test. We must not only ask whether a test has been shown to possess some validity for a known group of subjects, but also must investigate many other questions bearing on the particular circumstances surrounding the application of the test.

THE RIGID USE OF TEST SCORES. Test scores provide one opportunity or data base for the arbitrary classification of individuals. Anyone interested in labeling people can have a field day with test results. This fact notwithstanding, the properly trained user of tests is supposed to know that test scores are not fixed measures, that they are estimates of human attributes at best, and that they necessarily encompass various kinds of sampling errors. But test scores are often applied in rigid and arbitrary ways. In schools, this can result in assignment of children to ability groupings based on measures which may be indefensible. In industry, the rigid use of "cut-off scores" for establishing selection criteria has generated much criticism and produced a variety of legal actions. As we point out throughout this report, the quality of professional practice associated with test usage leaves much to be desired.

ASSUMPTION THAT TESTS MEASURE INNATE CHARACTERISTICS. Some critics of ability testing have argued that tests provide scores that may be naively interpreted as measures of innate characteristics, such as "intelligence"; many harmful consequences are said to flow from this misconception. It has occasionally been assumed that, if tests were not available, people would not make arbitrary classifications of individuals. Tests are therefore condemned as antihumanistic and as fostering a view of mankind that sees human abilities as fixed or rigidly limited.

Even worse, some critics have reasoned that tests influence individuals to conceive of man in categorical terms, such as "mentally retarded" or "gifted"; they conclude that thinking of this kind is undesirable. At first glance this seems to be nothing more than a variation on the practice of making rigid use of test scores. The essential difference, however, as expressed by some critics, is that not only do tests foster the belief that man has fixed "intelligence" based on innate characteristics, but also the use made of test scores depends heavily on such a belief. The kind of school program offered and the energy invested in preparing a youngster for the future may be directly influenced by an educator's belief that tests measure innate intelligence. The egalitarian ethic in America frowns upon labeling based on some arbitrary measurement supposed to reflect innate characteristics.

TESTS AS SELF-FULFILLING PROPHECIES. In a classical study, Rosenthal and Jacobson (1970) showed that, when teachers' expectations regarding student potentials were based on fictitious information about the students' abilities, the actual achievement of students reflected these expectations. Those who were expected to achieve less actually did achieve less, and vice versa. Critics of ability testing have argued with considerable force that tests of "intelligence" have highly undesirable consequences for student performance because, at least in part, teachers tend to relate to students differentially, according to their supposed intelligence. Students who are singled out as "gifted" or "low ability" are given different assignments, different rewards, different teachers, and they are systematically taught what is expected of them. There seems little argument that teachers' expectations contribute to student performance. It is less clear what factors shape teacher expectations. Test scores may be important in determining differences among students for some teachers; however, we need to know far more about the entire matter of teacher expectancy, for many other variables may help to determine their attitudes.

Five Criticisms That Are Independent of Test Validity

TESTS HAVE A HARMFUL EFFECT ON THE SHAPING OF COGNITIVE STYLES. The widespread use of multiple-choice test items, matching items, and other test components with a single correct answer is said by some critics of testing to contribute to undesirable styles of thinking. Some claim that the young student is carefully taught that all problems must have a right or wrong answer, and thus the student is led to think in this manner about all questions.

TESTS SHAPE SCHOOL CURRICULA AND RESTRICT EDUCATIONAL CHANGE. When teachers know that the evaluation of their students will be based on a particular kind of test of some more or less predictable content, they make extensive efforts to assist their students to perform well on these tests. The proponents of state-wide testing programs would probably argue that this is exactly what they have in mind, that teachers ought to be encouraged to cover material which their colleagues consider essential. "What's wrong with this?" they ask. Critics of testing say that experimentation with new ways of teaching, the introduction of new subject matter, and the whole process of individualizing instruction in terms of the needs and interests of individual students are hamstrung by a slavish adherence to standardized achievement testing. The question seems to come down to finding an acceptable balance between the need to know what has been learned during a given period of time and the encouragement of innovation, change, and experimentation in the classroom.

TESTS DISTORT INDIVIDUAL'S SELF-CONCEPT AND LEVEL OF ASPIRATION. Of all the criticisms of tests, one of the most penetrating and difficult to dismiss is that young persons may generalize from test results and make conclusions about themselves which are not warranted or intended. For example, consider the teen-ager who may be struggling to establish a more positive and more realistic self-concept; how helpful is it for him to be shown his low test scores which may make him conclude that he is far less capable than his classmates? How many high school students have received brief and inappropriate counseling recommendations, usually based in part on test results, and have concluded from these recommendations that they are not "college material"? One large school district, for example, regularly presents junior high school students with test result summaries printed on cards that the students take home to their parents. These cards offer a lucid and easily understandable summary of what the various achievement and aptitude scores mean. Although the intent is to make information available to parents, there are obviously risks in terms of shaping the attitudes of students toward themselves. In our view, the proper handling of test results calls for neither a strategy of silence and secrecy nor for open distribution of data without discussion, clarification, and interpretation of meanings.

TESTS SELECT HOMOGENEOUS EDUCATIONAL GROUPS. A common procedure in organizing a school is to assign students to classes on the basis of estimates of learning ability. Very often these estimates are based on ability testing. It is a short step to conclude that tests have determined the organizational style of schools, and it may surely be argued that tests do indeed contribute to the way in which students are assigned. Criticism of the ability-track system, as this arrangement is often called, hinges as much on the basic assumptions underlying this approach to student assignment as on discontent with tests that may contribute to the accomplishment of such assignment. Presumably, were no test data available, an educational administrator dedicated to the principle that good educational practice required homogeneous student grouping could find numerous criteria such as grades, teachers' ratings of ability, and so forth for making these assignments.

Concerns about homogeneous grouping in schools have acquired strength with recent research which suggests that this allocation procedure tends to do more harm to the low groups than can be justified. The proponents of heterogeneous assignment to classes argue that children with lower ability need the stimulation and the role models provided by higher-ability students if they are to achieve as much as they possibly can.

Contemporary approaches to school organization stress the importance of providing a program of individual instruction for each child, regardless of the range of competences within a class. Educators are now stressing the positive influences of heterogeneous grouping, with the result that the track system is generally thought to be on the way out. But for the parents of children who are assigned to low groups, the track system is an unpleasant reality based primarily on test results. Hence, since tests are often painted as the villain in the situation, it is assumed that banning tests will eliminate the track system. For the school district set on the perpetuation of homogeneous ability grouping, the problem is not so much one of testing or not testing, but rather the adherence to an outmoded concept of educational organization.

TESTS INVADE PRIVACY. School attendance is mandatory for young children. Once in school, the children are generally required to participate in activities, including testing, which some parents consider to be invasions of privacy. Certainly few would argue against allowing schools to give tests to determine what a student has learned in some course of study; but should schools be allowed to require students to take intelligence tests? What good is such information to a school? Can data from some tests be used to the disadvantage of a student without his knowledge that such information even exists? How can the line be more clearly established between information that a school or an employer requires to help reach a legitimate decision, and information that such organizations have no business acquiring in the first place? The right to privacy is precious to the citizens of a free society; where tests invade privacy, there must be a compelling justification for their use.

Criticisms of Personality Testing

Compared to ability testing, personality testing represents only a small fraction of assessment work in schools, industry, government, and clinical work. There are a number of reasons for this, including the problem of developing personality tests that are considered satisfactory from a technical point of view. For example, one immediately encounters the dilemma that personality theorists do not agree on fundamental questions concerning what should be measured in order to describe the components of personality.

The testing of personality in schools is virtually taboo in America, for it smacks of invasion of privacy. The ground rules have been somewhat looser in business, particularly where the selection of salesmen and executives is concerned; nonetheless, testing professionals disagree about the merits of personality assessment as an aid in predicting success on the job. Though some aspects of personality, such as interests, may touch directly on satisfaction in a job or even on the ability to perform a job well, very little personality testing is used in the typical selection battery. This has long been the case. It is curious, therefore, that some of the early anti-testing books hold up personality testing in industry as a prime example of what is wrong with testing in general (Gross, 1963). While shoddy practices involving personality testing must not be shoved under the table, it is important to keep in mind that personality assessment is an extremely small part of the testing scene. To give some rough perspective here, we would estimate that more ability and job-knowledge testing is done every day in schools, industry, and government than the total personality testing carried out for an entire year.

One of the major sources of criticism about personality testing has been the Congress. Both Congressman Cornelius E. Gallagher (D.-N.J.) (1965) and Senator Sam J. Ervin, Jr. (D.-N.C.) (1965) have held congressional hearings to review various charges about personality tests. Although in one way or another these charges incorporated many of the ten criticisms listed above, the invasion of privacy issue was stressed most heavily.

Tests as Gatekeepers: The Central Criticism

At the heart of the criticisms about tests and testing programs is one fact that is likely to help perpetuate at least some of the criticism: tests are often used as tools for the allocation of limited resources or opportunities. Put another way, educational and psychological tests are frequently designed to measure differences among individuals so that one person receives a reward or privilege which another person is then denied. We see this in the assignment of elementary school children to classes for the gifted, in the selection of students for college admission or for advanced professional study, and we see the stark implicit power that tests may have in job-selection procedures. Tests are likely to stir strong emotions, for they serve in many different ways as gatekeepers, opening and closing pathways of human opportunity. When the opportunities available (e.g., job assignments) are not sufficient to meet the demand, the wrath of those who lose may be directed toward whatever procedure was used for selection.

Are tests necessarily the kind of gatekeepers we want? This is a question involving individual values, organizational goals and, increasingly, laws and regulations designed to assure equal access to educational and employment opportunities. One thing is certain: tests are no longer granted any immunity or magical status, or are they assumed to be good simply because of their objectivity or psychometric purity. The lawmaker as well as the man on the street has a skeptical eye on educational and psychological testing.

There have been too many serious lapses of professional judgment, not only by those who are using tests without the proper qualifications, but also by professionals who should know better. And minority groups' intense concern for fair play relative to testing are not going to evaporate; they will probably be expressed with increasing vehemence. If this sounds too pessimistic, perhaps we need to remind ourselves that some of the most extensive testing programs currently in use have come in for very little criticism. This is especially true with regard to armed forces selection-and-classification testing. Thus, while we may anticipate continued criticism of tests for a variety of reasons, testing programs that measure up to high professional standards and can be shown to make constructive contributions to human assessment may well be regarded as beneficial by most people.

In the chapters that follow, we will examine the criticisms discussed here in the light of our research and that of others. We will briefly describe the characteristics of tests, delineate the criteria for a competent testing (or assessment) system, and show how various kinds of testing organizations relate to these criteria. We will then discuss the more serious testing issues and make recommendation for actions by governments, organizations, and individuals.

REFERENCES

Black, H. *They Shall Not Pass*. New York: Morrow, 1963.

Cooper, G. "Legal Implications of the Use of Standardized Ability Tests in Employment and Education," *Columbia Law Review*, 68 (1968), 690–744.

Enneis, W. "Misuses of Tests." Unpublished report presented at the 1969 Annual Convention of the American Psychological Association.

Ervin, S. J. "Why Senate Hearings on Psychological Tests in Government," *American Psychologist*, 20:11 (November 1965), 879–880.

Gallagher, C. E. "Why House Hearings on Invasion of Privacy," *American Psychologist*, 20:11 (November 1965), 881–882.

Goslin, D. A. *Teachers and Testing*. New York: Russell Sage Foundation, 1967a.

Goslin, D. A. "Criticisms of Standardized Tests and Testing." Unpublished report, CEEB, New York, May 20, 1967b.

Gross, M. L. *The Brain Watchers*. New York: New American Library, 1963.

Pasanella, A. K., W. H. Manning, and N. Findikyan. "Criticisms of Testing: I." Unpublished report, CEEB, New York, May 19, 1967.

Rosenthal, R., and L. Jacobson. *Pygmalion in the Classroom: Teacher Expectation and Pupil's Intellectual Ability*. New York: Holt, 1970.

2

What Are Educational and Psychological Tests?

Human behavior may be described and measured in many different ways. The novelist, the schoolteacher, the poet, the shop foreman, and your next-door neighbor all have an impressive array of descriptive adjectives which may be assembled to offer a vivid picture of human characteristics. One of the problems, however, is that these several observers usually provide quite different descriptions of the same person, depending on the vantage point from which observations are made. One way of getting around this sampling error is to use a standard set of observations and to provide unambiguous scoring for them. This is one of the design requirements for an educational or psychological test.

But information is collected and scored by many standard procedures that are certainly not educational or psychological tests. For example, applications for credit cards or for admission to college are standard ways of acquiring necessary information about many different people, but they are not tests. What makes a test different from procedures of this kind? In *Psychological Testing* (1968), Anne Anastasi has defined a psychological test as ". . . essentially an objective and standardized measure of a sample of behavior. . . . The diagnostic or predictive value of a psychological test depends on the degree to which it serves as an indicator of a relatively broad and significant area of behavior (pp. 21-22)."

Psychologists have agreed on a set of standards for the development of educational and psychological tests and have published them as the *Standards for Educational and Psychological Tests and Manuals.* Whether a measure-

17

ment procedure should be called a test or something else depends on the extent to which the procedure is in accord with these standards. The major characteristics that psychologists look for in a good test are: validity, reliability, and norms.

VALIDITY. Use of a test must be based on evidence that it actually taps those human attributes it claims to measure. Many ways have been developed to establish the validity of tests; the method used depends on the purpose for which a test has been developed. Since the same test may be used for various purposes and for different populations of subjects, a single test may have many different kinds of validities. It makes little sense to speak of the validity of a test as if this is an absolute property of a measuring instrument; we have to ask instead, what is the validity of this test when administered to these subjects relative to some particular criterion or purpose?

RELIABILITY. A test must be consistent in what it measures, given standard conditions of measurement. As with any measuring instrument, an inconsistent test is not likely to be of much use. But unlike rulers, scales, or volt meters, educational and psychological tests are applied to people who are changing over time. It has long been recognized that numerous situational factors can play an important part in determining test performance. These include, for example, not only various changes that may be seen in the person tested, but his attitude toward the person who is doing the testing. As in our discussion of validity, it is essential to consider the many kinds of reliability that a test may have, rather than to assume that any single measure of reliability covers all test-retest possibilities.

NORMS. A test must permit individual results to be compared with comparable test data derived from other known individuals or groups so that there is a foundation for asserting what some particular test performance means. The development of norms is the heart of test standardization.

These characteristics of a good test—validity, reliability, and norms—re-enforce the point that a test is more than a collection of standard procedures. Psychologists insist that these characteristics are essential attributes of competently constructed tests, and that human assessment strategies lacking these attributes should not be called tests.

Criteria for a Competent Assessment System

It is meaningless to ask if a test is any good. More appropriately, one might ask: Will this test correlate highly with certain criterion measures (e.g., success in training) when administered and used under these conditions with this particular group of subjects?

Here we see a major difference between objective physical measures and psychological measurement. People may disagree on the ideal temperature for a bath, but there is little room for argument concerning the temperature of the bath water at some point in time. We may read thermometers a little differently, thereby introducing the inevitable "human error"; however, this source of variation is not attributed to either the water or the measuring instrument. If the measuring device is checked against an independent standard from time to time, thereby re-establishing its calibration and accuracy, there is likely to be no complaint concerning its functioning. But this is not true with regard to psychological and educational tests, for these measures are not predicated upon the *direct* assessment of the attributes they attempt to quantify; instead, tests involve a variety of intervening variables which complicate the measurement process. For example, in the measurement of intelligence, it is not "intelligence" as some tangible thing that is being assessed; rather, intelligence is inferred from our observations of behavior that is said to reflect intelligence.

In order to create a test to measure intelligence, we must devise various opportunities for a subject to demonstrate those kinds of behavior that are said to require intelligence. But having done so, we still do not measure intelligence; rather, we infer intelligence from our evaluation of performance on a set of tasks. The behavior shown by an individual on these tasks obviously depends on his capability to comprehend the instructions, his rapport with the test administrator, his previous experience with similar tasks, and his eagerness to perform well in the test situation. If these and many other determinants that contribute to test behavior are not taken into account, the inferences drawn from any individual pattern of test performance may be highly misleading. The same rationale obtains for tests designed to predict success on a job or in training.

In order to evaluate whether a test is "any good," it is imperative to consider many other kinds of information and to assure that the procedures and personnel involved in all aspects of the testing process measure up to certain criteria of competence. Some of these criteria involve the technical aspects of test administration and scoring; others involve professional competences which are very difficult to assess, such as the ability of a test administrator to establish rapport.

Whenever tests are used, there exists not only a "testing" program in the narrow sense but, more importantly, an assessment system of interdependent parts. We believe it useful to develop criteria for the components of such assessment systems and to define the subsystems of greatest importance. We hope this will be helpful as a guide in the evaluation of specific assessment systems. We shall discuss the following six subsystems:

Subsystem 1: Definition of assessment-system requirements
Subsystem 2: Test development and standardization
Subsystem 3: Definition of subjects and test administration
Subsystem 4: Scoring and preparation of feedback documents

Subsystem 5: Feedback of test results

Subsystem 6: Evaluation of the assessment system.

Subsytem 1: Definition of Assessment-System Requirements

The requirements of an assessment system must be stated with sufficient specificity that they may be used for selection or development of tests which will contribute to the achievement of the objectives of the testing program. The first thing that must be done in connection with any kind of measurement is to define just what an assessment program is supposed to accomplish. Is it expected to predict success in military aviation training? If so, what kind of training? How standard will the training be? How will the results of the training program be measured so that the predictive value of the test results can be checked? Until the definition of objectives has been worked out very carefully, there can be no sound basis for advocating any kind of testing.

Given clear statements of objectives, the specifications for a test or a test battery can be designated. If the necessary tests are not available, a decision will have to be made concerning the desirability of developing the necessary measures.

The primary responsibility for this subsystem is with the test user. The authors and publishers of tests have virtually no functional control within this subsystem, although they play a vital role by making explicit in their test manuals the particular applications for which a test is offered and the subject-population constraints applicable to the norms provided. In the typical testing program in schools, industry, and government, more information is provided in test manuals than is properly used by those who buy commercially available tests. Extensive opportunity exists for the improvement of testing practices through insistence that the users of tests demonstrate more conclusively that tests have been appropriately selected and used, and that objectives of a testing program which are alleged to be met through such testing are in fact accomplished.

Subsystem 2: Test Development and Standardization

Tests must be developed in accordance with the Standards for Educational and Psychological Tests and Manuals. Whether a new test is developed for a special purpose or an established test is applied, the competent assessment system must require tests that measure up to professional standards. The principles of test development have been forged over the past half century, and have been endorsed by those who know test development best.

It is a matter of great concern, therefore, that so many unvalidated tests are applied in situations with such great potential to affect people's lives. We have observed many testing programs in which tests are used inappropriately or for which a technically deficient test was selected in the first place. While the well-established and professionally respected organizations in the test-development area condemn these practices, little has been done to change matters except through the pressures exerted by federal agencies concerned with civil rights and education.

It is likely that the production of a sound test is one of the easier elements to demand in the competent assessment system. Much has been learned about the construction of tests, the creation of test items, the design of test formats, and the effects of different kinds of answer sheets. The general improvement of assessment systems will proceed most rapidly if society demands the same kind of professional standards in test utilization that are required in most other matters intimately touching people's lives. But having a sound test does not ensure a sound assessment system. What concerns us most is not what tests are like, but rather the enormous deficiencies in the human side of too many assessment systems.

Subsystem 3: Definition of Subjects and Test Administration

Tests must be administered in accordance with standards set forth in the test manual; information concerning subject variables essential to the interpretation of the test results must be acquired. Although it seems modest to ask that tests be administered under reasonably standard conditions, what little evidence exists from field studies of testing in industry suggests deplorable practices (Rushmore, 1967). No assessment system can function competently if, for any reason, the subject is not able to render his best performance. Similarly, proper attention must be given to the formal conditions of testing, such as time limits and the reading and clarification of instructions. This seems easy to do, but when testing programs are carried out by persons not properly trained to discharge these obligations, it should be no surprise that shoddy and unprofessional practices come to light.

Subsystem 4: Scoring and Preparation of Feedback Documents

Test scoring and the preparation of feedback documents must be reliable and objective. Much test scoring is still carried out "by hand" rather than through electronic scoring and computing devices. No matter who does this work and regardless of what device may be used, the scoring of tests must be done with care and objectivity. Despite the growth of automated procedures for test scoring and for the preparation of feedback materials, individuals will probably continue to score many tests. In every assessment system, someone must take responsibility for assuring the integrity of the feedback process and for establishing with certainty that persons who score tests have whatever training and supervision may be required to assure that this activity is properly conducted.

As machine scoring and computer preparation of feedback materials become more available and more versatile, some of the possibilities for human error or lapses of judgment may be decreased. Undoubtedly, industry has the technical capability for carrying out machine scoring with very high accuracy, speed, and efficiency. But even more important is the capability of tying in computer utilization to make possible the interpretation of test results in whatever formats are desired. This often includes a summary of results for each individual tested, reports to teachers, personnel workers, administrators, or whoever has a need to know.

Subsystem 5: Feedback of Test Results

The assessment system must provide for information feedback to persons using the tests; this information must be communicated effectively, and the importance attributed to test results relative to personnel decisions should be clarified. Regardless of the original purpose of the testing program, feedback of test results should be given to the persons the program is serving and should be presented relevant to the purpose for which the program was designed. Sometimes the person taking a test is the user of the test results; sometimes he is not. Nonetheless, feedback should be given to the testee unless it is not in his best interest or the best interests of the testing program. People resent being tested and then not hearing what the results are.

It is common practice in industrial-selection testing to provide the most superficial test feedback possible (e.g., "You scored too low."). This may have the short-term advantage of obviating the necessity to explain or justify test results, but it has the very serious long-term disadvantage of discrediting the user of tests. Whenever tests are given, it may be well to start with the assumption that people have a right to know the results and how those results are to be used. People tested for various purposes will undoubtedly require different kinds of feedback; test scores are not necessarily the best unit of measure for communicating test results.

Subsystem 6: Evaluation of the Assessment System

Assessment systems must be objectively evaluated to determine the extent to which their objectives are being met. Like physical masses, assessment systems that have been set into motion tend to continue in motion until something stops them. Much of the educational and psychological testing carried on today is not directly tied in with evaluation of its effectiveness. The problem of evaluation takes us back to Subsystem 1, which deals with the objectives and requirements of an assessment system, for unless the purposes are explicit and unambiguous, no objective way can be found to support or denounce an assessment program.

A reasonable point of departure in the examination of most testing programs is the assumption that no suitable evaluation has ever been conducted. If this is true, and it often is, then the proper basis for responding to the critics of educational and psychological testing would be through a sound program of assessment-system evaluation whenever testing goes on. A testing program that has not been evaluated in the particular setting in which it is being used cannot claim to be a competent assessment activity until the data to support a thorough evaluation have been acquired.

Responsibility for Testing Programs

Although all the components of a competent testing system need not be under the supervision of a single person, the responsibility for establishing the adequacy of a testing program should be clearly established. When a competent system cannot be demonstrated, the use of tests is unjustified. We encourage the discontinuance of all testing programs that fail to measure up to these criteria for a competent assessment system.

How Competent Are Assessment Systems?

It is one thing to offer a format for the evaluation of assessment systems; it is another to attempt any global judgment of these systems. The following is a summary of our impressions of how various kinds of testing programs seem to be carried out and what some of their strengths and weaknesses may be. These impressions are based on our own career activities as psychologists who have used tests in many different settings, and also on the opinions and comments of those we interviewed throughout the course of this project. The bulk of new information about the testing industry comes from questionnaires and interviews with test distributors and developers.

Our evaluative impressions offer a bird's-eye view of contemporary testing practices in three areas of test utilization: (1) testing in counseling, guidance, and clinical work; (2) testing for educational achievement; and (3) selection-and-placement testing. Let's consider the adequacy of assessment systems in these three areas, keeping in mind that the competence of any particular assessment system can be established only through study of that individual system.

Counseling, Guidance, and Clinical Assessment Systems

Although the objectives of testing in the counseling, guidance, and clinical areas are primarily centered on individual services, the kinds of services and the functional objectives of testing are often vague. In these testing areas we have seen many examples of routine testing programs which are supposed to provide "screening" or early detection of some human characteristic. On balance, we believe too much testing continues to be carried out in the name of counseling and clinical services without the necessary conceptualization and definition of what this testing is supposed to accomplish. This point has been made with considerable force by Dr. Karl U. Smith in his testimony before a congressional committee (1965).

Individually administered tests, such as those often used in clinical work, represent a very small proportion of total test sales. Very few test publishers, therefore, are investing in the development of materials designed for clinical applications. A far greater market exists for school-based counseling and guidance materials and, as might be expected, substantial high-quality test-development work is carried out in this area. Clinical psychologists have been hard at work studying the applicability of tests for various clinical purposes. Their research has led to the reduction of much preliminary testing in mental health consultation work.

Professional standards requiring control of testing practices are substantially superior in the counseling, guidance, and clinical areas (compared with educational and industrial uses); as a result, we see a comparatively sophisticated level of practice. Tests are generally administered in a professional manner, and while examples occur of tests being given to individuals for whom such materials were never intended, such as bilingual youngsters, these practices are uncommon. There are generally adequate practices in the scoring of tests and in feeding back test results. A major weak spot, however, is in the evaluation of assessment systems in counseling, guidance, and clinical settings. This ties back to the need for careful definition of the purposes of a testing program, for without this it is not possible to evaluate an assessment system.

Testing for Educational Achievement

At first glance, the objectives of educational achievement testing seem clear enough, for the basic goal is to determine whether students can demonstrate proficiency in different subject-matter areas. If this is, in fact, the total objective, as it may be for some users, the topic may be quickly closed. But the justification for educational achievement tests is founded on a considerably more challenging question: How can achievement test data be used to improve the effectiveness of our educational activities? If achievement test results which are acquired annually do not have much impact on educational programs, they are a costly form of irrelevance at best. Many testing professionals are skeptical about how achievement tests are actually used by teachers and administrators. They suspect, as we do, that much of the test data is quietly filed away and is of little or no consequence to instructional practices. But when the spotlight shines on test results, such as in the assessment of reading ability in inner-city schools, the tests may have great impact on the allocation of resources and in the facilitation of new approaches toward increasing the effectiveness of educational activities.

With regard to the adequacy of test development, there is not only a large market for achievement tests, but also intense competition among many publishers. Coupled with continuing research on basic psychometrics, this has resulted in high-quality test-development practices.

Because it is very easy to administer most achievement tests, no major problems occur in this subsystem. The scoring of these tests is gradually being transferred from the hands of the classroom teacher to computer-controlled machines. The resulting advantages both in speed and accuracy make possible the preparation of test results in various forms for teachers, students, parents, and administrators. We shall probably continue to see advances in data-handling procedures which will make possible highly diverse kinds of feedback of test results. In turn, diverse kinds of feedback may have the potential for influencing the use of test results by teachers and administrators. If so, a giant step may be taken toward more thorough evaluation of the effectiveness of educational achievement testing.

Testing for Selection and Placement

Most selection-and-placement testing is aimed toward the prediction of success in a given job or training program. One problem is the definition of what is meant by "success," for jobs change and so do training programs; also, different supervisors and trainers have various ideas of what constitutes successful performance. But even with the many difficulties associated with the establishment of criterion measures whereby the predictive validity of an assessment program could be determined, the objectives of selection-and-placement testing in business and industry are typically far easier to define than they are in an educational setting.

Whenever testing for selection and placement is carried out, there is an urgent requirement for the careful designation of what this testing is supposed to accomplish. Many of the most disturbing examples of unprofessional uses of tests have come from applications involving selection and placement.

The quality of test-development work in this area is extremely uneven. At the one extreme are outstanding examples of high-quality programs, such as we see in some of the military selection-and-placement work and in some industrial assessment systems. At the other extreme are hundreds of tests used in civil service testing programs plus many other tests of questionable value that are used in business and industry. The tests cover many different assessment objectives including motor-performance measures, job-knowledge tests, general intelligence, and personality and attitude surveys. The major difficulty is not related to the technical merits of tests, but rather to the continued unprofessional use of tests by personnel who are inadequately trained and supervised for the responsibilities they attempt to shoulder.

Too many tests continue to be applied to subjects not adequately represented in standardization samples, such as Negroes and Mexican-Americans. In addition, some preliminary evidence (Rushmore, 1967) exists that the conditions under which tests are administered in many personnel departments are highly unsatisfactory. Poor practices in test administration and scoring are not likely to be overcome unless industry makes a much stronger commitment to carry out testing programs with competent personnel and adequate supervision.

While feedback of test results is generally available in selection testing required by academic institutions, this is usually not the case in industry. Feedback to a person who has been tested as a job applicant is typically given in the form of a personnel decision: testees are told whether they are to be hired, and little else. From the employer's standpoint, little is gained by presenting in detail all the reasons for such a decision. Many employers would no doubt conclude that they are not in the vocational counseling business, and therefore it is not their responsibility to interpret test results to applicants. Such an attitude tends to re-enforce the aura of mysticism and black magic that some associate with tests. Not surprisingly, individuals who are not adequately informed about their employment-test performance and who are subsequently not hired conclude that tests are unfair and harmful. If the veil of mystery concerning tests is to be lifted, it would be helpful to start telling job applicants how test data are used.

The Office of Federal Contract Compliance and the Equal Employment Opportunity Commission have issued regulations and guidelines requiring the use of tests to be limited to those job situations for which job-related validity data have been acquired. Many testing professionals acknowledge that tests have been used extensively to predict job success or training aptitude, even though sufficient evidence of appropriate validity studies has not been available. Such practices are considered unprofessional, but the requirement that validity data be acquired is the only demand that has any teeth in it. When there is an absence of data demonstrating that tests are actually helping to predict criterion performance, then no argument would appear to justify the continuation of selection-and-placement testing.

Why Study the Testing Industry?

The developers of tests play a crucial role in the assessment system, for if a testing program is founded on measurement procedures that are technically deficient, there is no way to compensate for such shortcomings. We need to know, therefore, who the developers of tests are, how they operate, and whether they are responsive to professional standards for the development of tests. Of the six subsystems that should be considered in evaluating the competence of an assessment program, the test-development subsystem is the primary one in which the testing industry is directly involved. There are, however, some contract testing programs in which the testing industry is significantly involved in all six subsystems. When computer-based scoring and interpretation services are offered, the industry contribution to a program is far greater. While such services are growing rapidly, they are largely relevant to educational-achievement testing and, to a smaller extent, educational selection and placement.

In conducting the present study, our main concern was to dissect the elements of the testing industry both in terms of the kinds of services offered and the quality of those services. We wanted to know, for example, how often different publishers issued updated revisions of their tests, how scoring services were staffed and operated, and what kinds of differences, if any, might be seen among large and small test publishers.

Major Elements of the Testing Industry

Despite the diversity of the testing industry, we believe it can be described in terms of seven major elements. Our classification is offered purely as a convenience in considering different kinds of companies within this industry. Sometimes this classification is based on the size of the organization, and at other times on the kind of service rendered; testing organizations can also be categorized according to their publishing and distribution practices. Each of the following six sections describes one major element of the testing industry. The classification is as follows:

The six largest testing companies
Medium-size and small test publishers
Government-employment testing
State educational testing programs
Contract and proprietary testing
Test scoring and interpretation companies

The Six Largest Testing Companies

The predominant organizations in the testing field are the six educational publishers (see Chapter 3 and Appendix) who together account for at least three-quarters of all tests sold. These organizations have five common characteristics:

1. Their major market is educational institutions.
2. All of these companies have been engaged in the testing field for a considerable length of time.
3. They all sell a wide variety of tests and test services in addition to having a large volume of sales. Most companies list in their catalogues a hundred or more tests, the majority of which are owned by the company. They generally do not sell tests owned by other publishers.
4. They employ fairly large numbers of persons who are well trained in testing and who are leaders in the professional organizations involved with testing.
5. With one exception, their test sales are not their major source of income.

At the beginning of our study, we were anxious to find out whether the testing industry included an organizational "model," i.e., a set of organizations that were employing high professional standards, making available a variety of high-quality products and services, and earning enough money to continue to develop tests and improve products. The existence of such a model could encourage organizations that have not yet achieved such status to realize their potential by offering quality products and services.

This core group of six educational test publishers appears to meet the criteria of the organizational model. Test sales of these publishers are increasing, but their services are increasing even faster. They devote considerable amounts of time and money to the development and improvement of their own products and to the technology on which the products are based; their prosperity and growth rate indicate that their professional excellence does not preclude reasonable economic returns.

In terms of the assessment-system model discussed earlier, these companies are primarily concerned with the test-development subsystem, although some of them offer services in all six subsystems.

Medium-Size and Small Test Publishers

The second group of test publishers consists of twenty-two publishers (see Chapter 4 and Appendix) that also produce most of their tests for the educational field; some of these organizations sell a substantial portion of their products to industry. Unlike the large organizations for which testing is an activity supporting the major business (e.g., textbook publishing), the medium-size publishers tend to be primarily in the testing business. They also tend to be somewhat more recent; for the most part, they are owned and managed by their founders, who have good reputations in the testing profession. The middle-size companies have limited catalogues which generally offer from five to fifty items. Though their smaller volume of business makes it more difficult for them to meet the same standards as their larger competitors, these organizations employ good professional help and make a serious attempt to meet established standards of test development.

Though this group of companies offers for sale tests developed by other testing companies or individuals, it does show considerable involvement in the development subsystem. Some of these organizations assist in requirements and evaluation work for their clients, and at least one provides test administration, scoring, and feedback services.

Small test publishers are also included in this group of testing organizations. Although most of them publish only one test, some publish two or three related tests. The small publishers present quite a different picture. Most of these persons and organizations are engaged in test publishing in support of some other activity; in this way they are more like the large publishers than the medium-size ones. Some provide a valuable service by publishing new kinds of tests, and most show concern for meeting test standards. Nevertheless, many interviewees in this group expressed the wish that someone else would do the test publishing since it was taking more of their time than it was worth in terms of the return. In many cases, the operation was not a profitable one. Most of these publishers serve only a part of the development subsystem, and almost none provides the full range of subsystem services.

Government-Employment Testing

The third group of testing organizations (see Chapter 5) consists of federal, state, and local agencies that have testing programs (particularly the military services, but including federal civil service examinations) and the U.S. Employment Service examination programs for guidance and placement purposes. The federal agencies have often pioneered new kinds of tests, test uses, and improved standards for test development and use (Uhlaner, 1967; pp. 7–47).

Because of the large numbers of people affected by their programs and because of the sensitivity of federal agencies and Congress to any possible infringement of rights through testing, these federal agencies are now moving rather slowly and cautiously. They do not appear to be innovating as rapidly as private industry, although they have made important changes in some federal civil service exams. These organizations either provide part of or all of complete testing systems; they have frequently set an example for other organizations in the evaluation of testing programs.

State and local government agencies generally follow the federal merit-system employment practices, including testing, to the extent permitted by their local laws and employment conditions. To a much greater extent than at the federal level, they are assisted by commercial organizations (either profit or nonprofit) in many of their tasks. Because these organizations are faced with unique objectives and constraints, they deal with testing problems quite differently from the groups primarily involved with educational and private-employment testing. Their emphasis is on item development and re-use of good items, with validities based on logic and internal consistency rather than on statistical relationships to criterion group performance. They make extensive use of job-knowledge tests. These organizations work in all six subsystem areas, although they are least involved in test administration.

State Educational Testing Programs

The fourth group of testing organizations includes state educational testing programs (see Chapter 6). At least thirty states carry out state-wide educational testing activities. Also well known, but with a smaller volume, are testing programs for licensing and certification of various professionals. The nature and method of operation of the state agencies vary greatly from those that depend entirely on nationally standardized instruments on the one hand to those that make no use of them at all. Their programs also range from mandatory to optional. Most of these programs have responsibilities encompassing all six subsystems.

Contract and Proprietary Programs

Many different kinds of organizations contract for the development, evaluation, or operation of testing programs (see Chapter 7). These organizations develop college- and other school-selection testing, applicant testing for employment in the insurance industry, and large national programs concerned with assessment of educational progress and related goals. The majority of services provided by these organizations relate to at least three of the six testing subsystems defined earlier: (1) definition of assessment-system objectives, (2) test development, and (3) scoring and preparation of feedback documents.

Although contract or proprietary testing is primarily developed by the companies described in this group, it is also conducted by the large educational publishers, the nonfederal public-employment testing companies, and the private-personnel test companies.

Test Scoring and Interpretation Companies

The newest testing organizations in the field and the fastest growing are the test scoring and interpretation companies (see Chapter 8). Capitalizing on the improvement in optical scanning and digital computer techniques, they have developed and produced machines that can score thousands of answer sheets per hour and yield large numbers of scores per sheet. These machines can also provide instant statistical summaries of results. One highly innovative activity of this group is computerized test interpretation. Test-scoring organizations seldom offer any services other than scoring and preparation of feedback documents. They participate with publishers on scoring and interpretation aspects of test development, including design of test booklets and answer sheets. They are also extending their activities into such related fields as attitude-survey work which uses a similar technology.

Establishment and Control of Testing Standards

Who is concerned with the quality of testing products and processes? How do they influence test publishers and test users? Has the "consumerism" movement in the United States had an effect on testing practices, or only on publications about them? The principal opportunity for control of testing practices is through the professional and paraprofessional persons involved in test development, distribution, and use. These persons can be influenced by legislation and by peer-group pressure generated by professional associations. The role of government and of people and organizations influencing testing will be discussed in Chapters 9 and 10. Not all influence exerted on testing programs is control oriented, however. The role of test reviews and advertising in making information about tests available is discussed in Chapter 11.

REFERENCES

Anastasi, A. *Psychological Testing.* New York: Macmillan, 1968.
Rushmore, J. E. "Psychological Tests and Fair Employment: A Study of Employment Tests in the San Francisco Bay Area," State of California Fair Employment Practice Commission, 1967.
Smith, K. U. Testimony, *American Psychologist*, 20:11 (November 1965), 907–915.
Uhlaner, J. E., ed. *Psychological Research in National Defense Today.* Washington, D.C.: U.S. Army Behavioral Science Research Laboratory, June 1967.

3

Large Commercial Test Publishers

The six largest sellers of educational and psychological tests are the California Test Bureau; Educational Testing Service; Harcourt Brace Jovanovich, Inc.; Houghton Mifflin Company; the Psychological Corporation; and Science Research Associates. These companies account for approximately three-quarters of the total test *sales* in the country and for probably a higher percentage of the educational test sales.

The six organizations share a number of characteristics: (1) They have all been engaged in the testing business for a long time; most of them helped pioneer the testing field in the 1920's. (2) The companies all sell a wide variety as well as a large volume of tests; most companies list more than one hundred tests in their catalogues. (3) They provide extensive services to test customers. (4) The organizations employ many individuals who are well trained in testing and who are leaders in professional organizations involved with testing; further, these persons are in the top management of the company or are influential in the company management. (5) With one exception, test sales are not the major source of income for these publishers.

History of Test Development

Harcourt Brace Jovanovich

World Book Company, one of the oldest testing organizations, merged with Harcourt Brace, Inc., in 1962, to form Harcourt, Brace & World, Inc., which is presently known as Harcourt Brace Jovanovich. The new organization is primarily engaged in educational publishing for the primary grades through college. The company, even before its recent purchase of the Psychological Corporation, was one of the largest of the Big Six publishers. In 1966, approximately $6.5 million of tests and test services accounted for a little over 10 percent of the company's total sales.

Probably the first successful commercial test publication in the United States was done by World Book Company which published the Courtis Standard Research Test in Arithmetic in 1914. In 1918, the company made arrangements with Arthur S. Otis, a former student of Lewis M. Terman, to issue the first of the historic series of Otis Intelligence tests under the title Otis Group Intelligence Scale. The youngest descendant of this family is the Otis-Lennon Mental Ability Test which was published in 1967. World Book Company began publication of standardized achievement tests in 1920, personality tests in 1921, and tests of mechanical and clerical aptitude in 1922.

In the early 1920's, testing was a sufficiently large activity within World Book Company to require establishment of a test-service department. In 1923, the Test Department began publication of its well-known test-service bulletins which provided simple, nontechnical discussions of test topics and practical examples of effective uses of tests. In addition, World sponsored an early series of books on measurement theory and practice.

Test-development activities in the 1920's were primarily the responsibility of the test author; however, during the 1930's and 1940's, the Division of Test Research and Service of World Book Company began taking over those aspects of test development, such as development and standardization tests, which were beyond the resources of individual authors or groups of authors.

A company history of standardized testing (World Book Company, 1954) describes this change as follows:

> The Test Division increasingly assumed responsibility for experimental work on problems of validity, reliability, equivalence of forms, norms, and the like. Staff and equipment, including scoring and tabulating machines, were expanded to handle these operations. In effect, the Company moved in the direction of a partnership with test authors in which the authors provided thoroughgoing subject matter knowledge and psychological expertise, and the Company's staff provided the technical and experimental facilities. The Company set a new pattern for standardization with its development of the 1940 edition of the Stanford Achievement Test (pp. 13–14).

That standardization effort, recognized for its excellence throughout the testing industry, was the forerunner of some portions of the present *Standards for Educational and Psychological Tests and Manuals.*

Houghton Mifflin Company

In 1916, Houghton Mifflin entered the testing field with publication of the Stanford-Binet test. The company's other early tests included the Lorge-Thorndike and Henmon-Nelson group tests of intelligence, the Iowa Tests of Basic Skills, and a number of academic-achievement tests.

Psychological Corporation

Another early test publisher was the Psychological Corporation, founded in 1921 by James McKeen Cattell, formerly of Columbia University, Edward L. Thorndike, and Robert S. Woodworth, both also of Columbia. The corporation's directors' lists have consistently read like a "Who's Who" in psychology.

Originally the company was to act as a clearinghouse to render expert services involving the application of psychology to education and business. The clearinghouse plan did not work well, so in the late 1920's, the corporation, under the leadership of Paul Achilles, became a supplier of psychological services and then of psychological tests. So that the American Psychological Association (APA) could exercise ethical control over the company's operations, it was given the perpetual right to buy all the company's stock. The need for APA monitoring evidently decreased until, in 1947, the APA waived its option rights in favor of a provision limiting stock ownership to psychologists. In late 1969, Harcourt Brace Jovanovich purchased the corporation's stock and made it a subsidiary.

Currently, tests are not only developed by the company's professional staff but are also purchased, commissioned, or published in partnership with test authors. For many years, the company also has had a significant contract testing activity.

California Test Bureau

The California Test Bureau (CTB) was founded in 1926 by Mrs. Ethel M. Clark, who was its president until it was sold to McGraw-Hill Book Company in 1965. McGraw-Hill was already somewhat involved in testing through its ownership of Educational Development Laboratories of Huntington, Long Island, and through some tests that the Psychological Corporation had developed under contract. CTB now ranks third or fourth in test sales. It is continuing to grow, especially through the development of new tests, but also by broadening its scope to include evaluation services.

Science Research Associates

Science Research Associates (SRA), founded in 1938 by the late Lyle Spencer, was acquired in 1963 by IBM Corporation. SRA is one of the three largest test publishers; yet tests account for only about 30 percent of the company's sales. Instructional materials comprise the remainder of the sales. In addition to developing and publishing test and guidance materials, SRA offers automated scoring services.

Educational Testing Service

Educational Testing Service (ETS), the newest of the large testing companies, was founded in 1947 by the American Council on Education, the Carnegie Foundation for the Advancement of Teaching, and the College Entrance Examination Board. The organizations founding ETS primarily served the major university and private college and university markets; generally they did not deal with state universities or with the smaller colleges. The new organization was given responsibility for conducting the testing activities of the three founding organizations and for providing leadership and dependable research in a rapidly growing field of educational measurement.

The company's three main areas of activity (testing, research, and advisory services) were spelled out in the statement of purposes by the first Board of Trustees. With respect to testing, the trustees said (Educational Testing Service, 1947) that the new organization should "attempt to continuously improve existing programs . . . undertake from time to time such new testing services as may be requested . . . [and] initiate new projects in the educational testing field . . . in collaboration with the groups for whom the service is to be provided (p. 7)."

As for research, ETS should "attempt to chart the major areas in which testing research is desirable, encouraging, conducting, or arranging for research in those areas . . . (p. 7)." The trustees also urged that the research be conducted "in areas in which no fundamental work is being done," stating that "areas such as motivation, personality traits, emotional adjustments, as well as certain intellectual quality, are still relatively unexplored and call for the most painstaking research and critical analysis (p. 10)."

Advisory services were also considered important by the early trustees, who said that they hoped to "stimulate research and sound testing procedures everywhere and to help educators who felt a need for guidance in the selection, use, and interpretation of tests (p. 10)." Thus, the word "service" in the organization's title was reflected in greater detail in its statement of objectives. The trustees also stated their belief that ETS must "be constantly sensitive to the needs and desires of educational institutions at all levels" and must always recognize "the diverse interests of the institutions using its services (p. 8)."

Because of the large number of persons taking the College Board Admissions Tests, the Preliminary Scholastic Aptitude Test, the College Board Advanced Placement Examinations, College Placement Tests, and the Graduate Record Examination, Educational Testing Service is probably the best-known testing organization in the United States. Test volume of ETS makes it one of the largest testing companies. In addition to test publication, the company sustains an extensive program in psychometric research.

Ownership

The six large companies differ from each other in type of ownership. Two of the companies are publicly owned, profit-making organizations: Harcourt Brace Jovanovich and Houghton Mifflin. Three are subsidiaries of profit-making organizations: Science Research Associates was purchased by IBM in 1963; California Test Bureau was purchased by McGraw-Hill Book Company in 1965, and in late 1969 the Psychological Corporation was purchased by Harcourt Brace Jovanovich. Only Educational Testing Service is a private, nonprofit organization.

Primary Business

These large test publishers differ slightly with respect to their principal business. Harcourt Brace Jovanovich, Houghton Mifflin, and McGraw-Hill are all general book publishing organizations. For Science Research Associates, which is heavily involved in the educational materials and services field, testing is a significant but still minor part of the company's total business. Only Educational Testing Service and the Psychological Corporation are primarily in the testing business.

Company Characteristics and Testing Subsystems

Let us next look at these organizations in terms of how their organization, staffing, and activities relate to the subsystems described in Chapter 2.

Subsystem 1: Definition of Assessment-System Requirements

In order to take an active part in assisting test users to define their objectives, companies must communicate with users before the users select their tests. For the most part, this communication must be done through the field representatives of the test publishers. The main alternative is for a test user to arrange for independent consultation; this may be desirable, but it is rare. In order to assess the capability of test publishers to provide early consultation, we shall examine the sales and distribution organizations of the large test publishers.

Harcourt Brace and the California Test Bureau have active field sales and distribution staffs. At Harcourt, all testing activity is handled by the Test Department under the direction of Dr. Roger T. Lennon. His staff of 135 includes field representatives throughout the United States, Canada, Central America, Europe, New Zealand, and Australia. The representatives, typically trained in educational measurement, are members of the professional associations. Most members of California Test Bureau's 22-man field staff have either a Master's or Ph.D. degree; all are members of educational or psychological professional organizations. Both to stimulate the sales of new products and to provide consultation on the uses of material already available, the field consultants at these two organizations travel extensively, meeting with present and potential users of their products and services.

Houghton Mifflin has a 150-man staff of textbook and test salesmen. Since most of the salesmen are not testing specialists, their activities in relation to testing are coordinated by 5 testing coordinators who serve as resource people. The coordinators also assist customers with testing problems. Similarly, Science Research Associates has a sales organization of approximately 250, primarily former teachers well acquainted with the personnel and the problems in the schools to which they provide sales and services. Because of the variations in educational background and qualifications of SRA's sales representatives, there is a wide variation in the extent to which they interpret technical aspects of the tests to the people with whom they deal. The company generally requires that persons who counsel customers on the interpretations of test materials have a Master's degree in testing and guidance.

Two of the six companies have essentially no field representatives. These are the Psychological Corporation, which has no field offices and no outside salesmen, and Educational Testing Service, which has no sales staff but does have seven regional offices for professional consultation. Harcourt's extensive field sales and consulting staff will undoubtedly assist in marketing Psychological Corporation products in the future.

All of these companies carry on extensive correspondence with test users concerning appropriate uses of their tests and methods of evaluating testing programs. The large companies and their customers are fortunate in that better-known tests are usually reviewed in the *Mental Measurements Yearbook*, in textbooks, and in technical journals; thus, users of the tests published by the six big publishers can be readily referred to a large amount of material on test use. Nevertheless, the quality of testing programs would be significantly improved by a closer relationship between the testing professionals in these large testing organizations and the customers whom they serve. The large test companies provide considerably more consultation of all kinds to their customers than do the medium-size and small test publishers.

Subsystem 2: Test Development and Standardization

Although all the large testing companies support test development activities, they handle these activities differently. Historically, much early test development took place on university campuses, and the test publisher ordinarily took responsibility for printing, advertising, and distributing his tests. More recently, the publishing companies have taken responsibility for a much higher proportion of test-development activity. Because extensive work is involved in test standardization, an experienced organization must carry out this phase of the development process. After a test author has developed preliminary forms for a new test and evidence that the test is likely to be of value, the test publisher ordinarily arranges for the selection of sample populations to whom the test is administered; an analysis of the resulting data; and publication of the validity, reliability, and normative data resulting from the standardization process. The final step is preparation of the manual for test use.

The present trend in test development is toward increased "in-house" test development by the test publisher's professional staff. Examples of tests developed in this way are the Differential Aptitude Test Series developed by the Psychological Corporation, the later versions of the Stanford Achievement Tests published by Harcourt Brace, and the TOBE Series recently published by the California Test Bureau.

Two of the large companies represent extremes in their methods of handling test development. Houghton Mifflin is the only large test publisher that does not employ personnel to develop tests. This company relies on independent test authors. Educational Testing Service, on the other hand, develops almost all its own tests. Since a high proportion of ETS testing activity is related to contract programs for such organizations as the College Entrance Examination Board, this company's development activities will be discussed more fully in the chapter on contract testing.

The other four large testing companies construct their own tests and also acquire tests from independent test authors. The Psychological Corporation has long had test-development staffs both in its Test Division and in its Professional Examinations Division. Although the Test Division, which publishes tests for general sale, began with tests initiated by authors outside the company, it has moved toward publishing materials developed within the company. In all cases, however, the company frequently revises old tests to update their content and to provide standardization data that is relevant to the problems of the test users.

Science Research Associates involves more than a hundred of its staff of fifteen hundred in test development and innovation. The amount and variety of development carried on by SRA is indicated by the fact that the company's Test and Guidance Catalog lists a wide variety of tests in such areas as ability and aptitude, achievement, interests, attitudes, and temperament. Further, approximately three new tests are developed each year. The company operates contract testing programs that call for annual test development and revision; it also publishes a number of well-known standardized tests which must be updated periodically. SRA tries to revise each test every five years, but it revises major tests more often.

Test development, standardization, and revision, clearly key activities in the test departments of the six largest test publishing companies, probably account for three-quarters or more of the total professional activity within these organizations. Most of these organizations involve at least three and perhaps as many as fifteen people at the professional level in test development for each one involved at the professional level in test sales. This suggests that the test-development capability of the large companies is probably one of their strongest contributions to assessment systems.

Subsystem 3: Definition of Subjects and Test Administration

Houghton Mifflin, California Test Bureau, and Harcourt Brace are minimally involved, if at all, in test administration. Involvement is greater on the part of Educational Testing Service, Science Research Associates, and the Psychological Corporation, because these companies engage in contract testing activities in which the organization either takes responsibility for or establishes standards for test administration. In some of the contract testing programs, test administration is done by the client, but in the large programs, such as the various school admissions testing programs, test administration is handled by the testing organization.

Probably the most innovative recent development in the test administration area is that by the Psychological Corporation, which has developed some equipment and processes known as CAST (Central Administration of Standardized Tests). CAST makes it possible for an examiner to present as many as three different testing programs simultaneously, routing each program to any of ten different locations. Individual programs are contained in tape cartridges which include directions and timing signals; this ensures standardization of instructions and accuracy of timing.

None of these test publishers claims to exert direct control over test users concerning either administration of tests to persons for whom the tests were intended or control of the conditions of test administration. Test manuals and other materials describing the tests generally offer explicit directions for the use of these materials; however, the publishers have no means whatever to assure good practice by those who acquire their tests. Spokesmen for these six large organizations are quick to acknowledge that they typically do not have a hand in the test-utilization process.

Subsystem 4: Scoring and Preparation of Feedback Documents

All the large testing companies are significantly involved in one way or another in scoring and preparation of feedback documents. Companies involved with contract testing programs prepare feedback documents which ordinarily go both to the person taking the tests and to the agency holding the testing contract.

Test scoring and preparation of feedback documents are conducted in a variety of ways by these organizations. Harcourt Brace and Houghton Mifflin do not operate scoring services but maintain arrangements with the Measurement Research Center (MRC) in Iowa City, Iowa, to score their tests. In fact, the majority of Harcourt's and Houghton's tests were developed and normed using MRC answer sheets and scoring. Science Research Associates is also primarily tied into the MRC services. MRC performs mechanical and computational tasks to the specifications of the test publisher.

For a number of years the Psychological Corporation experimented with various techniques for mechanical scoring and related problems; however, that work seems to have come to a close. A number of Psychological Corporation personnel were founding stockholders of National Computer Systems, which produces and sells equipment for automated test scoring. Psychological Corporation and California Test Bureau tend to be more closely tied to the National Computer Systems' (NCS) test-scoring operations.

In order to handle the vast volume of tests in its various entrance and admissions programs, Educational Testing Service ties its own scoring machinery to a large computer.

Subsystem 5: Feedback of Test Results

Two different kinds of test users must be considered with regard to the feedback subsystem. First, some test users are also test takers; this is true of those taking tests for guidance or appraisal of vocational interests. A second kind of user includes school systems, admissions officers in colleges, and individuals or institutions using tests that have been administered to other people. In some cases there are two test users for a single test application; in fact, this is the rule where many contract testing activities are concerned.

All the large testing companies provide feedback to the organizational test users who are their principal customers. Feedback is provided primarily through published reports and professional staff consultation with staff members of the client organizations. Feedback to the individual test takers is a more complex problem, however, and one that is often criticized.

It is difficult to prepare feedback documents suitable for all test takers. For example, interpretation that may be too simple for some may be too complex for others. Our personal experience (and that of many other professionals involved in testing activities) indicates that even many well-qualified professionals are unable to understand the complex feedback documents designed to provide many answers to many people. There is undoubtedly a need for simpler material to supplement these documents.

Subsystem 6: Evaluation of the Assessment System

The six largest companies have competence and experience in evaluating assessment systems developed by them or which use their tests. When these companies have contract testing programs (discussed in Chapter 7), evaluation is an integral part of the system. In connection with continued standardizations of the tests they sell, all of these companies do some evaluation of the uses of their products. In addition, several companies are undertaking evaluation of assessment of educational programs as a service offered to clients.

There is some merit in broadening the responsibilities of test publishers to include evaluation of how their materials are contributing to assessment systems. From a practical standpoint, however, it is far from clear how this might be accomplished. One problem is that many test consumers do not rate evaluation procedures highly enough to support assessment activities. Further, since there are thousands of testing programs in operation throughout the nation, test publishers cannot be directly involved in the evaluation of all the programs, even if test consumers called on them to do so. A more appealing strategy would require test users to take greater responsibility for the evaluation of their assessment systems.

Because of their ability to make extensive research commitments designed to keep their product line up-to-date and responsive to changing needs in the testing field, the large companies differ from the smaller companies in the quality of their efforts. These large organizations have often taken part in pioneering new test-related services, such as the rapidly developing test-scoring-and-interpretation field. Another significant contribution the large organizations make to the testing industry as a whole is the participation of their staff members in professional societies concerned with standards of test development, ethical practices, and resolution of public and professional issues concerned with the application of tests.

In many ways, these six testing organizations provide models of comprehensive technical and professional service which represent very high standards of professional practice within the testing industry. The companies compete actively to win contracts, which are awarded on a competitive basis, and to develop new tests as market conditions demand new measurement procedures or materials. Generally they do not interact with persons tested, either during the administration or the feedback activity. Uneven quality of test use results from this lack of involvement and from the failure of test users to evaluate their assessment programs.

REFERENCES

Educational Testing Service. *Establishment of the Educational Testing Service: A Statement by the Board of Trustees.* New York: ETS, Dec. 27, 1947.

World Book Company. *Standardized Testing: An Adventure in Educational Publishing, 1905–1955.* New York: World, August 1954.

4

Other Commercial Test Publishers

Although the six largest test publishers account for more than three-quarters of all tests sold commercially, at least one hundred other persons and organizations offer tests for sale to the general public. These publishers are of two general types, the medium-size commercial publishers that actively engage in the testing business and the one-test publishers that sell tests in addition to, or in support of, some other principal activity.

Medium-Size Test Publishers

The medium-size test publishers include twenty-two organizations that are smaller and more limited in their product line than the largest testing companies, and yet are significantly different from the large number of people and organizations publishing only one or two tests. Most of the medium-size organizations are principally in the testing business rather than in some other field with testing only an adjunctive activity. They advertise, publish catalogues, and display material at professional meetings. These twenty-two companies account for about 5 percent of the test sales made by the testing industry; their annual sales for tests and test services range from approximately $25,000 to $1,000,000.

Origins

While the medium-size organizations vary considerably in company history, some share similar reasons for their existence. Many of the companies originated as a consequence of test development undertaken or sponsored by the founder of the company. Other testing organizations were established when a parent organization purchased a series of tests or acquired other testing companies. For example, The Bobbs-Merrill Company purchased two older testing companies and their inventories as part of its acquisition of book publishing organizations; thus it entered the test distribution business. Though Consulting Psychologists Press was set up to publish the California Psychological Inventory, its growth was stimulated by arrangements to market tests controlled by the Stanford Press.

Organizational Development

The organizational development of these companies has been markedly different. Some companies, such as Psychological Test Specialists, were set up as nonprofit organizations; most, however, were organized as profit-making companies. The medium-size organizations vary significantly in their aggressiveness in developing new products. Some have hired professional staff competent to develop new test materials and weed out outdated tests; others have merely sustained an inventory and continued to offer it so long as a market existed. Some companies, such as American Guidance Service, appear highly motivated to acquire new test inventories and to expand into the instructional materials field. Others, such as Stoelting, maintain no staff of test experts; they depend entirely upon test authors to request inclusion of their materials in the company's catalogues.

Merchandising

Medium-size organizations merchandise their test products through direct-mail advertising, catalogues, and presentation of merchandise at conventions of professional associations. Unlike the larger testing organizations, these companies typically do not employ sales representatives in the field. An exception is Bobbs-Merrill. In their interviews with school district representatives, Bobbs-Merrill's salesmen can also promote test materials; Bobbs-Merrill is, of course, primarily a publishing house with an extensive line of educational materials.

Scoring Services

With regard to test-scoring services, the medium-size companies do not maintain their own computer-based scoring facilities. Some companies offer answer sheets printed in formats that permit machine scoring; the actual work of scoring is typically carried out on contract basis with an independent scoring agency. However, several of the testing organizations offer hand-scoring services which are often related to the handling of test booklets rather than answer sheets.

Similarity of Publishers

Fifteen of these organizations can be discussed as a unit: Consulting Psychologists Press; Educational and Industrial Testing Service; Educators/ Employers Tests and Services Associates; Industrial Psychology, Inc.; Institute for Personality and Ability Testing; University of Iowa Bureau of Educational Research and Service; Personnel Press; Personnel Research Associates, Inc.; Psychological Services, Inc.; Psychological Test Specialists; Richardson, Bellows, and Henry; Scholastic Testing Service; Sheridan Psychological Services, Inc.; Slosson Educational Publications; and Western Psychological Services. Most tests published by these organizations are owned by the test companies. Although few of these organizations have a sales staff as such, all actively market their products, and most distribute some other tests along with their own line. While eleven of the fifteen companies appear to sell more tests to educational institutions than to other customers, four of them (Industrial Psychology; Personnel Research Associates; Psychological Services; and Richardson, Bellows, and Henry) sell primarily to industry.

Resemblance to Large Publishers

At least three of the twenty-two companies (American Guidance Service, Inc., Personnel Press, and The Bobbs-Merrill Company) bear considerable resemblance to the larger test publishers described in Chapter 3. American Guidance Service (AGS) is primarily in the educational publishing field; tests and test services comprise only about one-third of its total business. Its principal customers are schools, which account for approximately 85 percent of its test sales. Shortly after its inception, AGS purchased most of its test inventory from one of the oldest organizations in the testing industry, the Educational Test Bureau. The Bureau had been selling tests, including the Kuhlmann-Anderson Test, since the early 1920's.

Personnel Press develops some of its own tests. Personnel Press was purchased in 1962 by Ginn and Company, a major publisher of educational books and materials; Ginn has recently been purchased by Xerox Corporation. During the past few years, Personnel Press has developed and released several new tests which are distributed through the national sales organization of Ginn. Other new tests, especially textbook-related tests, are currently being developed. Though Personnel Press offers scoring services, either the Educational Records Bureau in New York or Kent State University in Ohio actually performs the scoring.

The Bobbs-Merrill Company entered the testing business through its acquisition of two small publishing companies which owned some tests. Bobbs-Merrill does not maintain a test-development staff.

Some Unique Organizations

The remaining medium-size companies must be considered separately. Dr. Martin M. Bruce's test-publishing activities arose primarily from his own research and consulting work rather than from procurement of tests developed by others or from commercial development of tests (as is true of most of the organizations just discussed).

Family Life Publications, Inc., of Durham, North Carolina, is one of several organizations which publish materials that are not actually tests; however, these materials are sometimes used as tests by schools and counseling agencies. They included a dating-problems check list, marriage-adjustment form, role-expectation inventory, and sex-knowledge inventory.

Two companies active in the medical and scientific field are also test distributors. The first of these, Grune & Stratton, Inc., of New York City, distributes some tests but does not develop tests or provide testing services. Similarly, the C. H. Stoelting Company of Chicago specializes in graphic recording, lie detection, and similar laboratory equipment and also distributes some tests; the company does not do any test-development work of its own.

Guidance Testing Associates of Austin, Texas, is a small nonprofit corporation primarily engaged in the publication and distribution of the Inter-American series of tests which includes parallel English and Spanish editions of the same questions.

Sheridan Psychological Services in Beverly Hills, California, publishes approximately a dozen tests, many of which have separate subtests. All of the tests were developed by Professor J. P. Guilford and his students and associates at the University of Southern California. Most of their tests are sold to universities and clinics, although some are also sold to industrial companies. Unlike other publishers, this company makes almost no sales to elementary schools and few sales to high schools.

The Bureau of Educational Research and Service, a nonprofit subsidiary of the University of Iowa, publishes its own tests and distributes tests published by others. At one time, the Bureau was very active in the development and distribution of tests. It operated without a professional testing activities director for about ten years, during which time the Bureau essentially provided a mail-order sales and scoring service, but did not revise old tests or develop new ones. In 1967, however, the Bureau acquired a new professional director and dropped twelve tests from publication and distribution. The Bureau is now updating all tests that it expects to keep in its battery and is providing current norms for these tests.

Technical Competence

A central question concerns the ability of these medium-size companies to produce and distribute test materials that meet established professional standards. In our opinion, many of these organizations have an adequate capability.

Those companies actually engaged in the development or revision of tests usually employ technical personnel on their staffs or retain professional consultants to ensure test products that will enjoy good reviews. As may be expected, the more aggressive and rapidly growing companies tend to have stronger professional staffing.

A problem of some importance is presented by those organizations that merchandise tests produced by others but do not provide professional editing or reviewing to the test authors. For example, Stoelting, which does not see itself as a testing company and does not wish to expand its test inventory, has for many years published a test catalogue. The selection of materials for inclusion in the company's catalogue appears to be based entirely upon the marketability of the instruments. Stoelting depends on the test author to back up the company's claims for a given test offering. Nevertheless, test materials merchandised through organizations identified only casually with the testing industry represent a very small part of the tests sold annually in the United States.

A further problem develops because not all materials published and used as tests are actually tests. Family Life Publications, for example, produces testlike instruments, primarily inventories and check lists. When these materials are used as tests, the instruments should be evaluated against the *Standards for Educational and Psychological Tests and Manuals*. Of course, *Mental Measurements Yearbook* includes some reviews of materials that are not, strictly speaking, tests; the reviews evaluate the instruments against accepted testing standards.

ATTITUDES TOWARD PROFESSIONAL STANDARDS. Can the medium-size companies afford to invest in the kind of test-development process that will yield instruments to meet the demanding criteria of existing test standards? Some organizations in this group provide clear examples of extensive commitment to measure up in every possible way to the currently recognized standards for test and manual development. Others, however, regard the test standards as somewhat unrealistic, overly demanding, and impossible to meet without unwarranted investment. This point of view is characteristic of organizations that primarily issue individually administered tests for which there is a far more restricted market than for group-administered academic-achievement or ability tests.

A major factor that motivates the medium-size companies to strive to meet professional test standards is that tests enjoying positive reviews appear to have far greater sales potential than those that receive critical reviews. Further, at least two-thirds of the medium-size companies employ staff personnel who are identified with professional associations, such as the American Psychological Association, the American Personnel and Guidance Association, and the American Educational Research Association, that have long encouraged high standards for test development and ethical advertising practices. Additionally, companies with diverse product lines cannot afford to be identified with weak or inadequate testing programs, for a poor reputation in the testing area could detract from a reputation for quality in other areas, such as publication of educational textbooks or instructional materials.

Company Characteristics and Testing Subsystems

The medium-size testing companies differ greatly in their relevance to the six assessment-system criteria previously identified. But the following generalizations point up how limited most of these organizations are, except in the test-development area.

SUBSYSTEM 1: DEFINITION OF ASSESSMENT-SYSTEM REQUIREMENTS. These companies are rarely involved in the early stages of formulating an assessment program and seldom take an active part in the definition of program objectives. Similarly, it is rare for them to be called in on a consulting basis to help restructure a total assessment system. There are exceptions, but most medium-size companies do not have enough qualified personnel to carry out more than very limited consultation.

SUBSYSTEM 2: TEST DEVELOPMENT. Several medium-size companies have continuing relationships with well-qualified test authors whose testing materials they publish; others rely entirely on test authors who may have no continuing relationship with any particular publisher. Most of these organizations do not retain personnel to build tests.

SUBSYSTEM 3: DEFINITION OF SUBJECTS AND TEST ADMINISTRATION. Very few of these companies offer test-administration services. Where such services do exist, they are most likely associated with testing in industry and thus are part of a comprehensive program of testing activities. It is not uncommon for industrial consulting organizations to develop a special set of testing materials which then becomes a part of an assessment battery used by the organizations' consultants.

SUBSYSTEM 4: TEST SCORING AND PREPARATION OF FEEDBACK DOCUMENTS. With very few exceptions, the medium-size companies do not offer scoring services; therefore they do not prepare feedback documents. These companies generally do not have the resources or the personnel capabilities to compete in the automated scoring field.

SUBSYSTEM 5: TEST FEEDBACK. Some medium-size companies that offer direct services, often to industry, become involved in providing feedback of test results to test takers. With these exceptions, the companies in this group are not involved in providing test feedback.

SUBSYSTEM 6: EVALUATION. The medium-size companies that are primarily in the test-publishing business do not become involved in the evaluation of assessment systems. Where direct-testing services are involved in addition to test publication, the evaluation of assessment programs is often a part of the services offered; this is especially true with regard to industrial uses of tests. Some medium-size companies have excellent capabilities for conducting evaluative research.

To summarize, these twenty-two companies are competently and seriously in the testing business. With few exceptions, and most of these highly debatable, the companies do a good job of meeting the requirements of the *Test Standards Manual*. Almost without exception, they appear to be profitable operations. Thus, we may expect that in the future most of them will continue to grow and a number of them will be targets for purchase activity by larger corporations which either want to diversify or to get into the testing field or some branch of the commercial education market.

Small Test Publishers

The testing industry includes many small operations. More than one hundred persons and organizations distribute one or two tests each; to the best of our knowledge, none of them employs even one person full-time to develop and sell tests. The Appendix contains brief descriptions of thirty-six organizations that are typical of this publishing group; however, in view of the variety within the group, it is unlikely that all variations have been listed. Many of these publishers entered the test-publishing field in ways that lead us to consider them "unintentional test publishers." All the small publishers are primarily engaged in some other activity, such as teaching in a university, conducting research, operating a corporate personnel department, or running a professional association. Apparently, the small organizations' involvement in, and commitment to, the psychological testing industry is often minor and is always secondary to some other line of endeavor.

It is important to realize that many of the small companies concerned with the sales of testing materials are not offering tests at all, despite inclusion of the materials in such authoritative reference works as the *Mental Measurements Yearbook*. Often the product line of these organizations is limited to health inventories, check lists, brief questionnaires, and similar materials which technically do not qualify as tests.

In terms of annual sales, we estimate that the typical small company is generating less than $25,000 from test products; altogether, these companies account for less than 5 percent of the total market. The financial facts of life, therefore, make it unlikely that a small test publisher can make a large investment in the standardization, renovation, or redevelopment of his products. The overwhelming majority of the small test publishers do not appear oriented toward growth.

Development of Tests

Many test instruments sold by individuals and organizations in this group were originally developed in connection with research projects such as doctoral dissertations or research on mental health. Once a test has been developed for a research project, publication of information about the research often leads to requests for the test. If the test author does not make his material available, then his research or development work has been largely wasted; most professionals consider this an undesirable situation. Thus, the test author begins to produce copies of the instrument and to give them away or sell them, generally at minimal cost, to interested research workers. Should the author find that his test appears promising for use in personnel selection or medical diagnosis, he may feel some pressure to provide a useful instrument as soon as possible.

If the author wishes to make his material available to others, he can do so in any of three ways: (1) He can market the material in its preliminary form, preferably designating it an experimental test. (2) He can rapidly collect additional data and provide a manual of instructions, validity and reliability data, and test norms that will meet the requirements of the *Standards for Educational and Psychological Tests and Manuals*. (3) He can contract with a larger test publisher to handle his test. Since costs for the extensive work necessary to standardize a test, prepare manuals for it, and conduct the required validity studies typically range from $25,000 to $250,000, major test publishers are unlikely to be interested in a test unless it shows a great deal of promise.

Tests published by members of this publishing group generally are first offered without complete reliability or validity data and often without an adequate manual. The inadequacy of data provided may earn negative reviews for the tests; however, the reviews may stimulate interest in the test or motivate others to use it. Professional and scientific interest, and perhaps even financial interest, in the test may be sufficiently high that an author cannot completely ignore the possibilities his test presents. Thus the cycle continues, usually at an economic level too low to support adequate test development.

Test instruments sold by this group of publishers have sometimes been designed and developed by the personnel department of an organization for personnel selection and similar programs. Such tests are sometimes offered for public sale more or less as a consequence of demand for the materials. Small test publishers also develop some tests in connection with special scholarships or educational programs. One of the best examples of a testing program created for special use is the annual Westinghouse Science Search which utilizes the Science Aptitude Examination published in a different form each year by Performance Research.

Some tests published by small companies are part of a fairly complete testing system, most often a system developed for scholarship selection and language proficiency. Other tests, such as Dr. H. C. Tien's Organic Integrity Test and the tests of the Winter Haven Lions Research Foundation, are used by people who provide the publisher with a continuing source of validity data.

Technical Competence

Some persons who develop and publish a limited number of tests lack formal training in educational and psychological measurement; other small publishers, however, are highly respected members of the testing profession. Because of the vast differences in requirements for test development, some limited-purpose tests developed by persons with little test training may be as useful for their specific purposes as are the more complex and sophisticated tests designed by persons with greater technical training.

Organizations such as the Winter Haven Lions Foundation establish testing programs with the guidance of professionals who serve as consultants. The Foundation primarily concerns itself with research on blindness; however, it makes available a reading test which uses geometrical forms developed by Dr. Arnold Gessell of Yale. Competent consultants supervise work on the test, which is used by over two thousand schools.

Company Characteristics and Testing Subsystems

The small test companies are related to the educational and psychological measurement process exclusively as suppliers of tests; they offer virtually no other services. If we evaluate these companies in the framework of the six assessment subsystems described earlier, we find that most small test publishers contribute only to the test-development subsystem. A few also provide consultation on use and interpretation of their instruments.

The range of technical competence exhibited by this group of organizations is very great; some are highly qualified test developers but, at the other extreme, many claim no psychometric expertise whatever. From the standpoint of adherence to the usual professional standards, this situation is clearly undesirable; but whether any substantial harm is done remains open to debate. Most critics of testing have focused their attacks on the major producers of tests and the large-scale testing programs. The small test publisher has rarely been singled out for criticism. Although this may be due in part to the very small contribution such publishers make to the testing that goes on nationally, the lack of criticism may also be attributed to the relatively innocuous nature of their products.

Most products of the small testing companies do not shape decisions concerning employment or educational opportunities, nor are they engaged in gatekeeping functions; thus, their activities do not have broad social implications. Nevertheless, although many of these organizations may do no great harm, they are detached from the mainstream of professional work in the field of human assessment, and they are extremely limited in their capability to contribute to the elements of a competent assessment system. These factors concern us as evaluators. The small test publisher is obviously not in a position to exert leadership, to underwrite research, or to require high standards of practice of those who buy his tests. We can hope that the more significant products of this group will receive the attention and developmental efforts given the better products of the larger organizations described earlier.

5

Government Use of Tests for Employment

Federal, state, and local governments become involved in testing primarily through their roles as employers and educators. Some government agencies develop their own tests, but many purchase testing materials from organizations specializing in public personnel work. To a limited extent, government agencies also sell tests. This chapter discusses government use of tests for employment of both military and civilian personnel.

Selection and Classification for Military Service

The American military services make extensive use of testing procedures. From the standpoint of personnel matters, the problem faced by the military services is this: Given a large pool of manpower, how can individuals be sorted out according to aptitude for participation in the military services? Concerning inductees, a more refined question on classification and training is raised: What kind of school or job assignment is most suitable for a given individual? These fundamental and highly practical questions regarding personnel selection and classification were the foundation blocks for major personnel-program developments within our military services.

As background for the major personnel-research commitments currently made by the military services, it is instructive to consider a brief history of personnel testing and research within the Army. The scope and depth of personnel research activity have broadened extensively since World War II. Army researchers have gone beyond test development, administration, interpretation, and reporting of results to investigate areas of motivation, leadership, training, and morale.

History of Personnel Testing in the Army

At the time of the declaration of war in 1917, the Army had no systematic testing program for selection and classification. Initiative was taken by a group of distinguished psychologists who, offering their services to the government, quickly put together adaptations of the group tests by Otis. These tests, the Army Alpha, designed to be used with literate recruits, and the Army Beta, a performance test designed for use with men who could not read or write English, were the principal examination tools. Assessment of aptitude for training or job assignment was emphasized.

During World War I, the foundation was laid for systematic and objective procedures for classifying and selecting Army personnel. From 1921 to 1939, the Army resumed pre-World War I procedures, which amounted to use of an apprenticeship system for selecting and assigning recruits. But, during these years, there were many advances in the field of ability, achievement, and vocational testing. By October 1940, the Army's new General Classification Test (AGCT) had been prepared and standardized; additional and improved forms appeared a year later. Nonlanguage tests for illiterates, tests of mechanical and clerical skills and aptitudes, and tests of vocational knowledge were also prepared. The emphasis of classification and testing strategy was on measurement of "trainability," i.e., whether a person will benefit from an Army training program. While testing programs in the military services have changed over the years, the basic concern for predicting success in training remains a major objective of selection and classification programs.

The current Army classification battery employs eleven tests which are highly successful in predicting "trainability." In accordance with previous national policies, little systematic information is available concerning performance of different racial groups on these tests. The Army, however, has a considerable interest in reaching a better understanding of the relationships between race, socioeconomic background, rural vs. urban upbringing, and other variables that may be important factors in determining training or job success.

Most frequently, complaints about testing in the Army and other military services are caused by misunderstandings about the purposes of tests or their content. For example, after taking a series of tests that evaluated his visual *judgment,* one man complained that he was being subjected to inadequate and superficial techniques for measuring his visual *acuity.* Similarly, another man, after taking an information test on knowledge about helicopters, complained that he could not be expected to know the answers prior to completion of a training program about these aircraft (Uhlaner, 1966). Despite occasional protests, the Army has successfully convinced millions of inductees that they are being given an objective opportunity to "show their stuff" in order to qualify for the jobs or training assignments most suited both to the needs of the Army and to the interests and abilities of the inductees.

Since World War II, we have seen increased commitment within the Army to provide a research base not only for classification and assignment, but also for a broad array of other human concerns. These have included, for example, systematic research on how people learn to perform various tasks vital to the Army. The Army's commitment to generate useful research information in such areas as motivation, leadership, training, and morale seems far afield from the earlier concentration on aptitude testing. The implications of this research are quite clear, however, for the results of such research often find their way into test batteries. Several major units within the Army Behavioral Science Laboratory, an activity of the Office of the Chief of Research and Development, are responsible for carrying out military-selection research.

In summary, the Army has an extensive and historic commitment to test development and related personnel research. The extent and comprehensiveness of these research commitments and the general acceptance of testing programs sponsored by the Army are particularly noteworthy.

Testing in the Navy and the Air Force

Both the Navy and Air Force also have extensive organizations concerned with systematic assessment of job specifications, training requirements, and description of aptitudes and achievements appropriate to selection and classification. Like the Army, these services have been primarily concerned with initial screening with respect to ability and subsequently with classifying personnel into training programs. Ability assessment has been standardized across the services through the use of a common Armed Forces Qualification Test (AFQT). But the Navy and Air Force have developed their own special test instruments for classifying personnel. In addition to publishing the officer and airman qualifying examinations which are the backbone of pre-enlistment testing, the Air Force publishes scores of language and proficiency tests and batteries of examinations which cover knowledge in vocational areas.

One of the most extensive personnel research and development programs ever conducted for the purposes of trainee selection and classification was the air-crew-selection program carried out during World War II. The major objective was to make the best possible selection of men for placement in various training schools. The testing program proved very successful in increasing the prediction of success of men assigned to various training units.

Since World War II, there has been a need for human-factors research that would provide a better foundation, not only for selection and classification research, but also for redesign of training programs. Both the Navy and Air Force have operated research centers concerned with these functions and have contracted extensively with individuals and organizations to carry out project research.

Evaluation of Military Testing

Our impression of testing and personnel research in the Army, Navy, and Air Force is that the military programs are quite effective. Their procedures appear to be technically sophisticated, and their staffs are highly qualified from a professional standpoint. Their orientations are increasingly directed toward a systematic view of personnel selection, classification, training, and evaluation.

Selective Service Tests of College Aptitude

During periods of national emergency such as the Korean and Vietnam conflicts, the Selective Service System has contracted with large national testing organizations for the development of tests intended to assess aptitude for college success. Both the Educational Testing Service and Science Research Associates have taken this responsibility, using procedures described in Chapter 9, which concerns contract testing programs. The results of these tests and the basic normative data essential to interpret the meaning of the results are made available to local Selective Service boards. Local boards have been given considerable autonomy in their use of these test results.

U.S. Civil Service Commission

In filling a job vacancy, a government organization must deal not only with the general problems of selecting the best-qualified person but also with problems related to the organization's role as an agency that must serve citizens who are also potential employees or job applicants. Public-employment testing is carried out by federal, state, and local governments as part of an attempt to fill job vacancies on the basis of merit rather than patronage. Because of public concern for fairness in public employment, the testing and other employment activities of government agencies are generally open to public scrutiny and challenge by any unsuccessful job applicant.

The U.S. Civil Service Commission, created by act of Congress in 1883, has major personnel responsibilities covering nearly all federal jobs. These responsibilities include the establishment of standards for job classification throughout the federal government, the establishment of competitive examination procedures for filling job openings, and the establishment and implementation of personnel policies regulating practices of government agencies. Thus the Commission operates not only a complete testing system as we have defined it, but operates it within the context of an integrated personnel system as well.

Most test construction for competitive examinations is carried out by personnel on the staff of the Civil Service Commission. In the past, the Commission made very limited use of commercial tests, mainly on a pilot basis; however, recent regulations have reduced this practice. Occasionally, the Commission contracts with outside organizations for special research. For example, a current project involving the study of test bias in relation to the assessment of minority-group applicants is being conducted jointly with the Educational Testing Service.

Changes in Testing Practices

During the past five years, revolutionary changes have taken place in the role assigned to formal testing in the appraisal of job applicants. The scope of these changes can be appreciated when one looks at government testing practices as they existed until very recently. A review of this topic by Goslin (1963, pp. 101–120) is summarized below.

Until the mid-1920's, the typical applicant for an entry level position in the lower classification grades was faced with filling out a Form 57, the basic application for federal employment, and then with taking at least one battery of tests designed to establish his qualifications in a competitive examination. For example, an applicant for a stenographic or clerical position would be asked to take both a performance test and a written examination which encompassed such skills as spelling, work knowledge, and basic arithmetic. An applicant for a position involving a trade skill might take a similar test battery plus a specialized job-knowledge test.

Recent national policies which encourage the greatest possible job opportunities for minority group members have created pressures to evaluate the appropriateness of job-application testing. As a consequence of these pressures, the government has adopted a more flexible procedure for appraising an individual's competence to fill a specific position. For example, a so-called job-element system of applicant appraisal is now in use to fill all trade jobs in government agencies. This system employs the following steps.

First, an analysis of the elements of each job is made. Basically, this involves preparing a detailed statement of job requirements for the separate elements that comprise a total position or set of work responsibilities. For example, the following job elements might be specified for the position of offset printing press operator: (1) sets up offset printing press and makes it ready to run, (2) adjusts inking controls in accordance with requirements of various plates and papers, (3) replaces "blankets" and other components that are required, (4) monitors and adjusts press operation to maintain consistent quality throughout run.

Second, the ability of an applicant to fulfill these job requirements is evaluated in terms of evidence of competence rather than number of months or years of work experience in a related position. The job-element system requires the applicant to offer evidence of his ability to fill the demands of a given position. Such evidence of ability could be obtained from letters of reference, telephone checks with former supervisors, a certificate of completion of a training course, or demonstrated ability to perform job elements in an actual work situation.

This greater reliance on demonstrated ability to cope with specified job elements rather than on formal training, years of experience, or performance on a written aptitude test reportedly evokes more public acceptance of the civil service examination procedure and greatly improves the chances of minority-group members to qualify for federal positions.

Another example of the same trend is the recently established policy of accepting proficiency certification in lieu of formal examinations conducted by the federal civil service. Such a means of establishing competence is preferable for individuals who, though quite capable of performing the task to be evaluated, find examination situations threatening.

Generally, formal testing and examination procedures are being replaced with other techniques designed to assess as directly as possible an individual's competence to perform a specific task or set of tasks. For example, the Federal Civil Service Entrance Examination has long been used to evaluate the college-equivalent training and experience of those who apply for administrative positions; the examination has also been used to test many college graduates seeking federal employment. Now, although the examination is still given, the Graduate Record Examination or a high-grade point average in college work can substitute for the civil service examination.

This reduced emphasis on aptitude testing is not so much a totally new policy within the federal civil service as it is an extension of long-standing policies concerning evaluation for promotion or appointment of applicants for higher-level government positions. In these cases, aptitude tests have for many years been supplanted by evidence of job performance, work-history information, and ratings of supervisors. Evaluations of this kind, together with such related test data as may be needed, are now being required for most of the entry-level positions in the federal civil service. At the lowest end of the job classification spectrum, some trainee positions require no testing of any kind.

In summary, the Civil Service Commission is still concerned with administering merit examinations and with opening job opportunities to those most successful in a competitive examination. However, in response to dissatisfactions expressed by minority-group spokesmen, the Commission has made major changes in the structure and character of civil service assessment procedures. The current emphasis is on flexibility in the assessment of job-related competences as evidenced by work history, job performance, life experiences directly related to a job requirement, and other evidence of ability to perform a given set of assignments. The Civil Service Commission is deeply concerned with avoiding possibilities of built-in bias in the process of evaluating minority-group members for employment.

It is far too early to evaluate the effectiveness of these new procedures; data necessary to make such an assessment are not currently available. But if the new, more flexible evaluation procedures hold up, and there are reasons to believe they will, the trend may well bring more flexible evaluation procedures to local and state government merit programs. In any case, it seems clear that written tests designed to measure job-rated abilities, interests, or competences are going to have to show greater predictive value than they have in the past, or they will lose their central position in some evaluation programs.

U.S. Employment Service

The U.S. Employment Service (USES), a part of the Department of Labor's Bureau of Employment Security, develops tests primarily for use by state employment service agencies which are affiliates of USES. This work is carried out by research psychologists on the staff of USES and by groups with which USES has contracts. USES publishes the well-known General Aptitude Test Battery (GATB); it makes available tests of proficiency in dictation, typing, and spelling, and also a series of Oral Trade Questions. Because USES cannot directly control the sale and use of its tests, its activities are probably less system-oriented than are the activities of any other agency discussed in this chapter. However, they are more system-oriented than are many programs using tests for selection in industry.

State agencies typically use the testing materials to provide vocational guidance and counseling information for persons seeking employment. To some extent they also use the tests as a basis for making job referrals or recommendations for participation in training programs. In addition to providing these tests to state employment services, USES makes the materials available to schools and other organizations, both public and private, which have appropriate professional staffing and USES authorization for use of its tests.

From the technical standpoint, the research base for this battery is extensive. Efforts have been made over several decades to generate validity data relating GATB scores to a variety of criterion variables. Despite this, opinions about the tests range from antagonistic to enthusiastic. Commercial publishers of competing batteries are least enthusiastic.

Representatives of some commercial publishers have been critical of the GATB on grounds that it is not a "secure" test; i.e., an applicant can obtain a copy of the test for practice purposes. Since some evidence exists that practice in test taking results in changes in scores, there is no assurance that a given set of scores is not attributable, in part at least, to practice effects (Dvorak, 1968). Those who use the test and produce it seem to be aware of this particular difficulty; they have taken what steps they can to sustain the confidentiality of the test content. In at least two states, however, coaching services are reportedly available to assist job applicants to earn high GATB scores.

Another criticism of the GATB has been that it is not a fair test from the cultural standpoint; of course, many familiar psychological tests have also received such criticism. In any case, efforts are now underway to produce a more culture-free version of the GATB which would, presumably, overcome at least some of the objections that have been raised by spokesmen for minority groups. We shall be discussing the general problem of testing and discrimination in Chapter 12.

Evaluation of Federal Government Testing

Federal government testing programs generally provide a good example of system-oriented assessment with all subsystems monitored by administratively responsible and technically competent people. These programs are exemplary, especially with respect to the evaluation subsystem. They are becoming increasingly sensitive to problems of personal and minority-group rights because of the political pressures to which they are subject. Fortunately, those political pressures do not seem to have led to technically inadvisable compromises in test-system design and implementation.

State Civil Service Testing Programs

The pattern which the federal government established for selection and promotion based on education, experience, and objective examinations has been generally adopted by the states in their efforts to fill job vacancies on the basis of merit rather than patronage. Federal procedures have been emulated, both because of their popularity with voters and applicants and because of the assistance given by the federal government. The Division of State Merit Systems of the Department of Health, Education, and Welfare provides consultation and other services to help state government administrators develop and strengthen merit systems of public employment.

In addition to the state civil service commissions, thousands of municipal agencies at local levels engage in employment-testing activities. The larger of these agencies operate much like the federal and state agencies; the smaller ones make greater use of outside help in test development.

Public-Personnel Testing

Because of the different needs they are intended to serve, the testing procedures of state and local governments differ from most other employment-testing procedures. First, because of the need for public knowledge of all aspects of the process, it is not possible to maintain secrecy of the test items; therefore, a test usually cannot be used for more than one hiring period. For this reason, it is difficult and generally not worth the trouble to validate the test against job-performance criteria. Second, since external validation is not used, selection of test questions and answers is based on "expert judgment" rather than on psychometric or statistical data. Finally, as a result of the preceding considerations, there is considerable reliance on job-knowledge questions. The procedures for testing in this area were recently described in great detail by Donovan (1968).

Typical Public-Personnel Test-Development Process

Forbes McCann (1968) described a set of procedures used in item and test development for public-personnel tests. We believe these procedures are typically followed by both government and private-personnel test-development agencies:

1. The occupation to be tested (policeman, nurse, fireman, etc.) must be defined.
2. A subject-matter index "of all the knowledge which falls within the periphery of the occupational area" must be developed. For example, "within 'Nursing,' a few of the subject-matter areas might be 'Bedside Care,' 'Feeding,' 'Maintaining Patient Morale,' 'Ward Supervision,' and 'Nursing Department Administration.'" The purpose of developing a subject-matter index is to define "with workable specificity individual subject-matter knowledge areas which might or might not be appropriately included in a test for any single occupation . . .
   "This subject-matter index serves many purposes. It provides defined terminology that is used in discussing and planning the content appropriate for any specific test. It is used to classify individual items. It provides a way to ensure that the necessary subject-matter knowledges have not been overlooked. It provides the tool by which to define the proportions of test questions on each subject-matter area.
3. "Once the subject-matter index is completed, the next step in developing a test for a specific occupation is developing the test plan." This is done in

cooperation with administrative personnel familiar with the positions to be filled by use of the test.

4. The test developer then prepares job-knowledge items which cover the specified number of items representing different parts of a subject-matter area. These items are referred to an item editor who reviews and edits test items for style, format, content, and technical accuracy.

5. A test is then reviewed, either by having subject-matter experts look over the items, or by administering the test to personnel currently working in a given occupation. The purpose of this is to discover ambiguities and factual inaccuracies, and to iron out other bugs in the first draft of a test.

6. "Responses are scored, and item analysis is made to identify questions and choices within a question that are not up to established standards." The object of this analysis is to improve or eliminate defective items or choices.

7. Test items are then assembled into a test which is administered to a group of job candidates.

8. "After the test has been held, we score it and make item analyses, using the split-halves technique or, if the competition is sufficiently large, split-quarters or the top and bottom 27 percent.

9. "On the basis of the item-analysis data, we may determine that items should be double-keyed or omitted or scored with a different key in the final scoring of the candidates' papers in the test for which the item was used. On the basis of the revised scores, we make our recommendations to the client."

Note that in this process no external criterion measure of job success is involved. The assessment of the extent to which items contribute to the success of the test is based on their relationship to the rest of the test items and on expert judgment of knowledge needed. We do not allege that the entire process is necessarily unsatisfactory but rather that, given this procedure alone, it is impossible to say whether the test actually measures what it purports to measure.

Perhaps two major factors are currently sustaining the present operational pattern of public-employment testing: (1) the consumers (users and takers) of these tests are often not specialists in test development or test utilization; (2) the procedures have apparently worked well enough to enjoy acceptable public evaluation over the years. Indeed, there are some parts of the country in which the image of civil service testing suggests that public employment testing procedures have an almost magical quality of objectivity and purity.

Government-Related or Supported Public Personnel Agencies

The government sometimes contracts with government-sponsored or private organizations which develop public-employment tests for use by various government agencies. Four examples of independent agencies follow.

PUBLIC PERSONNEL ASSOCIATION. The Public Personnel Association (PPA) is a national group of public officials responsible for a variety of personnel functions in civil service commissions, personnel boards, merit system councils, schools and colleges, and public utilities. Among the many services PPA offers member government agencies is an extensive testing program geared to public-employment selection and promotion.

Approximately fifty employees are concerned with PPA's test-development activity. The Association has never retained a doctoral-level testing specialist; however, a Master's-level test-development expert was responsible for some aspects of the testing program in the past.

For many years, PPA sponsored a Test Exchange Library which collected test materials supplied by various government agencies and held them in a central pool for cooperative use. In the early 1950's, PPA established a testing service and issued a series of objective tests known as the General Form Tests, which typically include from one to two hundred multiple choice items and cover a variety of occupations. The format for developing these tests appears to be very similar to that described by McCann (1968).

A second major series of tests, the Ready-to-Use Tests, is offered for the more common entrance-level positions, such as firefighter, accountant/clerk, truck driver, policeman, engineering aide, office worker, and mechanical handyman. Tests are also available for assessment of applicants to professional positions at all levels. Virtually every occupation is covered by one or more of the job-knowledge tests available from this organization.

A major question concerning this testing program involves the basic technical adequacy of the products. There are virtually no normative or validity data suitable for making a technical appraisal of the instruments. Although PPA does not carry out validity studies, the organization encourages local users to do so. Our impression is that little in the way of validity studies is actually done. Further, test revision by PPA seems to boil down to introducing new or altered job-knowledge items. In place of statistical or psychometric criteria for such modification, there appears to be complete reliance upon expert judgment.

Some of the materials that PPA issues for public-employment selection purposes are sold with the agreement that they will not be changed by the user. These tests come closest to having some semblance of standardization; still they are not represented as measuring up to the generally accepted criteria for standardized tests. There are no restrictions on reproduction of most of the PPA's tests and answer sheets. Hence, the Association does not know exactly how much utilization is made of testing materials which it generates. Nor is there any way to keep track of the kinds of changes and alterations introduced locally into its tests. Such practices are not discouraged, in spite of the fact that the organization's catalogue includes a sample test-security agreement requiring test users to express willingness to control and guard tests in a professional way.

In answer to a question concerning the methods used to evaluate the appropriateness of the tests issued to government agencies, the response was: "The only way we can evaluate our tests is through feedback from government agencies. We get very little negative feedback (Byerly, 1967)."

INDUSTRIAL RELATIONS CENTER: UNIVERSITY OF CHICAGO. A different model of personnel research and test application is offered by the Industrial Relations Center at the University of Chicago. Concern for public-employment testing is only a small part of the Center's over-all mission. The primary goal is to carry out research and training services and, on a consulting basis, to prepare and apply personnel tests for industries or organizations which contract with the Center. For example, the Chicago Police Department has contracted with the Center to develop a personnel-selection battery. The organization does not develop and publish tests for sale, however.

The unique feature of this organization is that it offers a truly comprehensive system-oriented service which may even be purchased by relatively small companies. The Center's activities typically begin with systematic job-and-worker analyses; only after completion of these analyses are tests developed or tried out. The results of testing and assessment procedures in organizations contracting with the Center are followed up over a couple of years. This makes possible the development of data pertaining to validation of selection procedures. The Industrial Relations Center's unique program points up both the opportunities and the needs for continuing research in this field of testing.

AMERICAN PUBLIC HEALTH ASSOCIATION'S PROFESSIONAL EXAMINATION SERVICE. The Professional Examination Service (PES) is concerned with the development and use of "written communications that measure the competence of professional people (APHA; p. 5)." For a single annual fee, state agencies may make unlimited use of the PES examination resources. These include access to over seven hundred examinations in twenty-five professional areas with new materials being produced annually; consultation services and scoring services are included.

Over the past quarter of a century, PES has pioneered in developing objective testing procedures for evaluating professionals in twenty-five professional fields. Representatives of the Professional Examination Service have been prominent as participants on national committees of health personnel. The director, Dr. Lillian D. Long, serves as a consultant to the Advisory Committee on Merit System Standards under the Secretary of Health, Education, and Welfare.

An amendment of the Social Security Act, passed in 1939, required states to establish merit-system procedures for certain programs receiving federal support. This action created the need for examinations to be used by the states in the selection of professional public health personnel; in response, a program for providing such tests was established within the American Public Health Association. Further, a program of field consultation was set up to assist government agencies in using PES and in interpreting the test results.

Recent legislative development in the health field, particularly the Medicare legislation, has had a tremendous impact on the activities of the Professional Examination Service. PES assists the states and the Medicare program in carrying out licensing programs and in establishing the qualifications and standards of practitioners in science fields. PES examinations are given in the areas of laboratory science, medicine, pharmacy, physical therapy, psychology, sanitation, veterinary medicine, and nursing-home administration. The organization is involved daily with the need for selecting, licensing, evaluating, and deploying health personnel in this country.

A rapidly expanding area of service involves development and validation of examinations used in university graduate programs. Testing projects in the fields of radiological health and vocational counseling have been applied in over seventy institutions throughout the country. PES is now working with appropriate federal agencies to develop nationwide examination programs.

Examination security is very highly valued. Thus, for a number of years the Professional Examination Service was unable to serve certain state civil service organizations whose local procedures required that examination material be open to public inspection.

MCCANN ASSOCIATES. McCann Associates, based in Philadelphia, is one of several privately owned organizations that develop and distribute public-personnel tests to government agencies throughout the nation. With nine employees, the company develops and offers tests covering hundreds of different employment positions, including policemen, automotive mechanics, clerical workers, electricians, mechanics, secretaries, and hundreds of other public employees. This organization will either sell materials to government agencies or rent test booklets. It also offers scoring and reporting services.

When special needs or secure tests are essential, McCann Associates undertakes a custom program of test development which ranges from job analysis through development of new questions, scoring, item analysis, and interpretation and reporting of results. McCann Associates does not supplement its testing programs with materials produced elsewhere, nor does the organization produce personality tests.

Evaluation of Public-Employment Testing

One of the peculiarities of public-employment testing is that the assembly of individual test units is often highly nonstandard. This results in a very large number of one-time only testing programs which are virtually impossible to evaluate. It is beyond the scope of the current report to attempt a quality evaluation of the thousands of tests currently in use for public-employment purposes. However, it is our impression that the technical adequacy of many of these instruments is open to serious question.

While standardized performance procedures, as in the case of tests of typing, plastering, or motor-vehicle operation are generally adequate, there appear to be many unanswered and important questions concerning what is actually measured by many of the so-called job-knowledge tests. These instruments appear to rely almost entirely on the assumption that high job knowledge necessarily implies a competent employee and screens out an unsatisfactory applicant. Also, it is highly questionable that a job-knowledge test can assess some of the more essential or critical aspects of job performance. Further, from the variety of opinions on what constitutes a good policeman, social worker, or telephone operator, one can see that it is often debatable what the critical aspects of performance may be.

If the experience of the military services can be used as a rough basis for making judgments about the probable job-related validity of public-employment tests, we may estimate that less than 10 percent of the variance associated with job success in public employment is actually measured by tests or test batteries. At least this is approximately the best that testing programs have been able to do in predicting job success in the Army. (Note that this is substantially lower than the predictability of success in Army training programs.) If we are highly concerned about selecting the most appropriate applicant for a public-employment position, we shall have to give far greater attention to measuring the remaining 90 percent variance of job success. One of the complicating factors here is that, given the same occupation, radically different criteria of job success may be appropriate under two different supervisors.

System Analysis and Evaluation

Tests used for employment by state and local governments generally are part of a system-oriented selection-and-placement process; further, all elements of the process are generally under the control of a single person or agency. Although these organizations tend to lump all similar jobs together, they do study the job requirements more thoroughly than is the case in industrial personnel selection. At the federal and state level, test development is usually competently done by professionals in personnel testing. At the local level, there is much more emphasis on test items than on tests; in fact, tests are most often simply assembled from previously used items which appear useful for a job or job family. New items are developed to test for any unique aspects (such as geography or specialized equipment) of the job for which the test is being developed.

Administration of the tests, usually well conducted, is done by the "merit system" or by the personnel office of the government body that is doing the hiring. Either the personnel office or the test developer, if a contract developer is used, can score tests. Scoring is usually done by hand, since most tests are used only once. There is probably no area of testing where less preparation of feedback documents is done; feedback is usually limited to publishing the list of test takers and their scores. The usual feedback consists of a list of test takers, rank-ordered by final score, with scores shown for those who passed the test; diagnostic or predictive feedback is almost nonexistent. Much more interpretation may be done later if someone protests the test or some of its items. Test items are generallly evaluated rather than tests themselves. However, a test answer key may be changed if it appears from the item analysis that a change is desirable.

Government employment is clearly an area in which the quality of the process varies according to the funds available and the qualifications of the administrators. Federal-employment testing, both military and civilian, has generally been considered a model for other governments; it is based on good research and evaluation. A similar pattern is found in many states, especially the larger states with mature merit-oriented personnel systems. The methods used at the local level, though well adapted to the administrative and political problems faced by test administrators, are less satisfactory technically because of the lack of validation of most tests used at this level.

REFERENCES

American Public Health Association. Professional Examination Service brochure.

Byerly, S. Interview, Chicago, Illinois, July 19, 1967.

Donovan, J. J., ed. *Recruitment and Selection in the Public Service*. Chicago: Public Personnel Association, 1968.

Dvorak, Beatrice. Interview, Washington, D.C., August 9, 1968.

Goslin, D. A. *The Search for Ability*. New York: Russell Sage Foundation, 1963.

McCann, Forbes. Personal correspondence, February 8, 1968.

Uhlaner, J. E. Personal correspondence to Dr. Launor Carter, Chairman, Committee on Assessment, July 22, 1966.

6

State Educational Testing Programs

In addition to their sponsorship of employment testing, states conduct educational testing programs, generally under the auspices of state departments of education. For the most part, the state departments of education have administrative control of state educational testing programs, whether the programs are voluntary or compulsory. These programs are informally coordinated by an Annual Conference of Statewide Testing Program Directors sponsored by Educational Testing Service. The annual conferences provide a forum for discussion of major testing programs and problems. *State Testing Programs: A Survey of Functions, Tests, Materials, and Services*, published by Educational Testing Service, Princeton, New Jersey, in 1968, contains a valuable and comprehensive description of the state testing programs.

Earlier in this book we noted the significance of academic ability and achievement testing. Most tests falling into this category are selected by individual school districts on the basis of their own needs; however, a large part of the educational testing market is controlled or directly influenced by state testing policies. Of the thirty states that carry out some kind of academic ability or achievement testing program or testing service, the overwhelming majority administer either one or two state-wide tests.[1] Five states administer compulsory testing activities, and one state has a partly voluntary, partly

[1] The states include Alabama, Arkansas, California, Colorado, Delaware, Florida, Hawaii, Idaho, Illinois, Indiana, Iowa, Kansas, Kentucky, Maryland, Michigan, Minnesota, Missouri, New Hampshire, New Jersey, New York, North Dakota, Ohio, Rhode Island, South Dakota, Tennessee, Texas, Virginia, Washington, West Virginia, Wisconsin.

compulsory program.[2] A substantial part of this testing activity was stimulated by provisions and funding under Title V-A of the National Defense Education Act (NDEA) which concerned counseling and guidance in the secondary schools. In all states, testing is mandatory for schools participating in NDEA Title V-A programs.

Guidance and counseling procedures that make heavy utilization of test results are not typically found in elementary schools. In the lower grade levels, the primary purposes of testing programs tend to be centered on student evaluation and evaluation of instruction and curricula.

Test Development

Most of the states rely heavily on nationally standardized instruments for use in their testing programs; however, some state agencies or school districts either do their own test development or make some kind of contract arrangements with an outside agency. At least twenty-seven testing programs rely upon specially prepared materials, although many of these combine custom testing with use of nationally standardized tests.[3]

Examples of State-Wide Testing Programs

State-wide testing programs vary widely in size, competence, and types of testing activities. Below we discuss five different kinds of state educational testing programs which illustrate most of the characteristics of programs in the various states.

New York and Ohio provide diverse examples of states extensively committed to custom test development. California exemplifies a more typical state program in which the state purchases tests from commercial test publishers. Minnesota's program is unique in that it is administered by the University of Minnesota rather than by the state department of education. West Virginia illustrates the testing practices of a small state-wide testing program.

New York State Department of Education

For over one hundred years, the New York State Department of Education has been responsible for major test-development activities. Its program of

[2] The five states are California, Hawaii, New York, Rhode Island, and Virginia. The state operating the voluntary/compulsory program is West Virginia.

[3] The states are Alabama, Arkansas, California, Delaware, Florida, Hawaii, Illinois, Indiana, Iowa, Kentucky, Maryland, Michigan, Minnesota, Missouri, New Hampshire, New Jersey, New York, North Dakota, Ohio, Rhode Island, South Carolina, South Dakota, Tennessee, Texas, Virginia, West Virginia, Wisconsin.

test development and testing services is in dramatic contrast with most other state programs which undertake virtually no test development. Currently, eighty persons are employed by the Department of Education to assist in testing work; in addition, committees of teachers and other professionals are used on a consulting basis to prepare test items. Tests developed under the auspices of the New York State Department of Education are not sold or distributed outside the state.

NEW YORK REGENTS EXAMINATION. Best known of the New York programs are the New York State Regents Examinations administered in grades nine through twelve. According to ETS (1968, p. 79), the major purposes of these examinations are: (1) "to furnish schools with a yardstick for evaluating academic progress"; (2) "to establish a uniform State standard of achievement that is fair and equitable for students in all schools, large or small"; (3) "to provide a strong supervisory instrument by which high academic achievement and quality teaching can be stimulated throughout the State"; and (4) "to predict success in further study, both in high school and college."

The New York Regents Examination, originated in 1865, is probably the oldest state-conducted testing program in America. The original goal of this testing was to screen high school applicants to be sure that appropriations for state aid were not given to high schools that admitted students who were inadequately prepared for this level of education. Basically then, the original function of the Regents Examination was certification for entrance into high school. Some colleges felt there was merit in this type of testing and eventually established admissions testing standards for college entrance.

Gradually, as the high school changed from a select academy to a more comprehensive educational institution, and the character of the student body and the range of curriculum broadened greatly, the scope of the Regents Examinations also changed. Now the examinations, structured more as end-of-course achievement tests, are given in January, June, and August in twenty-five different high school subjects. The major areas in which these achievement tests are offered include business, English, foreign languages, mathematics, science, and social studies (SDE, 1965). These tests are required in all public high schools in New York; however, since the tests are intended for average or above students, only about 65 percent of the students actually take the examinations (USNY, 1966; p. 26). Students not enrolled in an academic program are not required to take the Regents Examinations.

Both essay and objective questions are included in these instruments, about 40 percent and 60 percent, respectively. The basic philosophy behind development and establishment of criteria for successful performance on the tests is founded on the desire to offer a baseline or floor of adequate performance rather than a ceiling. After test committees generate a pool of items, extensive pre-testing establishes item difficulty. When the final test is assembled, after field trials, it is possible to define "satisfactory" and "unsatisfactory" performance based on both the professional judgments of teachers who constructed the original test items and on the normative data which reflect a range of student performance.

These state-wide tests have a powerful influence on school curriculum changes and on instructional practices. For example, in the area of foreign language competence, stress was shifted from emphasis on grammar and vocabulary toward emphasis on the contemporary instructional method of teaching reading and speaking of foreign languages. As would be expected, the gradual inclusion of Regents Exam questions involving translation and related language-usage skills is said to have accelerated changes in classroom procedures by foreign language teachers. The testing system here helped serve the objective of changing language instruction.

INVENTORY OF PUPIL ACHIEVEMENT. The State Department of Education in New York also develops and administers a very comprehensive annual pupil achievement inventory which is based on New York State courses of study. The inventory is administered at the beginning of each school year to pupils in every school in the state. In first grade, measures of school readiness are administered; in grades three, six, and nine, reading and arithmetic achievement are evaluated.

The potential impact that this mandatory testing program can have on educators differentiates it from the more familiar voluntary achievement testing programs seen throughout this country. This program includes acquisition of systematic data which have implications for everyone connected with the educational system, from the classroom teacher to the State Commissioner of Education. We shall not debate here the many issues raised by proposals for mandatory evaluation of education; rather, we shall simply point up the strong commitment that one state has made toward system-wide evaluation of educational programs.

OTHER TESTING PROGRAMS. Other testing programs developed within the New York State Department of Education include the College Proficiency Examinations, High School Equivalency Tests, Regents Literacy Tests, and the Regents Scholarship and College Qualification Test.

The Ohio Testing Services

The Ohio Testing Services, a part of the Division of Guidance and Testing of the State Department of Education in Ohio, also develops tests and testing programs specifically for use by the state. To supplement their custom-made tests, this group contracts with national testing organizations for development of instruments which meet specifications for state-wide application.

Diagnostic and achievement testing for educational purposes, and development and supply of materials necessary for counseling and guidance in Ohio schools, are the primary concerns of the Ohio Testing Services. The group also carries out a state-wide program of testing for high school equivalency and for selection of outstanding students of Ohio history. Recent installation of a computer scoring facility will permit Ohio Testing Services to provide a more sophisticated form of test-score feedback to schools in Ohio.

One of the major differences between the New York and Ohio programs is that Ohio's state-wide activities are not compulsory. Since there is a substantial tradition for participation in these programs, however, the state conducts extensive testing annually. An additional difference in the programs is that the Ohio Testing Services issue a catalogue of materials which are sold to educational institutions in other states.

California State-Wide Testing Services

The state-wide testing program of the State of California typifies the kind of testing program maintained by most states. The principal characteristics of California's program are these:

1. The state testing program is mandated by action of the State Board of Education.
2. Several alternative nationally standardized tests are approved for application in the school districts of the state.
3. The state may reimburse the school district for some of the costs of testing materials and answer sheets.
4. The state does not provide scoring and reporting services to local school districts.

In California, mandatory testing is carried out in grades one, two, three, six, and ten. In an effort to improve reading instruction, the legislature provides supplementary funds to school districts and requires use of standardized tests in the lower grades. State-wide norms are prepared by the Bureau of Educational Research within the State Department of Education and are made available to local school districts for comparative purposes.

Minnesota

The state-wide testing program in Minnesota is unique in that it is administered by the Student Counseling Bureau, Office of the Dean of Students, University of Minnesota, rather than by the State Board of Education. Costs of Minnesota's program are sustained by local school districts or by members of the Association of Minnesota Colleges.

The Minnesota Committee on High School–College Relations serves in an advisory position on the high school testing program. Major policy for the college testing program is established by this committee, a committee of the Association of Minnesota Colleges, and the Minnesota Association of Secondary School Principals with representatives from other Minnesota educational organizations.

Small State-Wide Testing Programs

West Virginia provides a good example of a small state-wide testing program. Beginning in 1958, a state-wide program was established to provide for testing in grades three, six, nine, and eleven. Both mental ability and achievement tests were given with school districts participating on a voluntary basis. During the past decade, all districts have joined the program; currently, approximately 134,000 students are tested annually. The basic objective is to provide an evaluation of the educational programs offered throughout the state. The program is centered in the offices of the State Department of Education and is supervised by a staff of three. In addition to providing scoring and reporting services, these personnel train teachers in test administration and interpretation. All costs of this program are paid for by the State Department of Education.

Through their state-wide testing activities, most states show a growing commitment to systematic evaluation of educational progress; however, at least twenty-one states either have no such programs or have extremely limited testing services.[4] South Carolina, for example, provides only a free scoring service for school districts; Washington conducts only a pre-high school graduation scholarship examination.

Effects of Testing on Educational Practices

We may ask whether large testing programs are better than small ones. The evidence is by no means clear. We have cited the kinds of gains achieved in New York schools which accelerate curriculum revision to meet the level of test content. Clearly, state-wide testing-program information concerning educational progress can be useful to public policy makers. For example, when supplementary funding is provided for reading instruction, some comparative measure ought to be used to determine whether additional funds are making any difference.

Those who believe a serious commitment to educational evaluation is at the heart of the problem of changing and improving our schools will argue

[4] The states having no programs are Arizona, Arkansas, Alaska, Connecticut, Georgia, Louisiana, Maine, Massachusetts, Mississippi, Montana, Nebraska, Nevada, New Mexico, North Carolina, Oklahoma, Oregon, Pennsylvania, South Carolina, Utah, Vermont, and Wyoming.

strongly for state-wide testing programs. Others will point out that much of the testing in schools today simply does not make much difference to individual youngsters. It is important to keep in mind, however, that much of the state-wide testing that is conducted is not intended to serve a diagnostic requirement. The most common purpose for such testing is to provide some kind of comparative measure among schools and school districts throughout a state.

State Testing Programs in Relation to Six Assessment Subsystems

Subsystem 1: Definition of Assessment-System Requirements

Despite considerable variation across the nation, most states have developed competently stated goals for their testing programs in employment and in the schools. We believe these goals are generally stated with sufficient specificity to permit substantial argument concerning whether some of the testing programs aimed at meeting these measurement goals are in fact doing so. But the problem is complicated by the fact that often multiple objectives, some of which may not be fully compatible, are behind state-wide testing activities. This may be seen in educational achievement testing, for example, when teachers look to test results for helpful diagnostic information but administrators or elected officeholders expect the same tests to reveal which teachers or schools are doing an effective job. In any case, most states have a capability for providing a rigorous definition of assessment-system objectives; the trouble is that sometimes they have not done so. This omission permits wide-ranging interpretations of how effective a testing program may be.

Subsystem 2: Test Development and Standardization

Very few states are engaged in the development and standardization of their own tests, but where this is the pattern, we believe the work is being carried out in a highly professional manner. For the most part, the tests used in state-wide programs, for both educational and employment testing, are acquired from one of the larger test publishers. We see no significant difficulties with respect to the quality of this development and standardization work.

Subsystem 3: Definition of Subjects and Test Administration

The biggest difficulty we have seen in this area concerns the administration of tests to school children who have not been properly represented in the standardization of a given test. The subsequent publication of norms, school by school, leads some parents to conclude that the schools are accomplishing virtually nothing, and it leads teachers to argue that the use of inappropriate measurements is worse than no measurement at all. The problem is particularly acute with respect to bilingual children, with whom much questionable testing has been carried out. We have observed a substantial amount of state-wide testing involving bilingual and lower socioeconomic youngsters wherein neither parents nor school personnel are satisfied that the tests used contribute anything important in the way of educational diagnosis or evaluation. Publishers seem to have clung rather tenaciously to the idea that a single test or test battery ought to be so standardized as to be applicable to any school population. In our view, this is unlikely to be a sound strategy.

Subsystem 4: Scoring and Preparation of Feedback Documents

Test scoring seems to present much less of a problem than the preparation of feedback documents. First, most states do not do their own scoring unless computer-based scoring apparatus is available. If it is, the technology for doing this in a sophisticated manner is now available, and the problems are few. On the other hand, if the program relies on the classroom teacher to administer and score her own tests, the possibility of error is considerably increased. As far as the preparation of feedback documents is concerned, most states have not developed much capability in this area and they rely, therefore, on the large commercial scoring and interpretation services.

Subsystem 5: Feedback of Test Results

In many state-wide testing programs for both educational and employment testing there is virtually no feedback to the test taker. Equally unfortunate, many teachers do not receive much feedback on test results, at least not at a time when they are interested in acting upon this information. This deficiency is not attributable so much to inability to provide such information as to unwillingness to budget the cost for such a service. With the emergence of computer scoring and test interpretation, it may be anticipated that the potential for an important breakthrough is now at hand. Whether such progress really has much impact upon the behavior of teachers remains to be seen. Certainly there is room for considerable improvement in the packaging of test results as they are presented to teachers.

Subsystem 6: Evaluation of the Assessment System

State-wide testing programs have not been evaluated as rigorously as they deserve and, as a consequence, some of them go rolling along year after year with little improvement. In our opinion, the place to begin in the strengthening of these programs is with a commitment to a competent assessment system as we have presented it here, or to some similar systematic format for evaluation. Based on our meetings with school personnel throughout the country, evidence indicates that many teachers simply do not get much good from some very expensive educational testing programs. But this is certainly not to suggest that objective assessment does not have a central role to play in the educational process. What we are saying is that administrators charged with responsibility for building and carrying out excellent assessment programs have their work cut out for them, and that a more systems-oriented approach to the evaluation of testing activities sponsored by the states is very much in order.

REFERENCES

Educational Testing Service. *State Testing Programs: A Survey of Functions, Tests, Materials, and Services.* Princeton, N.J.: ETS, March 1968.

State Department of Education. *Regents Examinations (1865–1965): 100 Years of Quality Control in Education.* Albany, N.Y.: SDE, 1965.

University of the State of New York. *Annual Report, Regents Examination and Scholarship Center, 1965–66.* The State Department, Regents Examination and Scholarship Center, Sept. 1, 1966.

7

Contract and Proprietary Testing Programs

The preceding chapters have described different elements of the testing "establishment." This chapter, while describing other organizations involved in testing, focuses on relationships between test users and test producers, particularly those in which the test users rather than the producers have initiated the programs and relationships. It indicates many different organizational arrangements for developing and operating testing systems. The chapter title reflects the fact that contracts between organizations typically provide the "glue" that binds the subsystems together into testing systems. The wide variety of apparently successful arrangements should be encouraging to persons interested in creating a testing system.

What distinguishes "contract" testing programs from others? Though the distinctions are not clear-cut, contract testing programs generally are initiated by the user or an organization of users. The programs usually contract with established test producers for development and administration of testing programs to serve the needs of the user organization or its members. Since the tests developed are the property of the user organization, they are generally not sold by the test producer to other users. The arrangements between the user and the testing organization tend to be fairly permanent, although some of them are handled on an annual, biennial, or similar contract, subject to competitive bidding.

Arrangements described in this chapter include those initiated by the College Entrance Examination Board and the American College Testing Program to provide academic-selection testing systems and related services to colleges and universities. Educational Research Bureau, described as an example of an organization primarily concerned with procurement of good testing services for its member schools, is also engaged in providing some services to its members and to test users generally.

The selection testing system developed for life insurance agencies provides a business model that other associations may wish to emulate. Descriptions of such large special-purpose testing programs as Project TALENT and the National Assessment of Educational Progress indicate other contract testing arrangements.

Smaller testing programs ordinarily associated with universities are discussed as are private-personnel testing companies which ordinarily provide selection-and-placement testing services to industry.

College Entrance Examination Board

The College Entrance Examination Board (CEEB), established in 1900, is probably the oldest and best known of the organizations involved in testing for college entrance and related programs. It is a nonprofit association of almost 1,000 member organizations, of which approximately 700 are colleges, 250 are secondary schools, and 50 are associations. Its staff consists of approximately forty professional and administrative personnel in the central office in New York and thirty representatives in the Washington office and five regional offices. CEEB founded the Educational Testing Service (see Chapter 3) which administers all of CEEB's programs.

During the 1890's, educators evaluated and debated the fact that educational institutions had widely varying requirements for admission. On this issue, there was a general lack of cooperation among colleges as a group, and between colleges and secondary schools. With the support of Harvard President Charles W. Eliot, Columbia Professor (and later President) Nicholas M. Butler worked to solve these problems. The solution seemed to require the establishment of a college examining board that would be an instrument of the Association of Colleges and Secondary Schools of the Middle States and Maryland. Regarding the purposes of such a board, Butler stated (Fuess, 1967; p. 43), "The main purpose . . . is to ascertain whether a pupil is well enough equipped for more advanced study in college or scientific school . . . [and] to secure, by means of cooperation between all those vitally interested, that uniformity of standards which is essential for the general systematic improvement of the conditions of secondary education (p. 56)." To accomplish these goals, the Board would "so define the subjects of admission that they would be uniform, conduct examinations in these subjects at uniform times throughout the world, and issue to those who take the examination, certificates of performance, good, bad, or indifferent (p. 25)."

The Board, formed in 1900, operated in the face of considerable opposition from secondary schools. Of interest is the fact that, during the first year of operation, CEEB was aware that participating schools essentially suspended regular classes near examination time so that special coaches or "crammers" could work with the students to prepare them for the tests. Coaching is no less a problem today.

The number of persons affected by CEEB's programs is reflected in the following figures: the Scholastic Aptitude Test is now administered to almost 2 million students per year; the Preliminary Scholastic Test is administered to about 1.3 million students at 15,000 schools; the administration of Advanced Placement Program examination affects approximately 40,000 students from 2,500 secondary schools (CEEB, 1966). The number of parents' confidential statements processed for use in college scholarship programs exceeds a quarter of a million per year. Both the Scholastic Aptitude and the Achievement Tests are offered at about three thousand centers throughout the United States and in seventy foreign countries.

CEEB spends more than a million dollars a year on research; some of these funds come from foundation sources. Currently the Board is engaged in Project Opportunity, in which it is cooperating with the Southern Association of Colleges and Secondary Schools under a Ford Foundation grant. The aim of the project is to prepare potentially superior students from disadvantaged families for college or for other post-high school education. Other research projects are concerned with helping students become motivated to enter college and with helping them find access to higher education.

In 1967, the Board appointed a twenty-man Commission on Tests to "undertake a thorough and critical review of the Board's testing function in American education and to consider possibilities for fundamental changes in the present tests and their use in schools, colleges, and universities (CEEB, 1970a)." The Commission has recommended that CEEB broaden its services to assist students who are not planning to go directly into college from high school, as well as provide more services for those who do apply for college admission. Significantly, it recommended that "the Board regard all potential entrants in programs offering opportunities for post-secondary education as a clientele whose interests and needs are to be served and met as fully as are those of the Board's institutional clientele (p. 57)." If these recommendations are implemented, the action will provide a milestone, not only in American education, but in concern by "establishment" institutions for individuals who may never use their services. The use of the word "clientele" is significant, since it suggests that rather than view the actual applicant as a "customer," CEEB should accept both actual and potential applicants as "clients" to whom the organization has responsibilities similar to those it has to its member schools. Also illuminating are the discussions of educational assessment, written by members of the Commission (CEEB, 1970b).

American College Testing Program

The American College Testing Program (ACTP), a federation of state programs, was founded in 1959, primarily to serve the admissions-testing needs of state colleges and universities and private colleges whose needs were not being met by the College Entrance Examination Board. CEEB focused on the larger public and private universities, especially in the Eastern United States. ACTP now consists of approximately one thousand agencies and institutions nationwide, including all kinds of public and private educational institutions above the secondary school level.

As is true of CEEB, the governing board of ACTP consists of members selected by member-school representatives. ACTP's national headquarters is in Iowa City, Iowa; the program also operates five regional offices which consult directly with educational institutions using ACTP's services. ACTP contracts with Science Research Associates, which provides test registration, printing, and materials distribution services, as well as test construction and development. Also under contract to ACTP, the Measurement Research Center in Iowa City provides electronic scoring of the ACTP battery, distribution of reports and other interpretive material, and data processing services for the Research and Development Division of ACTP. The principal financial support for ACTP derives from the $4 fee that students pay when they register to take the ACTP battery.

ACTP is chartered as an independent nonprofit corporation and serves as a central agency for the collection, analysis, processing, and reporting of information for use in educational planning by college-bound students and those with whom they interact. Its centralized program replaces a large number of individual college testing programs. The ACTP assessment battery is administered five times a year at approximately fifteen hundred test centers in the United States and Canada and is administered twice a year at some ninety overseas centers.

Participating colleges may request special norms of interest and value to them, and special research services. Research services of various kinds are available to assist colleges in predicting the success of students who may, for one reason or another, need special attention; and to provide descriptive information to help the colleges better understand changes in their student populations. ACTP's extensive research program, which serves participating schools, generates more knowledge about higher education, develops new tools and techniques for the educational process, and improves assessment devices for inclusion in the ACTP.

Both CEEB and ACTP monitor all six subsystems described in Chapter 2. Generally, they perform the test specification and evaluation subsystems. They contract for part of the test-development subsystem and all administration, scoring, and preparation of feedback documents. Some feedback to test takers and users is done by the contractors and some by the user organizations. These organizations, fortunately, employ highly competent test professionals to interact with the organizations' members and the contractors.

Educational Records Bureau

One of the oldest and largest of the contract testing organizations is the Educational Records Bureau (ERB), headquartered in New York City. ERB is owned by approximately twelve hundred independent schools, public schools, and colleges across the United States and in foreign countries; member institutions elect a board of trustees to manage the organization. Nonprofit and independent, ERB is engaged in testing, consultation, and research.

In addition to its members, ERB has many affiliates who receive some services from the Bureau. These services are provided by some fifty full-time employees, plus one to two hundred temporary and part-time employees. The organization plans to open nationwide offices when it is able to staff them and to develop ties with the participating schools in the new areas.

ERB is self-supporting, primarily from testing and scoring programs and, to a lesser extent, from modest membership dues and the sale of educational services and publications. During the 1967–68 fiscal year, ERB scored approximately six hundred thousand tests, most of which were also sold by ERB to the participating schools. The majority of these tests were commercial tests sold to the schools for the price charged by the publisher. Thus, the Sales Division generally operates at a small loss, most of which is presumably made up by profits in the Scoring Division.

When ERB needs a new test or testing program, its staff members, working with a committee of school representatives, scan reviews of available tests. They then carefully examine the tests and the manuals; if they feel a manual is well done, a teacher committee assesses the test in detail. If the committee considers the test valuable for some segment of the ERB schools, it tries out the test in schools which collectively represent the larger group for which it is hoped the tests will be useful. If, after an item analysis, the test still appears good, it goes back to the committee; if the test is approved, information on what the test does and does not do is sent to the schools. About one-tenth of the tests reviewed by ERB for inclusion in its programs are now on the list of recommended tests for ERB participating schools. Not surprisingly, when a test enters that list there is generally a significant increase in sales for that test. When no appropriate test is available, ERB will develop and publish one, but it prefers to buy tests because of the time and expense involved in complete test development.

ERB assists member schools in specifying requirements for testing programs and in selecting or developing tests to meet them. The schools typically do their own test administration and send tests to ERB for scoring and preparation of feedback documents. As part of that task and as part of the evaluation subsystem, ERB computes and reports independent school, public school, regional and local norms. The Bureau evaluates tests and testing programs and also maintains educational research programs; one output of these efforts is professional consultation to members and affiliates on problems of guidance, curriculum development, and administration, in addition to testing. Thus, ERB is involved in a different mix of subsystems from CEEB and ACTP; this is traceable to differences in their member organizations.

Life Insurance Agency Management Association

Though Life Insurance Agency Management Association (LIAMA) is not, strictly speaking, a contract testing organization, it is included here because it is a business-world counterpart of CEEB and ACTP. As its name implies, LIAMA is an association of life insurance agencies, 350 of them in the United States and Canada, and 100 associates overseas. Its testing program, which is a complete assessment system, is operated as a service for the association's members and is subsidiary to LIAMA's major role in the research area.

The Research Division of LIAMA handles test development and scoring in addition to research on training, selection, supervision, leadership of sales organizations, job attitudes and morale, public opinion, and on the cost of marketing insurance. The Research Division employs approximately eighty-five people.

LIAMA's initial selection battery, developed in 1932, consisted of personality and personal-history items. The biographical items were rescaled after World War II, as there had been many changes in the U.S. economy and in the experience of applicants for sales jobs. The rescaled tests were used very briefly without proof of current validity of items. Personality data did not hold up, so personal history was the only base available. Other experimental items, added as rapidly as possible, were included in the scoring after validation statistics indicated their relationship to survival of the first year of selling life insurance and to production above the median sales level during that time.

Each test now contains some items known to be valid, some experimental items, and some items for which norms are being developed. The current Aptitude Index Battery has 320 items, over half of which are scored; most of the items are biographical interest or personality items.

The Aptitude Index Battery is not separately scored by race and sex since it has, until recently, been illegal in most states to collect and record information on items which might in any way bias employment or promotion. LIAMA is now requesting permission of appropriate agencies to collect data which will make possible the separate validation now preferred, according to EEOC guidelines.

Each member company in LIAMA is free to direct its agencies to use the test in any manner; such direction ranges from purely advisory to a policy of "If a man doesn't pass the test, you can't hire him." The value of this testing program is enhanced by the fact that the selection ratio in the insurance industry is about 10 percent; about half the applicants fail the test; another 40 percent are not hired for other reasons. The testing activity of LIAMA now grosses almost $500,000 a year and makes sufficient profit to support a test research program in excess of $100,000 a year. This program is partly sponsored by dues from members.

Paul W. Thayer, vice president and director of research for LIAMA, commented on test standards and equal employment opportunities. He mentioned that the Equal Employment Opportunity Commission (EEOC) guidelines fail to recognize the special test-retest problems that LIAMA has (Thayer, 1967). The standards permit concurrent validity studies, which LIAMA considers below its own standards.

Although the LIAMA testing system is apparently unique in that it is an industry-developed and managed testing program, it is a model that other industries or associations may wish to consider. It is obviously competently run and responsive to the needs of its industry members. The services LIAMA provides are similar to those provided by the Professional Examinations Division of the Psychological Corporation and the Cooperative Test Service of Educational Testing Service. Either model provides competent, conscientious testing for organizations and professional groups that wish to maintain selection standards or ensure efficient placement. Generally, these organizations provide all subsystems and work cooperatively with the user on specification of requirements, on evaluation of programs, and sometimes on development.

American Institutes for Research

PROJECT TALENT. The goals of Project TALENT are to establish (1) an inventory of human resources, (2) a set of standards for educational and psychological measurement, (3) a comprehensive counseling guide that indicates the patterns of aptitude and ability which are predictive of success in various careers, (4) a better understanding of how young people choose their life work, and (5) a basic understanding of the educational experiences that prepare students for their life work. Project TALENT was conceived and organized by John C. Flanagan, chairman of the board of the American Institutes for Research, which operates the program. The project costs about

$500,000 per year, most of which comes from the U.S. Office of Education.

In 1960, 450,000 students in secondary schools were tested by Project TALENT with a comprehensive, two-day battery of aptitude tests, achievement tests, and inventories. Project TALENT has retested, on a five-year follow-up, the majority of the students tested in 1960; additional five- and ten-year follow-ups on that group and others are planned. In general, Project TALENT has shown that U.S. education has not been very good.

The idea for Project TALENT grew out of Flanagan's development of the Flanagan Aptitude Classification Tests (FACT) for which he needed much validation and follow-up data. Although 15,000 of these tests had been administered, and data on the population had been collected, Flanagan felt that the data were still inadequate. Further, he felt that the effort required to obtain adequate data and make validity studies could be justified only if the data were made available to the general educational community. Costs of this effort would exceed the resources of any private organization; thus Project TALENT was proposed. So that the project could get support for the necessary validity studies, it was essential that the tests involved not be a proprietary test battery. Therefore, Project TALENT developed its own battery, which is in the public domain.

Data from TALENT, FACT, DAT, and similar batteries are now being correlated and analyzed. Data from Project TALENT are used mainly as a national data resource for behavioral, social, and educational research. Since the data bank was first announced in 1965, approximately one hundred scientists have utilized its data in studies of their own design.

National Assessment of Educational Progress

The National Assessment of Educational Progress (NAEP) is both a program and an organization. The goal of NAEP is the collection, analysis, and distribution of comprehensive, dependable data that can be used as a basis for public understanding of educational progress. Testing in connection with this program began in the early part of 1969. A review of some of the ideas and actions leading up to it may be of interest.

During the 1960's, organizations, agencies, and committees at national and state level were attempting to make predictions and influence the course of education in the United States. They discovered they had neither the data on which to base decisions nor a reliable means of collecting data which would indicate changes in the areas of interest to them. In addition, legislation providing federal funds for education has increasingly required evaluation of the effectiveness of education and of the expenditures of the moneys appropriated for it. The needs of these groups spurred the development of National Assessment. The Exploratory Committee on Assessment of Progress in Education was set up to consider development of an assessment program that would provide landmarks of educational progress as a basis for meeting the changing educational needs of society.

Following conferences and consultations with a wide variety of persons involved in education and related fields, the committee decided that a new kind of assessment device and a means of communication were needed. The committee established two guidelines for procedure development:

1. Reports should be made on the basis of age-level groups.
2. For each age group included in the national assessment, there should be an attempt to describe: (a) things that almost all persons of that age level have accomplished, (b) things that average persons have achieved, (c) things that most advanced persons at that age level have accomplished.

The committee, feeling that conventional, existing national testing programs would not be adequate for accomplishment of their objectives, sought the counsel and advice of both lay people and professionals with respect to problems of testing and sampling. This led to additional guidelines:

1. The reports of the national assessment activities must provide meaningful information on the progress of education to thoughtful lay people as well as to professional educators.
2. The design of procedures must be as practical and efficient as possible in producing and conveying this information (NAEP, 1967; p. 12).

The committee's report, submitted in 1968, recommended that assessments focus initially on four age levels. These were ages nine, thirteen, seventeen, and young adult. It was determined further that, for age seventeen and beyond, separate samples should be made for both school and nonschool populations; other subpopulation stratifications should include sex, region of the country, type of community, socioeconomic background, and race (which was further defined for the purpose of this program as Caucasian, Negro, and other). The proposed design called for complex and sophisticated sampling; the accuracy of the statements about educational progress would depend more upon statistical procedures than on mass data collection.

Ten subject-matter areas were selected, and assessment materials were developed in three of those areas in 1969. The specific goals for each of the subject-matter areas were developed under contract by four well-known testing organizations: Educational Testing Service, responsible for the bulk of the work; Science Research Associates; the American Institutes for Research; and the Psychological Corporation. These companies then developed specific test items for inclusion in the assessment batteries.

Such a large, long-term testing program as that envisaged by NAEP will undoubtedly have an impact on many aspects of the testing activity and on the testing industry in the United States. Already a group of government, nonprofit, and commercial organizations is working on the project. If new types of test items and assessment devices are developed, interesting questions about the ownership and use of such items may be raised. The impact that such a program may have on education is difficult to estimate at this time. There is undoubtedly some concern that this program could produce another organization like Educational Testing Service which would compete with commercial testing organizations in some areas. There are also opposite concerns that the large amounts of money spent on Project TALENT and NAEP may not have a significant impact.

Small Contract Programs

Not all contract testing programs are as large as those described above. Among the smaller ones are some discussed earlier in the book, e.g., the activities of the Professional Examinations Division of the Psychological Corporation and the Cooperative Test Service and other activities of Educational Testing Service. A description of some other programs follows.

Air-Crew Selection

The American Institutes for Research contracts to provide a program for the selection of air-crew personnel for commercial airlines. This project, started for United Airlines, has been extended to other airlines; a test battery for stewardesses will be added as soon as forward validation tests are completed. Since the Airline Pilots Selection Battery is a controlled test, no public information is available about the items, scoring, or validities. In view of the success of the aviation psychology program, no one appears to have questioned the quality or validity of the battery.

Industrial Relations Center, University of Chicago

The testing unit of the Industrial Relations Center at the University of Chicago performs a variety of research and training services; on a consulting basis the Center develops and applies tests for specific purposes in various companies.

Test sales are a very small part of the Center's activity. The organization does sell tests to its clients, but it does not publish a catalogue. The important distinction here is that the Center is not oriented toward merchandising, but only toward selling tests as a service, primarily to companies supporting the Industrial Relations Center.

This organization provides an interesting example of a consultation service model which incorporates a truly systematic approach to personnel problems. Not only will the Measurement and Research Division undertake job analyses and personnel-selection procedures, but it will also follow up with systematic research over a period of years in order to improve the assessment procedures and validate the instruments used. The Center's activities in the public personnel field are reported in Chapter 6.

Personnel Research Institute, Case Western Reserve University

The Personnel Research Institute of Case Western Reserve University is very similar to the Industrial Relations Center. The Institute, a division of the Psychology Department, is primarily concerned with training graduate students in research methods in personnel psychology. Total test sales, which constitute only 6 or 7 percent of the total income of the Institute, amount to less than $10,000 per year. Test consulting and test program development are contracted for on a limited scale and are usually done by graduate students under the supervision of the director or associate director of the Institute.

Language Institutes: University of Michigan, Georgetown University

Universities, like other organizations, frequently get involved in testing activities as a by-product of some other program. Two rather similar examples of this are the English Language Institute (ELI) at the University of Michigan and the American Language Institute (ALI) at Georgetown University.

The English Language Institute has been concerned for many years with research on the teaching of English and with development of programs and program materials for use in teaching and understanding English. ELI entered the testing field when it was asked by the United States Information Agency (USIA) to develop some tests which could be administered by USIA overseas to determine English-language competence for employment in USIA offices and for programs which would bring foreigners to the United States. The tests are also used for foreign-student applicants for the 175 institutions which accept ELI certificates of English for college entry. An interesting by-product of these testing programs is the development of an "advisory test" which an applicant may take to determine the probability of his success on the screening examination. Approximately twenty-eight thousand of these are administered each year, compared with about thirty-five hundred of the final form.

Robert Lado, who built the first testing programs at ELI, later moved to Georgetown University; this may account, in part, for the extension of testing programs there. The American Language Institute (ALI) at Georgetown University was asked by the Agency for International Development to prepare a simple English screening test for use in the overseas testing of applicants for grants and scholarship programs. Since then, ALI's English Usage Test and the scored interviews have been supplemented with listening and vocabulary and reading tests; the latter tests are used by academic institutions only.

The quality of assessment work done by the small testing contract programs described on the preceding pages is probably as high as can be found in any programs in the United States. The overseas programs, however, seem to face the usual U.S. testing problems of overinterpretation and difficulty of validation. Further, test-security compromise and overuse of tests with few alternate forms result in test passing based as much on repeated exposure as on language competence.

Proprietary Testing Programs

Another group of testing organizations provides services similar to those described earlier in this chapter, but different in that most of their clients are business organizations which use the tests and programs for personnel selection and placement. These "private personnel test" companies generally have five characteristics:

1. These companies develop and use instruments that are quite simple, i.e., easy to fill out and generally involving a considerable amount of self-report material.
2. They employ these instruments over a wide range of occupations.
3. These organizations frequently train employers' representatives to interpret the tests.
4. They are primarily concerned with providing services connected with their testing programs rather than with selling tests.
5. They are involved in employee selection and classification work.

Compared to most companies that focus on providing tests for sale, the organizations in this group are generally more thorough about determining the details of the jobs for which their tests are to be used and about ensuring good test administration and interpretation. Practices vary widely between clients using the same private-personnel testing services as well as between companies offering these services.

Lack of Validity Data

The principal reason for controversy surrounding these organizations is that they typically do not publish the validity data considered essential by most professionals. Professionals disagree, however, about the adequacy of the small amount of validity data provided. Generally, these organizations have indicated willingness to supply validity data; in one form or another, practically all do. Perhaps the best known example is Walter V. Clarke Associates which published in 1967 an annotated bibliography containing forty-eight studies on the Activity Vector Analysis.

Examples of Private-Personnel-Test Companies

Organizations in this classification are the aforementioned Walter V. Clarke Associates; John P. Cleaver Company of Princeton, New Jersey; the Marketing Survey and Research Corporation, which has its headquarters in New York City; and Humm Personnel Consultants of Los Angeles.

WALTER V. CLARKE ASSOCIATES. The oldest and best known of these organizations is Walter V. Clarke Associates of Providence, Rhode Island, and Fort Lauderdale, Florida. The organization operates a subsidiary in Canada.

Clarke's "total employment system," which he developed when he was director of industrial relations for a manufacturing firm, consists of job analysis and description, selection and placement, performance evaluation, and feedback; all of these center around the Activity Vector Analysis (AVA). The AVA system develops job requirements through systematic ratings of job activities and skill requirements from which a job description can be written. In order to get high reliability on these ratings, Clarke uses multiple ratings by people who supervise others on the job, by people who perform the job, and by others who observe the job. Applicants and employees fill out a form which is mostly self-report.

Clarke has modified his tests somewhat, particularly as word meanings have changed and thus have changed norms and interpretations. He has analyzed word meanings extensively, using S. I. Hayakawa as a consultant. Clarke, now working on some nonlanguage tests, continues to keep data, including both scores and original responses, from over seventeen thousand people; he continues to relate this to follow-up information from these people.

Clarke and his staff conduct training seminars for business and personnel executives; the seminars concern the use of materials and procedures, including methods for performance evaluation and feedback.

JOHN P. CLEAVER COMPANY, INC. The organization that most resembles Walter V. Clarke Associates is, not surprisingly, the John P. Cleaver Company, since Cleaver was previously associated with Clarke. John P. Cleaver Company employs twenty-five people in two offices in Worcester, Massachusetts, and Princeton, New Jersey. Three of the twelve professionals on the staff are psychologists. Cleaver's group is guided in part by a psychological advisory board made up of men from among his own client organizations and from Division 14 of the APA.

A human-factor job description is the major stock in trade of this company. Cleaver trains managers to specify the human behaviors required for a job and helps corporate officers evaluate the human criteria for jobs. Cleaver spends most of his time with top management in companies, teaching them to anticipate their personnel and management needs and to develop channels by which good managers can be hired and trained. A two-day intensive program is the major means for his interaction with these company officers.

Cleaver also has an evaluation-techniques program in which he teaches others to use methods and forms and provides general support to his client companies, so that any member of the company management may receive assistance on human aspects of organizational problems. Typically, Cleaver runs two executive training programs a month for top management personnel. He offers managers a four-stage program concerned with assisting people within companies to do a better job.

MARKETING SURVEY AND RESEARCH CORPORATION. Another aggressive organization whose methods bear some resemblance to those of Clarke and Cleaver is the Marketing Survey and Research Corporation of New York. The major activity of this company is assessment of job applicants, particularly for sales and sales-related jobs. Dr. Herbert Greenberg, an APA member, and Mr. David Mayer run the corporation. The company's test evaluators are not required to have psychological training or college degrees; however, a close record of the predictive accuracy of each grader is kept. Unlike Clarke and Cleaver, this company does not train others to make test evaluations.

Marketing Survey and Research Corporation provides client companies with copies of its tests. These are filled out by job applicants and mailed to the home office which makes a prediction of the applicant's probability of success on the job for which he is being considered, ordinarily a sales job. Since the tests provide clues for interviews, interviewing is preferably done after testing; the company feels it can obtain a better prediction from the Inventory than from interviewing.

This organization has done some contract work for the government in Puerto Rico where it tested 1,700 unemployed or underemployed and eventually placed 325 in professional sales jobs in good companies. At the time of our meeting, the company was negotiating a government contract to do selection on job opportunities in the business sector and was working on a larger management test scheduled for publication in the near future. Sales and sensitivity-training programs are also being developed, especially for poverty and minority groups.

HUMM PERSONNEL CONSULTANTS. One of the older but smaller organizations in this field is Humm Personnel Consultants of Los Angeles. Clearly a consulting organization with a proprietary product, the company makes no test sales in the usual sense. What test sales it does make are directed toward personnel selection, classification, and promotion in businesses. This organization works only with clients willing to pay for the training of the personnel who are going to administer the tests. One of the unique features of the Humm operation is that, in order to achieve a high degree of control over testing practices and utilization of the Humm-Wadsworth Test, the company rents its test booklets to client companies.

System Analysis and Evaluation

In many ways, the organizations described in this chapter are strong where the traditional test publishers may not be, and vice versa. Let us look at their activities by subsystem. These companies attempt, though not always with equal zeal, to assure study of the job requirements for which their tests are making predictions. Although these test publishers provide manuals listing uses for which validation data are available and provide advice and assistance when asked, most publishers depend on test purchasers to determine test requirements.

On the development subsystem, the other groups of publishers seem to do a better job than the personnel group. The test instruments of the personnel testing group appear to most professionals to be inadequate for the wide variety of jobs for which they are used. On the administration subsystem, the balance shifts again; it is typical for the personnel testing companies to train test administrators, though not typical for most test publishers to do so. On scoring and preparation of feedback documents, the personnel testing people usually depend on hand scoring by the test administrator, and do very limited, if any, preparation of feedback material. The larger testing programs of the major publishers depend almost entirely on machine scoring which employs many quality-control checks; they also provide considerable interpretive material to counselors, administrators, and others using the test results. On feedback, the two groups seem about even, with little help provided directly in either case.

There is no reason why the tests of the private testing companies should be inferior to those sold more broadly. Indeed, such batteries as AIR's Air-Crew Selection Battery are considered adequate for the job; AIR's battery, however, was developed by reputable professional people who had done similar work for the Air Force. More innovative approaches, especially by persons not in the "mainstream" of the testing movement, are not generally well regarded.

Wide use of standardized tests and of electronic scoring equipment, along with answer-sheet copyright problems, will make secure private-personnel testing programs more common than at present. Therefore, responsible professionals must not postpone dealing with the problems inherent in these programs. Standards for evaluating the program procedures and instruments in relation to their objectives must be considered. Such standards may or may not be the same as those applied to tests offered for relatively open public sale and use.

Perspective

Contract testing organizations are among the most highly regarded, and among the most criticized, testing companies. The professionals in the field criticize the small private-personnel testing companies for failing to follow accepted practice and to meet standards for tests and manuals. The same critics have very high regard for college-entrance and similar contract programs that are considered technically competent. Criticisms of these latter programs are most frequently voiced by persons who wish to gain access to the Establishment and who resent the purposes of testing.

The private-personnel testing organizations illustrate some of the problems involved in trying to innovate in the field of testing. New kinds of items, such as those developed by Paul Torrence for the creativity test published by Personnel Press, are acceptable if they are scored, validated, and normed in the traditionally accepted ways. Innovating with respect to procedures is less acceptable, however, generally for good scientific reasons. For example, Greenberg and Mayer's (1964) publication of validity data, based on "clinical" interpretation of test data, is not considered professionally acceptable, presumably because there is no assurance that future interpretations of the test will be done with equal skill. Though this is a valid complaint, it is not ordinarily used as a criticism of clinical use of tests or as a basis for refusing to sell tests for clinical uses.

Psychological and educational journals are generally unwilling to publish validity data developed by the organizations described in the latter part of this chapter; the company's tests are then criticized for lack of such information. The only significant professional involvement in this problem was a complaint against Walter Clarke Associates for unjustified advertising claims; but the complaint was dismissed by the APA Ethics Committee after extensive investigations and hearings. Some of the other private-personnel testing organizations have not been investigated because they are not run by APA members and thus are not subject to professional ethical standards. Undoubtedly, a general review of the standards and methods of all these organizations should be conducted by one or more of the professional organizations concerned with testing, so an evaluation of their tests and methods can be made available to potential clients.

We believe the testing programs described in the first part of this chapter provide a variety of excellent models for other organizations to emulate. The fact that the College Entrance Examination Board created a commission to study the Board's goals is encouraging for several reasons. It indicates that change can come from within testing organizations. It points the way for other publicly concerned groups to examine the goals as well as the methods of testing programs and similar gatekeeping devices in our society.

REFERENCES

CEEB. *The College Board Today.* New York, 1966.

CEEB. *Report of the Commission on Tests: I. Righting the Balance.* New York, 1970a.

CEEB. *Report of the Commission on Tests: II. Briefs.* New York, 1970b.

Fuess, C. M. *The College Board: Its First Fifty Years.* New York: College Entrance Examination Board, 1967.

Greenberg, H., and D. Mayer, "A New Approach to the Scientific Selection of Successful Salesmen," *Journal of Psychology,* 57 (1964), 113–123.

National Assessment of Educational Progress: Some Questions and Comments. Washington, D.C.: Department of Elementary School Principles, NEA, in cooperation with NEA Center for the Study of Instruction, 1967.

Thayer, Paul W., Vice President and Director of Research, LIAMA, Hartford, Conn. Interview, Aug. 1, 1967.

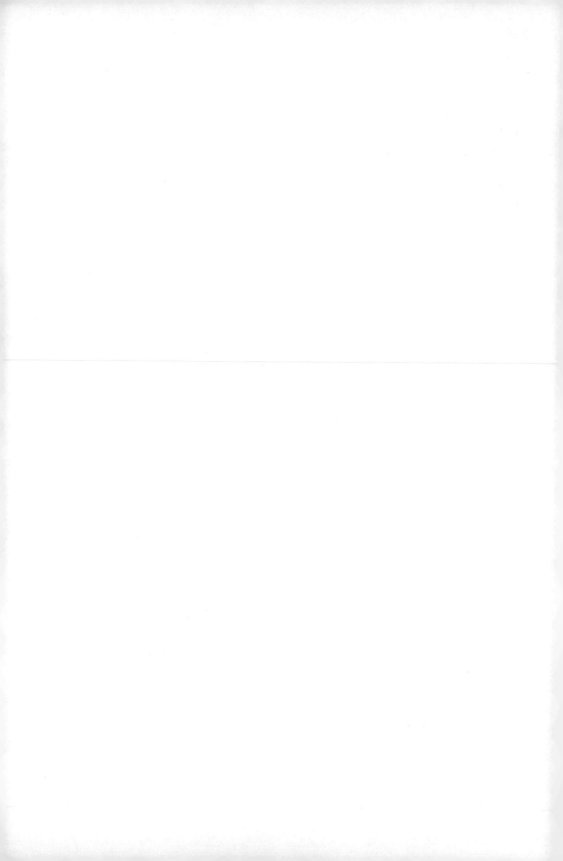

8

Test Scoring and Interpretation

For many years, tests have been scored and interpreted manually. Development of computer and advanced electronics technology has led to the development of machine scoring and interpretation and related services. The rise of such services has both benefited the testing industry and created new ethical problems for testing professionals to solve. This chapter discusses the use of machines for scoring and interpretation, and the problems and criticisms stemming from this use (Carter, 1966).

Test scoring, undoubtedly the largest and most rapidly growing test service offered, probably accounts for more income than does the sale of tests and answer sheets. For example, reusable test booklets range in cost from 8 to 80 cents, depending on the type of test involved; single answer sheets range in cost from 2½ to 12 cents, depending on the type of test involved and the quantity of answer sheets ordered. In contrast, scoring the answer sheets may run from 5 cents per side to 85 cents per sheet for machine scoring, or $.35 to $1.20 each sheet for hand scoring; again, cost is related to the type of test being scored. Scoring and interpretation services can reach $3 or more per test for the Minnesota Multiphasic Personality Inventory (MMPI); this price includes a computer printout of diagnostic and interpretive statements in addition to the scores and profile for the fourteen standard scales plus scores on eleven research scales and a special scale developed at Mayo Clinic. Optional services (such as reporting of means and standard deviations, frequency distributions, statistical analyses, item counting, and additional profiles) naturally increase the cost of scoring services; however, these are frequently provided in the basic scoring price for large school testing programs.

Growth of Machine-Scoring Companies

Machine scoring of tests began in the 1930's when International Business Machines Corporation (IBM) developed a machine designed principally to score locally developed objective tests in schools. This equipment, of course, was soon used to score achievement tests, intelligence, aptitude, clerical, and similar tests. The operator of the early scoring machine wired a plugboard to reflect the test key, placed the plugboard in the scoring machine, fed some quality-control sample sheets through the system, and when the system was checked out, fed sheets individually into the machine, read the answers off needle-type dials on the machine, and wrote them onto the test answer sheets. Although this process was obviously much faster than hand scoring, it had drawbacks. Since the machine had no memory, it could not generate any statistical reports. Because its operation depended on transmission of electricity through graphic marks, the machine performed inaccurately when there were changes in the humidity. Further, it could score only one scale at a time, unless the operator turned switches to get additional answers. Nevertheless, the machine showed the possibilities of machine scoring and stimulated greater test use.

Testscor

The next major development in machine scoring of tests was the result of work by Elmer J. Hankes, president of Engineers Northwest, an engineering consulting firm. About 1940, Hankes received a request from the Educational Test Bureau (ETB), then a test-publishing company in Minneapolis, to evaluate a design for a test-scoring machine which ETB wanted to build and use for scoring. In connection with this project, Hankes encountered the Strong Vocational Interest Blank which included four hundred items, each of which had three possible answers; each item could be scored over a nine-point range on as many as fifty different scales. Challenged by the problems presented by the Strong Blank, Hankes developed and built a machine to score Strong Blanks, which were sent to him by Strong and by many other persons using the Blanks. Use of the Strong Blank increased with the one-day turnaround that was possible by mail, or the turnaround in a few minutes for persons who brought in Strong Blanks.

About 1960, Hankes founded Testscor as a commercial scoring service and developed an additional machine which made no further use of analog circuitry, but rather employed digital photoelectric circuitry with a line printer.

Hankes is now using that machine to score Strong Blanks and MMPI's. The machines developed by Hankes have been used only in his own organization.

Quality-control processes are important in Hankes' operation, as they are for all other scoring services with which we are acquainted. Hankes' use of integrated circuitry rather than manual operation makes most of the quality-control checks automatic. No scores are mailed out until the checks for quality control have been processed.

Hankes does not score tests for unidentified practitioners and does not return answer sheets to test takers except as requested by a psychologist; in that case, the answer sheet is put in a sealed envelope. He does score for company personnel departments without ascertaining whether there is a qualified user to interpret the scores. Individuals who request scoring service are referred to professionals in their area.

National Computer Systems, Inc.

National Computer Systems (NCS) of Minneapolis was founded by Harlan Ward, who had been associated with Hankes for a number of years. The company, chartered as a Minnesota corporation in March 1962, became a publicly held corporation in 1968. NCS's principal business is the production, sale, and use of an optical-mark reading system by which data placed in the form of marks on specially designed and prepared sheets of paper are read photoelectrically and transmitted to a general-purpose computer. The computer's programs are set to score or otherwise record and organize the data from the forms. An NCS data-input system consists of input documents, an optical scanner interfaced with a computer, appropriate computer programs, and printing equipment for outputting the necessary information.

In 1962 and 1963, NCS primarily scored personality and interest tests; in late 1963 the organization began developing answer sheets in connection with new tests, especially in the achievement area. Since then, the company has expanded its activities to include analysis of research and survey data from market surveys, morale surveys, and the like. Test scoring now constitutes 70 percent of NCS's processing activity, and surveys account for the other 30 percent. The company has three divisions: the Test Scoring Division; the Forms Division, which produces the forms that are run through the machines; and the Equipment Division, which sells equipment produced by NCS. The company does not presently rent out any equipment.

NCS has developed a fan-fold answer sheet and has acquired data on its usefulness from a very large sample of pupils. The company found that 99.6 percent of the pupils were able to use the forms properly, even at the first-grade level (Ward, 1968). Use of multiple forms for the third-grade level required some assurance that the two different forms could be put together at some point in the interpretive process. According to the research, 99.3 percent of the pupils at this level fill out the forms properly. On the average, from sixth grade up, accuracy of usage was at the 99 percent level (Ward, 1968). Obviously, this kind of answer-sheet usability has a direct bearing on the validity of test norms and on the usefulness of both norms and tests.

NCS pays the test publisher a royalty on all answer-sheet forms it prepares; it also pays a commission on all tests scored. The company does not feel there is a legal requirement for this, particularly in the latter case, but considers it desirable to obtain a publisher's support and to encourage the publisher to continue development of tests which NCS scores. Publisher agreements also require that quality control be monitored and that feedback on quality be given to NCS. The company indicated that quality control is a major responsibility, as is assurance that completed NCS forms and NCS test scores are confidential.

One of the unique aspects of NCS's business is that, with the assistance of Howard Rome, the company prepares computerized interpretations of the MMPI, using the interpretations developed by Pierson and Swenson of the Mayo Clinic. This interpretation activity, begun in the late 1950's with a grant from the National Institutes of Health, was stimulated by psychologists who felt the tests were inadequately interpreted by many users, particularly medical users. Since NCS was already scoring MMPI's, the company contacted Pierson at the Mayo Clinic and worked out an arrangement for him to use the NCS interpretive scheme, which was operationally superior to the earlier scheme developed by Pierson and Swenson. The Mayo Clinic and Psychological Corporation then cooperated with NCS on the relevant financial and ethical problems.

Psychological Corporation, as publisher of the MMPI, announced the scoring service in June 1967. Since the Psychological Corporation is the publisher responsible for the test, it has also assumed responsibility for the quality control of interpretive programs. An agreement between the Psychological Corporation, the Mayo Clinic, and National Computer Systems specifies that, as a quality control measure of the work done by NCS, Psychological Corporation will periodically send in unidentified MMPI answer sheets for scoring and evaluation.

Measurement Research Center

Probably the largest scorer of tests in the United States is the Measurement Research Center (MRC) located in Iowa City, Iowa. This organization started as a part of the University of Iowa, but now belongs to the Westinghouse Corporation. The president and founder of the Center is Dr. E. F. Lindquist, who has been prominent in the testing movement almost since its inception.

The Measurement Research Center is involved in two ways in the test scoring business. First, the Center does a large volume of test scoring. One of its reports indicates that it scored tests for 7 million persons in a single year, and that it scored 100,000 tests in 10 hours (MRC, 1964a) ; thus, the company has both high total volume and capacity for additional volume. Major test publishers for which MRC processes standardized tests are Harcourt Brace Jovanovich, Houghton Mifflin, Psychological Corporation, and Science Research Associates. Second, MRC sells test-development services to publishers and test-consulting services to schools and other organizations.

The organization's equipment and processes are specifically designed to deal with large testing programs where the "get-ready cost" is high, but the unit-processing cost is very low. Where local test development and scoring are required, MRC can provide an optical card scanner with procedures for reading position-coded information from IBM-size cards and for feeding the information into a computer and onto magnetic tape directly from the source document. From a single card, the scanner will simultaneously read pencil marks, imprinted codes, printed marks, and punched holes, translating all of this information into appropriate form for on-line input into the associated computer.

The company also has an MRC Model 10 sheet scanner which reads position-coded information from 8½ x 11-inch documents and feeds this data into a computer just as it does with the cards. From the sheets, it will read pencil marks, imprinted codes, and printed marks simultaneously. Both of the company's systems bypass the need for punching responses onto cards, which was necessary in some earlier systems. According to MRC documents, one MRC-1501 can read in an hour a volume of data equal to the output of 1,440 keypunch machine hours (MRC, 1964b). It is likely that such increases in data processing speed will significantly increase the use of tests and computerized interpretations of answer-sheet profiles.

MRC scores material on either its own separate answer sheets or on disposable booklets. The latter form has three advantages: (1) it makes test taking easier for the person involved; (2) it eliminates problems of copyright, since there is no economical way to score these forms except at MRC; and (3) disposable test booklets allow greater design freedom relative to the content and structure of a test. Dr. Lindquist indicated that historically it has been typical to use answer sheets with multiple-choice responses; this precluded the use of promising procedures that did not lend themselves to machine scoring of multiple-choice formats. He believes that we are now on the verge of technological breakthroughs that will permit inclusion of new kinds of test materials in test booklets; answers will be marked directly in the booklet rather than on the answer sheet. For example, maps and other graphic materials, which cannot be used on most answer sheets, could be used in a direct-mark booklet in which marks on the map could be scored by MRC equipment. It is also possible, of course, to combine a great deal of additional information with the test data. Dr. Lindquist predicts an increasing use of the disposable-booklet format for tests. NCS has also started work on this format.

In the future, Dr. Lindquist believes it may be necessary to devise methods for assembling comprehensive information about students, assessing this information, and then feeding it back to users in a more efficient manner than we are presently doing. He is quick to point out that we may now have more capability to acquire information about an individual and his academic difficulties than to know what to do about the difficulties.

Automata Corporation

The Automata Corporation of Richland, Washington, is a small organization just entering the test-scoring field. Automata's principal product is a card reader known as the Automata 450 Test Scorer. Intended for use in local school systems, it uses a 4 x 11-inch card that can handle fifty student answers with up to five choices per answer. The scoring key for the test is prepared on a similar card and inserted in the machine, which will then score 450 of the 50-item cards in one hour and provide visual feedback on the kinds of errors being made by the students. Though this machine is evidently intended for about the same market as the MRC-1501, it appears to be slower and less expensive. There is no need to tie it to a computer; it operates independently. Motorola Corporation in Phoenix also has a card reader for test scoring, and IBM is developing one.

Roche Psychiatric Service Institute

Another kind of scoring service is the Roche Psychiatric Service Institute which is a part of Hoffman-LaRoche, Inc., of Nutley, New Jersey. This company provides computer scoring and interpretation of the MMPI using a computer program developed by Dr. Raymond D. Fowler, Jr., at the University of Alabama. The computer program was designed to simulate the decision-making functions of the skilled MMPI interpreter. Highly configural in nature, the program makes use of the existing MMPI literature, including current actuarial research. The service is marketed to psychologists and physicians.

Institute for Behavioral Research

Automated scoring service for the Holtzman Inkblot Technique is available from the Institute of Behavioral Research, Inc., a nonprofit organization in Silver Springs, Maryland. The computer-based system scores seventeen variables of the Holtzman Inkblot Technique. The system was developed by Dr. Donald R. Gorham, Dr. Edward C. Moseley, and Dr. Wayne H. Holtzman, with support from the Veterans Administration and a grant from the National Institute of Mental Health.

Data are submitted in the form of examinees' handwritten responses, typed responses, data-punched IBM cards, or as data transferred from cards to magnetic tape to facilitate transmission. The output is a computer printout which gives scores for each of the seventeen Holtzman Inkblot scales; it includes a table of means, standard deviations, and percentiles for each subsample of one hundred records. Published norms are based on over seven thousand subjects from the United States and a large number of foreign countries.

Development of Computerized Interpretations

The development of computerized scoring has also led to potential improvements in preparation of feedback documents, especially those based on complex score relationships. The landmark in the growth of automated interpretation was the development of interpretive feedback programs for use by physicians at the Mayo Clinic. J. S. Pierson and Wendell M. Swenson of the Mayo Clinic were responsible for the work. Recently, by agreement with the Psychological Corporation, which publishes the MMPI, National Computer Systems made the MMPI interpretation service available nationwide to professionals.

Pierson and Swenson undertook the development of a feedback program in order to solve a problem at the Mayo Clinic: many clinic physicians were not using psychological test data because of the time and cost of obtaining it. More often, MMPI's were not used because too much time was required to administer the test, send it away for scoring, and then have it interpreted by a psychologist. The feedback information was received by the physicians long after other diagnostic test data had been provided. Furthermore, the cost of individual psychological interpretation of each profile was quite out of line with the cost of other available laboratory procedures.

The two psychiatrists searched the MMPI literature and their own clinical experience in order to develop interpretive statements that could be derived from scale scores or combinations of such scores on the MMPI. They arranged for a computer to analyze MMPI scores and then print out the appropriate statements on the bottom half of a score feedback form which they had devised. To satisfy themselves that the reports made by the computer were as useful and valid as those provided by the typical psychologist-evaluator, the researchers compared the computer-printout responses with similar responses from psychologists who had interpreted the test. It is interesting to note that they avoided specific diagnosis and only used statements related to attitude and behavior.

MMPI's were administered to more than one hundred fifty thousand patients during the five-year period when norms were being developed for the various printout statements. The results of this research were published by the Psychological Corporation in 1967 (Pierson and Swenson, 1967). Thus, there are now norms based on age groups, sex, and so on, for all of the standard MMPI scales, plus a couple of new ones which were developed out of this research.

Several universities have experimented rather extensively with automated test scoring. Dr. Joseph C. Finney has been directing scoring work in the Department of Psychiatry at the University of Kentucky. Finney has extended the work on the MMPI to include the California Psychological Inventory; he has also added a large number of scales to the MMPI, since he used nineteen scales on which to base his interpretive statements. Similar MMPI work is being done by Dr. Raymond Fowler at the University of Alabama and by members of the faculty at the UCLA Medical Center.

According to officers of National Computer Systems, the major supplier of MMPI interpretations, the majority of users of the service are psychologists; the remainder are psychiatrists. Most of the interpretation services are provided to regular users who are evidently well pleased with the service they receive. In the near future, we may see computerized interpretations of Strong Vocational Interest Blank scores, since they are subject to the same kind of analysis; however, we are not presently aware of any work in this direction. This general technique will also very likely be applied to combinations of other kinds of less similar data, for example, the results of a variety of physical medicine and laboratory measures which would either provide interpretive statements to the physician or suggest additional questions and laboratory testing.

Reactions to Machine Interpretation

As one might expect, the response of psychologists to machine interpretation of tests has been mixed. Some psychologists feel that the really important part of an MMPI interpretation involves nuances that could not be readily programmed into a computer. It is entirely conceivable that other professionals feel threatened by this invasion of their professional bailiwick; they may be psychologically as well as economically threatened by the new developments.

The concern of the opponents of the computer process was heightened and given additional credibility because persons providing the service made a perhaps inadvertent misstatement regarding the basis of, or the development of, interpretive statements. Material on the back of answer- and interpretation-sheet forms which bear the name and logo of the Psychological Corporation says, among other things, "The various descriptive adjectives either were gleaned from the MMPI literature or grew out of the clinical experience of the developers. The statement library stored in the computer was developed at the Mayo Clinic in Rochester, Minnesota, over a five-year period, using MMPI records of more than 150,000 patients." Unfortunately, those two statements are inconsistent with each other. The norms are actually based on samples drawn from records of about twenty-five thousand of those patients. The quotation's first statement, regarding the source of the descriptive adjectives or descriptive statements, is correct. Users are referred to Pierson and Swenson's published manual and to other documents. It is indicated that the report is intended as an aid to the professional user, not as a complete analysis of the profile.

Development of computerized interpretation raises the question: Can a computer make as good an interpretation of a complex profile as an individual can? Some recent research work by Lewis Goldberg at the Oregon Research Institute (Goldberg, 1969) provides at least one answer. Goldberg had 25 clinical psychologists each analyze 100 MMPI profiles. He then had a computer analyze the relationships between the profiles and the interpretive statements that each psychologist made. From that analysis, the computer derived interpretive statements which best represented the "model" apparently used by each psychologist in his interpretation. Another 600 blanks were then analyzed both by the psychologists and by the computer, using the model developed for each psychologist. The diagnosis provided by the computer and that made by the psychologist were each correlated with clinical diagnosis based on more complete information on the same patient. Goldberg found that the computer, using a model derived from a psychologist's actual interpretations, was better able to predict the diagnosis than was the psychologist. Apparently, the psychologist is not as reliable as the computer.

Clearly, additional work of this kind is needed to substantiate further the claims of users of such programs. But the Goldberg work already seems to shift the burden of proof for the adequacy of such interpretations from the defenders to the attackers.

The technology now exists to improve testing systems through better feedback; using scores on tests or batteries, the computer can prepare natural language interpretation documents. Such documents may go a long way to overcome the deficiencies now caused by the lack of sufficiently trained counselors, the lack of time of those counselors available to integrate and organize the scores from several tests or batteries for each test taker, and the difficulty of direct communication with all the persons who may need to understand the implications of test-battery scores. Good work in the scoring and interpretation area can help overcome problems in some other testing subsystem areas.

REFERENCES

Carter, Launor F. *Annual Report of the Ad Hoc Committee on Assessment*, May 1, 1966, pp. 7–8.

Goldberg, Lewis R. "Man vs Model of Man: A Rationale, Plus Some Evidence, for a Method of Improving on Clinical Inferences." Paper, University of Oregon and Oregon Research Institute, 1969.

Measurement Research Center. *Automated Test Processing the Measurement Research Center Way!* Brochure, Iowa City, Iowa, 1964a.

Measurement Research Center. *1501 Optical Card Scanner.* Brochure, Iowa City, Iowa, 1964b.

Pierson, John S., and Wendell M. Swenson. *A User's Guide to the Mayo Clinic Automated MMPI Program.* New York: Psychological Corporation, 1967.

Ward, Harlan, President, Gerald F. Koch, Director of Processing Division, and Dr. William Moonan, statistician, National Computer Systems, Minneapolis, Minn. Interviews, 1968.

9

People and Organizations in Testing

The quality of an assessment system is dependent on the competence of many individuals; the adequacy of assessment systems nationwide is also dependent on the ways in which competence is evaluated and assured, functions typically performed by government agencies and professional associations. This chapter is concerned with the people actually involved in testing, and the legal and organizational means of assuring adequacy of professional qualifications and practice.

Subsystem 1: Definition of Assessment-System Requirements

A person who selects tests for testing programs must be able to derive specific test objectives from educational, employment, and other program objectives which the testing serves. He must have general knowledge of tests available in his area of work and must be able to understand such reference sources as research reports, test reviews, advertisements, and test manuals. He must also have a good understanding of the content area of which the testing is to be a part. This typically requires at least a Master's degree with emphasis on testing and related fields, plus education and experience in the field the testing serves, such as elementary education or industrial-personnel selection.

Subsystem 2: Test Development and Standardization

Work in the development subsystem requires the highest level of technical competence of any subsystem. The professional in the test-development field must be able to translate test requirements into test formats and items, supervise collection and analysis of data used to establish validity, reliability, and norms, and prepare test manuals that reflect purposes, population, and other information needed for test selection. These tasks require extensive knowledge of test-development statistics and related methodology, usually at the doctoral level, unless the individual is working under supervision.

Subsystem 3: Test Administration

The test administrator must be able to follow the instructions in the test manual and must assure appropriate physical and emotional environments for the testing. He must distribute materials, ascertain that examinees understand what they are to do, time the examinations, and collect materials. Test-administration duties probably require less training than responsibilities in any other subsystem, except for routine test scoring. Nonetheless, administrative procedures are critical, since the quality of these activities may significantly influence test results and test-taker's attitudes; further, problems in this area are difficult to detect later.

It is generally recommended that test administrators have at least a bachelor's degree in the behavioral sciences or in education and have supervised experience in testing. Even more important than formal education, however, are the requirements that the person responsible for administering tests be capable of establishing rapport with persons being tested, and that he be conscientious in following instructions in test manuals.

Subsystem 4: Scoring and Preparation of Feedback Documents

Most scoring of standardized tests is done by machine, so organizational as well as personal competence is necessary for quality assurance. Sampling and other quality-control procedures mentioned earlier are essential for machine scoring. Individuals scoring tests must understand the instructions to both test takers and scorers, have good clerical skills, and exercise care in their work. Although scorers are not required to have special schooling, they should work under the supervision of a person trained in test administration and interpretation.

Preparation of feedback documents, if separate from the feedback activity itself, is usually associated with machine scoring of standardized tests and batteries. The same high level of skill required for test development is needed for development of feedback processes and information formats.

Subsystem 5: Feedback of Test Results

The person giving feedback must be able to relate the test findings to educational, employment, or other plans and problems of the test taker or to other test uses. He must be able to answer questions on the meaning of test results. Feedback to the user requires about the same knowledge as is required for test selection, plus skill in counseling.

Subsystem 6: Evaluation of the Assessment System

The evaluation of assessment systems requires research competences similar to those called for in connection with establishing test requirements and with test development. Knowledge of experimental design, sampling theory, and statistical applications are essential.

Persons Performing Testing Work

What kinds of skills do various personnel have for test selection, development, use, and evaluation? Because people involved in administering and interpreting tests are not uniformly licensed, certified, or otherwise organized into discrete groups, it is difficult to determine what persons are involved in testing and what their qualifications are. We do know that most of these individuals may be broadly classified as educators, psychologists, and industrial or government personnel workers. By examining the organizations to which they belong, we can gain some clues to the number of persons engaged in testing activities and to their training and professional identifications. It is important to remember that many testing professionals belong to more than one organization and that, on the other hand, many test users do not belong to any organization.

Psychologists

We estimate that between ten thousand and fifteen thousand psychologists perform professional work involved with testing. Most psychologists have a doctoral degree, preparation for which included several courses in testing, statistics, and counseling. These people are primarily working in the fields of test development and clinical, counseling, industrial, educational, and school psychology. They are most often involved in the development, feedback, and evaluation subsystems, although some are responsible for the general supervision of testing programs in education, industry, and government.

Counseling, Guidance, and Personnel Workers

Judging from membership data of the American Personnel and Guidance Association (APGA), we estimate that between fifteen thousand and twenty thousand members are directly concerned with some aspect of testing. Their work typically involves test administration and daily utilization of test scores in individual counseling or personnel work. It frequently also involves test selection (especially in industry) and evaluation and often test development as well.

Although APGA members differ greatly in their professional backgrounds, a high percentage of them have had some formal training in testing principles; often this is graduate-level training. However, Black (1963; p. 169) charged that about 70 percent of the school counselors he studied did not know how to make validity studies appropriate to their own use of tests. He interpreted this as evidence of inadequate training and technical capability in school counselors. Although we have no reason to challenge Black's data, it is by no means clear that all school counselors must be capable of conducting studies of the predictive validity of tests in order to be effective in their work. They must, of course, be able to understand reports of such work by other professionals.

Teachers

The extent of testing in schools has been found to be related to such variables as grade level, size of city, socioeconomic level, and section of the country (Goslin, 1967; p. 18). Nevertheless, it is a rare school district that does not carry out some kind of standardized testing program at various grade levels. Classroom teachers are thus the largest professional group making regular use of standardized tests. They are most involved in test administration and feedback to students, parents, and others needing interpretation of test results.

How well are teachers prepared to make use of these test results? No simple answer exists, for it depends on the kind of test used, the information desired by the teacher relative to an individual child, and so forth. Certainly, the typical teacher might gain a better understanding of achievement levels of pupils without knowing many of the fine points about measurement theory. On the other hand, test results may be used for educational classification purposes even at the classroom level, as in assignment to ability groups of some kind. In such a case, it may be a matter of some concern that so many teachers have had virtually no training in tests and measurement.

Goslin (1967; p. 35) found in his sample of seventy-five schools that 22 percent of the public secondary school teachers reported having no undergraduate or graduate training in testing. A similar percentage was reported for teachers in parochial schools, but for private schools, the figure was reported as 63 percent. At the elementary level, 24 percent reported that they never had a testing course. If these percentages are roughly representative of the national population of teachers, it means we now have between three hundred thousand and four hundred thousand teachers who have had no formal training in measurement theory or methods. Such training would undoubtedly improve their capability for making effective use of test results.

Teachers who wish to do so can obtain information about tests from a variety of sources; in fact, most teachers can obtain help from other professionals in their school or their school district. On the other hand, reliance upon such sources of help concerning tests may not be adequate. There is a strong national trend toward more individual assessment and greater individualization in instruction and toward the continued use of standardized tests in classrooms. Thus, practically all teachers will need more training in tests and measurement than they have received in the past. Our impression, however, is that teachers are less well prepared in this area than was previously the case.

Industrial Users

Russell Sage Foundation is supporting a study by Stanley H. Udy, Jr., of Yale University, and Vernon E. Buck of the University of Washington, of testing-and-placement practices in American business and industrial organizations. Data from a sample of over three hundred business organizations are being used to test the efficacy of a model derived from trends in industrial development and the structure of the U.S. labor force, portraying differential recruitment problems by occupational categories and types of industry. The data were collected by a detailed mailed questionnaire, supplemented by telephone interviews and, in some cases, on-site visits.

At present, we do not know how many business organizations use training in personnel work. It is far easier to enter personnel work, which requires no credentials or formal training, than to become a school counselor or a psychologist, which almost universally requires credentials. Very little is known about the professional qualifications of many persons who use tests in industry. However, there is little doubt that a substantial number of this group are not members of any professional organization; many have not had any formal training in the theory or practice of testing.

Government Users

In general, the same questions that must be raised with respect to testing in industry apply to public-employment testing; foremost is the question whether persons using tests to aid in personnel decisions are appropriately qualified for this responsibility. Where civil service or merit systems exist for purposes of personnel selection and promotion in state and local governments, there are legal requirements or regulations which set standards for test utilization. Little is known of the predictive validity of these assessment procedures as typically applied; but there is, at least, assurance that merit-system selection will be carried out in accordance with basic principles of fair play.

Subsystem Analysis: Personnel Strengths and Weaknesses

The problems relating to qualifications of people in testing seem to focus on the lack of adequately trained workers at the point of contact with the test taker and user rather than on the area of test development. Lack of qualified paraprofessionals seems to be a more serious problem than lack of qualified professionals (if we assume that the unavailability and cost of fully qualified professionals generally precludes extensive use of their services at the point of contact with the test user). Governments at various levels can influence the quality of testing by prescribing or proscribing certain behaviors, by controlling distribution, or by controlling who enters the testing field; the latter is the means most used to date.

Government Quality Controls of People in Testing Systems

In view of the social implications of improper test utilization, controlling the quality of test usage may become an issue of increasing concern to public policy makers. Assuming that some proof of qualifications based on specialized training is important for those who use tests, let us now consider the present status of certification, licensing, and other quality controls affecting assessment systems.

Types of Licensing and Certification Relative to Testing

There are three major forms of legal control with respect to personnel who, among other things, utilize tests in connection with their professional activity. Insofar as they influence the employment or job assignment of personnel using tests, these controls may have an important effect on standard setting in professional practice.

LICENSING. Licensing provides for control of specific activities in some area of practice. These activities are restricted to one or more designated professional groups to which licenses are issued; for example, licensing laws governing the work of psychologists are in effect in seventeen states. We know of no licensing legislation covering counseling, guidance, or personnel workers. Licensing, in theory at least, can effect the highest degree of control over professional functioning.

CERTIFICATION. Certification provides for control of a professional designation or title; perhaps the best-known example would be "Certified Public Accountant." Certification laws regulating the title "Psychologist" have been passed in twenty-four states. Such laws do not provide any control over the function of an individual, but they do prevent uncertified persons from using the professional designation covered by the law. Therefore, certification may offer some protection to the public insofar as the public is aware of differences between certified personnel and others who may represent themselves as capable of carrying out some function whether or not, in fact, they have had the proper training and experience to do so.

CREDENTIALS. Professional credentials are required for employment in publicly supported or licensed organizations in most states. The standards of training and experience that must be met for the credential are ordinarily established by the state with the assistance of the relevant professional groups. Most familiar are credentials for public school teachers and vocational guidance workers.

Similarly, school psychologists in the United States typically obtain their positions after they earn a credential in psychological counseling. Although a credential does not assure a high quality of practice, it is an effective mechanism for setting minimum standards for employment. It may be a useful tool for assuring at least adequate formal training for responsibilities involving the use of tests.

Associations of Professionals in Test Work

It is evident that government control of persons entering testing does not affect many people in testing work. Professional associations, on the other hand, exert considerable influence over the testing practices of their members.

American Psychological Association

The American Psychological Association (APA) was founded in 1892; with over twenty-seven thousand members, it represents a high percentage of the psychologists in this country. Recent manpower data revealed that over 50 percent of the members of APA are identified with the fields of clinical, counseling, or industrial psychology (APA, 1968; p. 3). Judging from this, a high percentage of the membership is probably involved to some degree in the use of psychological tests. A much smaller percentage is represented by the membership of Division 5 (Evaluation and Measurement), which is concerned more directly with the theory and practice of test development.

APA holds an annual meeting, publishes psychological journals in virtually all areas of psychology, and works to strengthen standards for psychological training, service, and scientific development. The association does not in any way own any part of the testing industry, nor does it publish tests.

In its publication *Psychology as a Profession,* APA (1968; p. 2) lists the following four points as a summary of purposes for which it accepts responsibility: "(1) advancing basic knowledge concerning behavior, (2) setting standards for training qualified aspirants to professional competence, (3) cooperating with state associations and with governmental bodies in establishing and maintaining standards of professional competence, and (4) developing and enforcing a code of ethics."

APA has state associations affiliated in all states except Alaska; most of these associations maintain active committees on ethical practices. Similarly, the national APA ethics committee is backed by an extensive statement of ethical principles which includes considerable material bearing on proper uses of psychological tests and information derived therefrom. For the past five years, an assessment committee sponsored by APA's Board of Professional Affairs has studied and made recommendations on a number of policy issues directly concerned with testing.

With the American Educational Research Association and the National Council of Measurement in Education, APA sponsored and published the *Standards for Educational and Psychological Tests and Manuals.* This publication, probably the most significant technical contribution made by APA with regard to test development, is discussed in Chapter 10.

American Personnel and Guidance Association

The American Personnel and Guidance Association (APGA), comprising over twenty-eight thousand members, is made up of the following divisions: American College Personnel Association (ACPA), Association for Counselor Education and Supervision (ACES), National Vocational Guidance Association (NVGA), Student Personnel Association for Teacher Education (SPATE), American School Counselor Association (ASCA), American Rehabilitation Counseling Association (ARCA), National Employment Counselors Association (NECA), and Association for Measurement and Evaluation in Guidance (AMEG).

At the rate of about two thousand new members annually, the membership of APGA is increasing more rapidly than the membership of APA. The rate is attributed in part to recent heavy funding of counselor training programs and to American education's very high demand for personnel in the counseling and guidance field. To a great extent, this demand has been spurred by funds available under the Federal Elementary and Secondary Education

Act for employment of personnel in these professional specialties. Although a very high percentage of the membership of APGA probably has some college-level training in tests and measurements, hard data on such preparation are not available.

With the exception of members of AMEG, most personnel in APGA's other seven divisions are primarily test users. Most AMEG members are concerned with conducting testing programs, developing new tests and evaluating old ones, and teaching college courses in evaluation and measurement. The focus of AMEG is, as its name suggests, on the guidance area rather than on the measurement and evaluation spectrum in general.

While APGA itself does not currently carry out accreditation programs, it cooperates with the National Council on Accreditation of Training in Education (NCATE), and its members frequently belong to accreditation teams concerned with the counseling and guidance area. APGA does maintain a national ethics committee. To guide the work of such committees, the Association has published the extensive *Ethical Standards Casebook* which includes a section on testing. The *Casebook* provides broad coverage of a variety of ethical issues related to test usage.

American Educational Research Association

The American Educational Research Association (AERA), with about ten thousand members, offers an organizational framework for professionals concerned with educational research and development. Through papers presented at its annual meetings and through technical reports and monographs dealing with evaluation and measurement, this association has become an important contributor to the theory and practice of testing. AERA is not, however, involved in any way in the ownership or distribution of testing materials.

AERA has performed an important function as an intermediary between federal agencies, some of which have had considerable influence on testing programs and program evaluation policies. From time to time, AERA representatives and officers consult with both elected public officials and government administrators to interpret AERA recommendations on policy matters concerning measurement and evaluation and many other topics bearing on education. Increased commitments of federal funds for educational research throughout the United States may explain AERA's particularly rapid growth during the past ten years.

National Council on Measurement in Education

The National Council on Measurement in Education (NCME) has approximately seven hundred members; the organization's annual meeting is usually held in conjunction with the American Educational Research Association. NCME publishes the *Journal of Educational Measurement*. For over fifty years, NCME has provided a forum and a publication outlet for school district measurement and evaluation personnel who are often at a high administrative level, and for teachers of measurement and evaluation courses in higher education. The organization's activities are mainly addressed to the advancement of knowledge in the field of measurement in education and to efforts to contribute toward the improvement of training in this area.

NCME committees have developed training standards for college courses in the field of measurement and evaluation. They have also provided recommendations and materials pertaining to the evaluation of courses in these areas.

National Associations That Produce and Distribute Tests

Both the Public Personnel Association and the Professional Examination Service of the American Public Health Association are actively engaged in test development and distribution. We have discussed their activities in Chapter 5. The American Public Health Association is similar to the four organizations discussed above in that it is intimately concerned with training standards and professional development within the broad field of public health. Here we will merely underscore the organization's major contributions to the evaluation field through the work of the Professional Examination Service.

The Public Personnel Association (PPA), also described in Chapter 5, is both a test publisher and an association of persons and organizations producing and, particularly, using tests for selection and placement in civil service programs below the federal level. The PPA has not contributed significantly to the technical side of test development, except for its book *Recruitment and Selection in the Public Service*, edited by J. J. Donovan and published in 1968.

American Educational Publishers Institute

In addition to the professional associations described above, there is an organization of test publishers, the American Educational Publishers Institute (AEPI). This organization probably has less impact than any of the previously described organizations. Concern over restraint-of-trade prosecution appears to temper AEPI members' enthusiasm to engage in actions that might ensure quality in the development and use of tests. AEPI's Schools Division supports a test committee comprised of representatives of eleven educational publishers who also deal in testing. For a number of years, chairmanship of the committee has been held by senior test personnel of the largest companies.

The principal visible function of the AEPI test committee is the publication of an annual report on total test- and answer-sheet sales by publishers. Since AEPI is primarily concerned with educational publishing rather than with testing, it is not surprising that the majority of medium-size test publishers, primarily in the business of publishing tests, do not belong to the Institute. Similarly, small test publishers do not belong to AEPI. Both Educational Testing Service (ETS) and other members of the committee felt that it was not appropriate for a nonprofit organization to be a member of the AEPI, and so ETS resigned a few years ago. With Harcourt Brace's recent resignation from AEPI, the organization's influence in the testing area appears to be decreasing further.

Controls

Professional Association Controls

It is evident that there are many kinds and levels of control on people who develop and use tests, but there is no system of control. The most effective control may be that exercised by the professional organizations to which testing people belong. A number of these organizations have taken leadership in the recommendation of training standards relative to test development and use, and in the formulation of credential, certification, and licensing standards throughout the United States. Both the American Psychological Association and the American Personnel and Guidance Association have developed ethical codes, parts of which deal very specifically with proper use of test materials and with the control of test results.

Professional organizations, while highly interested in the professional activities of their members, have no jurisdiction over nonmembers; thus they are limited in the scope of their regulatory or quality-control function. Certain committees and staff members of these associations have been actively concerned about questionable testing practices, but none of the associations has any mechanism through which malpractice by nonmembers may be detected, evaluated, or regulated.

Until very recently, no government regulations have attempted to curb most of the poor practice in the testing industry. Although regulatory legislation has been instigated by some associations, the legislation covers professional activities, not test sales. Thus the concerns of professional associations have been limited to the practices of their members and to the development of certification, licensing, and training which enable consumers of testing services to make informed judgments regarding the qualifications of persons offering such services. Within the past decade, most of these organizations have become considerably more involved in protecting the public with regard to the use and misuse of tests. This involvement has been evident in the numerous presentations at annual meetings, in the forming of special committees and task forces charged with the review of special problems (e.g., testing minority-group members), and in the revisions and supplements to ethical codes.

American Board of Examiners in Professional Psychology

The American Board of Examiners in Professional Psychology, a part of APA, conducts written, oral, and field-work examinations which lead to a diploma for psychologists in the areas of clinical, counseling, industrial, and school psychology. Individuals who pass these examinations thus receive formal recognition that their professional colleagues consider their training and experience sufficiently appropriate so that they may take independent professional responsibility for work in their specialty area. Knowledge and experience with testing and evaluation procedures of various kinds are an important part of these examinations. The total number of diplomas issued through 1969 were 1,718 in the clinical area, 310 in counseling, 231 in industrial and organizational, and 15 in school psychology.

This kind of intraprofessional standard setting gives the consumer of services an opportunity to distinguish among professionals who have similar but different competences. But since professional examinations are intended only for highly qualified persons, such procedures have questionable impact upon the day-to-day testing practices of most of the people who use tests in this country. It may be important to examine the potential values of some form of national certification which would be available to qualified test users who could demonstrate their competence as testing specialists.

Industry Association Controls

Since control of test utilization is by no means complete, the industry attempts to regulate the distribution of certain types of tests. Unless a potential test purchaser can prove he is trained to use tests, he will find it difficult to obtain from test publishers materials for individual intelligence tests and to obtain projective tests such as the Rorschach and the Thematic Apperception Test. The testing industry does attempt to follow the ethical standards recommended by the American Psychological Association with regard to distribution of testing materials; however, distributors have virtually no control over what is done with the materials once they are mailed to an authorized user. If the purchaser chooses to make materials available to unqualified personnel, he can do so.

The development of industry associations or committees concerned with testing standards has been slow; it has come about largely as a consequence of pressures from minority groups and from state fair employment practice agencies. The impetus for improving testing practices in industry has clearly been related to legislation that requires employers to take actions furthering equal-employment opportunities for minority-group members.

Perhaps the best example of an organization concerned with testing standards is California's Technical Advisory Committee on Testing (TACT). This organization has conducted research and issued recommendations which help businesses measure up to professional standards in their testing activities. Also, TACT provides guidance so that businesses can carry out constructive and fair testing programs. The TACT committee has been able to fill the need of business and industry for information and consultation regarding recently imposed requirements for defensible and technically sound employment-selection procedures.

TACT provides an interesting model of cooperation among three groups: a state agency concerned with equal-employment opportunity, representatives of personnel departments of large industries, and private consultants in the personnel-selection field. This kind of collaborative effort appears very necessary if the quality of industrial testing programs is to be improved.

In addition to the formal organizational interrelationships described in this chapter and elsewhere, there is a significant informal organization. This structure is held together by the mutual interests, common educational backgrounds, and professional concern of the key members of private, educational, and governmental organizations concerned with testing. Such individuals exert a very strong influence in government, in professional societies, and in testing companies; further, they are well acquainted with each other, primarily through professional societies. Undoubtedly, those who comprise this vital informal organization can be counted on to continue to give their support and leadership to bring about improvements in testing systems.

REFERENCES

American Psychological Association. *Ethical Standards for the Distribution of Psychological Tests and Diagnostic Aids.* Washington, D.C.: APA, 1954.

American Psychological Association. *Psychology as a Profession.* Washington, D.C.: APA, 1968.

Black, H. *They Shall Not Pass.* New York: Morrow, 1963.

Goslin, D. A. *Teachers and Testing.* New York: Russell Sage Foundation, 1967.

10

Control of Test Standards, Distribution, and Use of Tests

Although control of testing practices is not the exclusive concern of any group or agency, controls are most effectively exercised by the professional organizations discussed in the preceding chapter.

The three principal ways in which professional organizations influence the quality of testing are: (1) by establishing standards for tests and related materials; (2) by recommending to test publishers the standards of education that should be met by persons to whom tests are distributed; and (3) by monitoring the professional practices of the organizations' members.

Test Standards

Development of Test Standards

The first organizational recommendations for test standards were the *Technical Recommendations for Psychological Tests and Diagnostic Techniques,* published by the American Psychological Association (APA) in March 1954. Shortly thereafter, *Technical Recommendations for Achievement Tests* were prepared by committees of the American Educational Research Association (AERA) and the National Council on Measurements in Education (NCME). The product of their efforts was published in 1955 and copyrighted by the National Educational Association.

The most influential document at the present time is a revision and combination of these two earlier publications. Prepared by a joint APA, AERA,

123

and NCME committee formed in 1963, the document was published in 1966. Since this manual, *Standards for Educational and Psychological Tests and Manuals* was copyrighted and published by the American Psychological Association; it is often referred to as the *APA Standards Manual.* This despite the fact that its editors were committee co-chairmen John W. French of APA and William B. Michael of AERA and NCME.

In preparing the *Standards,* the committee invited comments from members of the three sponsoring professional organizations and from test authors, publishers, and users. The current *Standards* are, of course, not only the result of the work of the committees formed in the early 1950's and 1960's; they reflect a long history of work by professionals in universities and within the testing industry.

Since testing is one procedure by which society regulates life opportunities, technical foundation for test development must be sound. The establishment of standards for tests and manuals is one of the hallmarks of a competent and self-critical profession. Interestingly, the impact of the *Standards* has been felt by others than psychologists, counselors, and personnel specialists who use tests. For example, both the Equal Employment Opportunities Commission and the Office of Federal Contract Compliance have adopted the *Standards* as criteria for professional test development.

Use of Standards

The breadth of application of the *Standards* is not evident from the book's title. Application covers "not only tests as narrowly defined, but also most published devices for diagnosis, prognosis, and evaluation (APA, 1966; p. 3)." The *Standards* apply to interest inventories, personality inventories, projective techniques and related clinical techniques, tests of aptitude or ability, and achievement tests, especially those administered in an educational setting.

Interviews with test publishers indicate that, with rare exception, publishers have not only found the *Standards* useful in preparation of their tests, but have followed them in the development of most tests and manuals. In fact, some test development organizations have actually converted the manual into a check-list form for use by their authors and editors. Several statements by publishers indicate that one or more of the aspects of the *Standards* are somewhat unrealistic, however; a case in point is the requirement for publishing validity data on a wide variety of populations for all scales on a test.

The *Standards* editors recognize that the publication of specifications for tests can have the effect of discouraging the development of new types of tests. The *Standards* do, to some extent, interfere with innovation, but they are written to preclude such interference as far as possible. Indeed, regarding one new test series, the test reviewer indicated that, while the tests did not meet all requirements of the *Standards,* they were, in fact, a model for other test publishers in preparing similar tests. The stated goal in the *Standards* is "to assist test publishers in bringing out a wide variety of tests that will be suitable for all the different purposes for which tests should be used, and to make those tests as valuable as possible (APA, 1966; p. 2)."

The *Standards* allow for the fact that some tests are still being developed and are thus considered in the experimental stage, while others are being published commercially for regular sale to the public. The manual recognizes that standards must be different in these cases. There are three levels of standards: those which are *essential,* those which are *very desirable,* and those which are *desirable.* Each requirement for a test is classified into one of these categories in terms of the importance and the feasibility of attaining the objective.

At first glance, the *Standards* appear to be much more concerned with information about tests than with the tests themselves. In fact, one critical reviewer commented that reading the *Standards* reminded him of the line in *My Fair Lady:* "It doesn't matter what you do exactly, so long as you pronounce it properly." Nevertheless, careful consideration proves the editors of the *Standards* correct in focusing more on reporting accurately how the test was developed than on putting developers in a straitjacket of standards not appropriate to new test forms.

The editors of the manual recognize that it is possible to produce a test that essentially meets all standards yet appears virtually worthless from the standpoint of fulfilling its intended or stated objective. Potential users of such a test should be able to discern its uselessness, however, either from their own experience and training or from reviews of new and existing tests. Generally, insofar as the reviews apply the *Standards* to tests under consideration, they assist test users in their evaluation of various instruments.

Content of Test Standards

The *APA Standards Manual* is divided into six sections. These are presented below with examples of representative principles quoted from the manual (APA, 1966).

DISSEMINATION OF INFORMATION. "When a test is published for operational use, it should be accompanied by a manual (or other published and readily available information) that makes every reasonable effort to follow the recommendations in this report (p. 7)."

"The test and its manual should be revised at appropriate intervals (p. 8)."

INTERPRETATION. "The test, the manual, record forms, and other accompanying material should assist users to make correct interpretations of test results (p. 9)."

"The test manual should indicate the qualifications required to administer the test and to interpret it properly (p. 10)."

VALIDITY. "The manual should report the validity of the test for each type of inference for which it is recommended. If its validity for some suggested interpretation has not been investigated, that fact should be made clear (p. 15)."

"The sample employed in a validity study and the conditions under which testing is done should be consistent with the recommendations made in the manual. They should be described sufficiently for the user to judge whether the reported validity is pertinent to his situation (p. 18)."

RELIABILITY. "The test manual should report evidence of reliability that permits the reader to judge whether scores are sufficiently dependable for the recommended uses of the test. If any of the necessary evidence has not been collected, the absence of such information should be noted (p. 27)."

ADMINISTRATION AND SCORING. "The directions for administration should be presented in the test manual with sufficient clarity and emphasis that the test user can duplicate, and will be encouraged to duplicate, administrative conditions under which the norms and the data on reliability and validity were obtained (p. 32)."

"The procedures for scoring the test should be presented in the test manual with a maximum of detail and clarity so as to reduce the likelihood of scoring error (p. 32)."

SCALES AND NORMS. "Scales used for reporting scores should be so carefully described in the test manual as to increase the likelihood of accurate interpretation and the understanding of both the test interpreter and the subject (p. 33)."

Note that the material on administration and scoring occupies less than two of the thirty pages in the *APA Standards Manual*. This is probably an accurate reflection that the *Standards* primarily influence development of tests and the collection and dissemination of information about how different populations perform on tests.

Ethical Standards

Another aspect of the development and enforcement of professional standards in connection with testing comes from the ethical standards established and administered by the American Psychological Association and the American Personnel and Guidance Association (APGA). In 1956, APA first published a complete code of ethics which included both statements of principle and illustrative examples. When the code was updated in 1963, some of the principles were restated; when it was again revised in 1966, a fairly complete statement of principles, examples, and cases was published.

The statements on ethical standards are fortunately at their best in areas where test standards do not apply or do not appear to be effective. The ethical standards deal primarily with the relationship of the psychologist to the client or to others who receive his services.

Comparison of Standards Manuals

The *APA Standards Manual* and the APA *Ethical Standards of Psychologists* touch a number of common areas. The first area involves the general statement in *Ethical Standards* (APA, 1963; p. 7) that tests and diagnostic aids can be released only to persons who can demonstrate the knowledge and skill necessary to use and interpret the tests effectively. That statement advances the same philosophy as the *Standards* (APA, 1966; pp. 10–11) which recommends (1) that tests be divided into three categories, depending upon the amount of skill required for the use and interpretation of the tests, and (2) that separate distribution standards be established for each of the three categories.

The *Ethical Standards* statements (APA, 1963; p. 7) require that the psychologist responsible for a testing program assume responsibility for the usefulness and appropriateness of the materials used and for an adequate interpretation of the results to those using the scores. This goes considerably beyond the statements in the *Standards* (APA, 1966; pp. 9–10) which require only that such information be available. Of course, the psychologist responsible for a testing program would be unable to carry out his part of the ethical standards if the test publisher did not carry out his part of the test-standards requirements for complete, relevant information about the test.

The two sets of standards also indicate a common philosophy with respect to test manuals, advertising materials, and other information that may affect peoples' decisions to use tests. Both guides require that the information provided be sufficiently complete and objective to allow adequate appraisal of the possible application of the specific test for the specific purpose for which it is to be used. A third common area concerns the responsibility for revision of test manuals and norms that influence the user populations and the test purposes.

In 1965, the American Personnel and Guidance Association published the *Ethical Standards Casebook,* which had been prepared by APGA's ethical-practices committee during the preceding two years. The *Casebook* provides illustrative examples of both ethical and unethical practices as they relate to each of the fifty-six principles in the APGA ethical-standards code.

Nine of the fifty-six statements in the code relate specifically to testing and show concern for essentially the same problems as those covered in the *APA Standards Manual*. They are, of course, expressed in terms that are primarily relevant for the typical school or similar institutional employment environment of APGA members.

Both APA and APGA have ethical-practices committees which police their members' performances. The only control available to these organizations, however, is the threat of expulsion from the organization. Although very meaningful to conscientious professionals, this threat has no impact on persons who are not subject to the ethical-practice sanctions. It is unlikely that such persons would attempt to join a professional organization, however; and many of them would not be accepted into one. In addition, these people might be less concerned with staying in the professional association than with increasing profit in their business activities. The result is that the *APA Standards Manual* and *Ethical Standards* are most effective for those least likely to need them; fortunately, however, this appears to be the majority of people involved in the field.

Distribution Controls

Following the recommendations of the professional organizations, most companies in the testing industry attempt to regulate the distribution of certain types of tests. Unless a potential test purchaser can prove he is trained to use tests, he will find it difficult to obtain from test publishers materials for individual intelligence testing and projective tests such as the Rorschach and the Thematic Apperception Test. The test industry does attempt to follow the standards recommended by the American Psychological Association with regard to distribution of testing materials; however, distributors have virtually no control over what is done with the materials once they are mailed to an authorized user. If the purchaser chooses to make materials available to unqualified personnel, he can do so.

There are two major ways in which distribution of tests can be controlled: (1) through laws that prevent their purchase by (or distribution to) unqualified users or that prevent their distribution for unapproved purposes, and (2) through voluntary control by test authors and publishers.

We expected to find that appropriate laws protected the public interest and that the industry did not restrict sales, for restriction would presumably result in reduced profits. We found just the opposite. Through the influence of professional organizations and their members in the industry, control of distribution at the point of sale has been significantly influenced. Apparently because it has been more concerned with the competitive rights of a few business organizations than with the rights of unsuspecting test takers, the federal government has discouraged attempts to keep tests out of the hands of the unqualified, or possibly unscrupulous, sellers of testing services.

Control by Test Publishers and Distributors

Enforcement of test standards at the point of testing is essentially impossible; thus the professional organizations involved with testing have recommended that the publishers and distributors of tests control sales so that only those qualified to purchase a given type of test can buy that test. Congressional committees have recently been critical of test publishers for distributing materials to unqualified persons. In part, this apparent lack of control by publishers and distributors may have stemmed from some actions of the Compliance Division, Bureau of Restraint of Trade, Federal Trade Commission (FTC). A discussion of these circumstances follows.

As they have in the past, most testing companies continue trying to police the sale of their tests; however, this is not always an easy task. The cost of determining qualifications of a potential purchaser is considerable, as is the problem of developing adequacy and reliability of data on which qualification evaluations are made. One short cut to establishing qualifications is to accept as properly qualified only those who belong to professional organizations involved with testing. The membership and ethical-practices committees of such organizations generally assure that their members are qualified. Potential test purchasers who are not members of such professional organizations are asked by test publishers to provide information on their qualifications.

For a number of years it was common practice in the testing industry, at least among the large companies, to exchange information on qualified purchasers. Thus, a person who had established himself as qualified with one company could indicate that fact when he attempted to purchase tests from another company. The prospective new seller could then check with the former seller; i.e., a reference system was established. This process was challenged in the fall of 1967 by a Federal Trade Commission complaint made in response to a reported violation of the Federal Trade Commission Act by a number of the larger psychological testing organizations.

Four organizations were named in the FTC complaint: Psychological Corporation, Science Research Associates, World Book Company (Harcourt Brace Jovanovich), and California Test Bureau. These four companies, called respondents in the FTC documents, were said to be the largest publishers and distributors of tests and related materials in the United States and the only source of supply for many of those products. Therefore, the FTC said (1967), they were in a position to control distribution of substantially all testing products. They were charged with actions in restraint of trade as follows:

> Sometime prior to March 1955, the respondents entered into and have since carried out understandings, agreements, and a planned common course of action to restrict and restrain competition and interstate trade and commerce in the sale and distribution of said product. Pursuant to, and in furtherance of said understandings, agreements, and planned common course of action, the respondents have been and are now doing the following acts and practices: (1) agreed not to sell to persons or firms who conduct tests by mail; (2) have refused to sell to persons or firms who conduct tests by mail; (3) have kept and maintained lists of persons and firms engaged in conducting tests by mail and exchanged such lists with each other; (4) investigated prospective customers as to their qualifications and methods used in giving tests, and advised each other as to the information obtained; (5) boycotted persons and firms engaged in conducting tests by mail (p. 3).

The companies involved were given the following year to enter into an agreement containing a consent order to cease and desist from the practices charged. Persons in the testing industry feel that, as a result of this complaint and the consent decree which followed it, tests were made available to persons not necessarily qualified to administer them. Further, the nonprofessionals desiring to purchase tests followed practices that were not in keeping with what is considered good practice in the field.

Details regarding the original complainant and other information about the case are not available from the FTC because the complaint resulted in a consent decree rather than in a public trial. Mr. Joseph J. Gercke, Chief, Compliance Division, Bureau of Restraint of Trade, Federal Trade Commission, and members of his staff provided copies of the public materials pertinent to this case. They indicated that no other case involving testing companies has resulted in the issuance of an FTC cease-and-desist order.

In response to our questions, FTC spokesmen stated that a small amount of activity relating to testing companies was alleged to be in violation of the Federal Trade Commission Act; all pertinent cases have been resolved without legal action, although the Commission is required to prosecute cases involving violation of the FTC Act. Evidently, when the Commission received an informal complaint from a test buyer or user, it began an informal investigation by corresponding with the potential defendant. Generally, the complainant was either satisfied with this or with resolutions achieved through other channels.

At the time of this writing, the case cited above was the only one the

Commission had prosecuted, an indication that the Commission was unaware of any other violations. In early 1969, another case was pending, but details of the matter could not be provided legally. It was indicated that some test publishers have engaged in activities that are not literally within the constraints of the FTC Act. According to Chief Gercke, these actions might relate more to price fixing than to restriction of sales; in fact, the FTC has ordered major test publishers to forward records of answer-sheet sales for the past five years.

There seems to be considerable agreement among testing professionals and test publishers that tests should not be distributed to unqualified users; the same viewpoint has been voiced in congressional hearings. This raises a question which should be reopened and considered more thoroughly: Is the *public interest* served best under present FTC provisions governing test sales, or should publishers be permitted to restrict sales to qualified test users? Since the present FTC position makes it rather easy for unqualified persons to acquire test materials, it also contributes to the possibility of invalid, unprofessional testing procedures and results.

Based on our discussion with publishers throughout the nation, we believe it extremely unlikely that control of test distribution can be effected through APA recommendations. Three reasons for pessimism about industrial controls: (1) their ineffectiveness (as indicated above), (2) the cost of administering a control program, and (3) the genuine concern of industry members that such actions would result in problems with the Federal Trade Commission.

Copyrights and Answer Sheets

Copyrights

Copyright laws and laws relating to purchase of test materials by public agencies have created problems for test publishers and probably for test users as well. All the large test publishers and most of the smaller groups indicated that copyright protection for tests and answer sheets is a major problem. The difficulty lies less with the copying of test booklets than with the copying of answer sheets; test booklets, clearly protected by copyright laws, are probably as expensive to reproduce as they are to purchase. Copyright protection for separate answer sheets, on the other hand, is doubtful; consequently, large quantities of answer sheets may be purchased at low cost from printers who generally do not pay royalties to the test author or publisher.

Legislation has compounded this problem. Administrative rulings in some states specify that answer sheets purchased with public funds must be bought from the lowest bidder, regardless of ensuing copyright problems. In 1962, for example, the California State Department of Education informed school districts that the State Attorney General advised authorization to purchase answer sheets from suppliers other that the test publisher; further, school districts were required to purchase from the lowest bidder if public funds were to be used. The exception to this requirement is the Differential Aptitude Test which must be purchased from the publisher (presumably because one test *question* appears on the answer sheet).

Answer Sheets

The problem of a separate answer sheet evolved slowly, along with the development of testing programs, scoring machines, and copying processes. It became a serious matter when IBM test-scoring machines became available in the late 1930's. Currently the problem increases as the use of electrostatic and similar copying processes make reproduction of answer sheets quite simple, although perhaps not justifiable economically. Such methods make it possible for a test user to reproduce a few tests or a few hundred answer sheets without resorting to telephone calls to the publisher and to expensive airmail delivery of materials.

Test publishers claim that one of their major concerns about separate answer sheets that are not identical to those provided by the publisher is that such sheets change the testing situation and thus require establishment of different norms. This claim has been considered specious by many test users. Nonetheless, the Minnesota Statewide Testing Program indicates that when Measurement Research Center (MRC) answer sheets were used for the Differential Aptitude Tests and the Clerical Speed and Accuracy Test, significantly different norms were required. Nonapproved answer sheets do lessen the probability that the person using the test scores is getting the most acurate evaluation of whatever he is testing (or tested) for.

The development of high-speed scoring devices which use either mark-sense cards or optical scanners and the effect of machine scoring on the norms and validity of established tests also create problems for test publishers. Since the use of optical-scanning equipment coupled with digital computers for scoring tests is increasing very rapidly, it seems likely at least half of all tests administered in the future will have special optical-scanning test forms or answer-sheet forms.

Generally, test-scoring and scoring-equipment organizations that print answer sheets feel that quality control of answer sheets is necessary to assure the accuracy of the scoring; test publishers, of course, are similarly concerned with quality of test administration and scoring. Thus, the larger test-scoring organizations have voluntarily entered into royalty agreements with the publishers, both to ensure continued production of good tests and to maintain good relationships with the publishers. It is not clear, however, that all scoring organizations pay royalties or license fees, or that they intend to continue paying them.

Responses to the Problem

Test publishers have responded in several ways to the answer-sheet problem. One of the earlier attempts to alleviate copying involved changing the pricing of their products, specifically by raising the price of answer booklets and by lowering the price of answer sheets and tabulator cards. A second approach to the problem was to arrange royalties between the test user and test publisher. For example, the Psychological Corporation is reimbursed for each MRC answer sheet for the Differential Aptitude Tests used in the Illinois Statewide High School Testing Program. Many large school systems and industrial organizations prefer to have their own names on the tests they use; thus, they have licensing or royalty agreements with the test publishers for both test booklets and separate answer sheets.

One of the newer arrangements is to print the test on the optical-scanning answer sheet; this results in a disposable, copyright-protected test and thus avoids the problem altogether. A similar solution is to print the answer columns on one side of the test booklet pages, then separate the booklet from the answers before the scoring process begins. Norms and validation are established for the machine-scoring forms. Thus, the needs of all parties concerned seem to be served. The publisher is assured that, when tests are administered, the answer sheet on which the norms were based will be used; copyright violation is not a problem since the test questions are printed on the answer sheet. The user receives fast, accurate scoring, and the scoring-machine company earns its income by providing a service needed by both test publisher and user.

As they attempt to resolve copyright and answer-sheet problems, both the testing companies and the scoring companies express some concern that any reasonable solution which requires agreement between the two sets of organizations might well be considered in restraint of trade by the Federal Trade Commission. For example, some companies are solving the copyright problem by selling test services rather than tests and answer sheets themselves. In this case, purchase of an answer sheet will entitle the purchaser to free test scoring. This solution, however, may be in restraint of trade; it resembles the problems of Eastman Kodak Company, which sold color-film development along with the film itself.

REFERENCES

American Psychological Association. *Ethical Standards of Psychologists.* Washington, D.C.: APA, 1963.

APA, AERA, and NCME. *Standards for Educational and Psychological Tests and Manuals.* Prepared by a joint committee, John W. French and William B. Michael, co-chairmen. Washington, D.C.: APA, 1966.

United States of America before Federal Trade Commission, *Complaint, Docket 6967*, Washington, D.C., Nov. 29, 1967.

11

Test Reviews and Advertising

In Chapter 1 we mentioned that critics of testing decried rigid use or interpretation of test scores, the assumption that tests measure innate characteristics, and the self-fulfilling prophesies that test interpretations may become. If these criticisms are valid, then we must determine to what extent problems are caused by incorrect or inadequate information available to persons using tests. Are there adequate reviews of tests to inform potential users? Can the typical test user interpret the reviews in terms of his problems? Does test advertising tend primarily to inform or to mislead? This chapter examines test reviews and test advertising in the light of these criticisms and in terms of the standards for tests and test information discussed in the previous chapters.

Test Reviews

The testing industry and profession are specialized organizations serving the public. They not only establish standards which provide outsiders the tools for criticizing their products, but they also publish reviews of their products in widely distributed journals. Thus, as the old cliché would have it, they are their own severest critics.

There are two major sources of reviews and one ancillary source. Probably the best known single source of reviews is the *Mental Measurements Yearbook*, edited by Oscar K. Buros. The second major source consists of approximately eighty-eight educational and psychological journals which publish reviews with varying frequency, among them: *American Educational Journal,*

American Journal of Mental Deficiency, Archives of General Psychiatry, Contemporary Psychology, Educational and Psychological Measurement, Journal of Consulting and Clinical Psychology, Journal of Counseling Psychology, Journal of Educational Measurement, Journal of Projective Techniques and Personality Assessment, Occupational Psychology, Personnel and Guidance Journal, Personnel Psychology, Psychological Bulletin, and *Quarterly Journal of Experimental Psychology.*

Many test and measurement textbooks contain descriptions of tests; these descriptions often provide test purchases with their major source of information about tests. Although textbooks do not review tests in a formal sense, they include substantial material on specific tests and their applications, as well as on test development and use.

Mental Measurements Yearbook

The *Mental Measurements Yearbook* and other similar information published by Buros is central to the whole field of test reviews. Buros began his series in 1935 with a book entitled *Educational, Psychological, and Personality Tests of 1933 and 1934.* This book, and the 1936 and 1937 publications that followed it, were primarily bibliographies of recently published tests. Although the 1937 edition included critical excerpts of reviews from technical journals, 1938 saw the first "frankly critical reviews"; subsequent *Yearbooks* have been comprised primarily of evaluative reviews.

The six *Mental Measurements Yearbooks* published to date contain a total of 3,936 original test reviews, and over 20,000 references to other material relating to the tests reviewed. For example, the *Sixth Mental Measurements Yearbook,* published in 1965, lists 1,219 tests, includes 795 critical test reviews by 396 reviewers, 97 excerpts from reviews of tests which first appeared in 30 journals, and 8,001 references for specific tests. This volume of over 1,700 two-column pages is virtually a bible for persons seriously involved in testing. Continuing interest in the reviews is indicated by a Buros report that sales of the 1965 edition were continuing into 1969, even though preparations were underway for the *Seventh Mental Measurements Yearbook.*

The reviews provided in the *Sixth Mental Measurements Yearbook,* as well as those published in most of the journals that review tests, contain two basic kinds of information. Summary information, ordinarily obtained directly from the test manual, indicates the name of the test, the number of forms, the number of pages, the kinds of norms available, and the price for various parts of the testing package. Descriptive and evaluative information, ordinarily written by professionals in the testing field, describe the test and its development; summaries and evaluative statements indicate the usefulness of the tests for various purposes and point out the tests' faults. If references to the tests have not been listed previously in one of the *Mental Measurements Yearbooks,* the references are listed with the test reviews.

OBJECTIVES FOR THE YEARBOOKS. Buros (1965) lists eight objectives for the test and review sections of his *Yearbooks.* We will attempt to evaluate the *Yearbooks* against those objectives.

The first objective is "to make readily available comprehensive and up-to-date bibliographies of recent tests published in all English speaking countries (p. xxviii)." There appears to be little question that this objective is being met, since over twenty thousand references have been presented in the bibliographies associated with the tests.

Second, Buros hopes "to make readily available hundreds of frankly critical test reviews, written by persons of outstanding ability, representing various viewpoints, which will assist test users to make more discriminating selections of the standard tests which will best meet their needs (p. xxviii)." The bulk of the material in the *Mental Measurements Yearbooks* is intended to satisfy this objective; undoubtedly the *Yearbooks* are primarily used for the intended purposes. Nevertheless, some publishers and authors feel that these "frankly critical reviews" more often appear to be negative than objective. Although most of the test authors and publishers with whom we talked felt that, on the whole, reviews in the *Mental Measurements Yearbooks* were quite good, they often criticized the apparent bias on the part of reviewers and the lack of explicit standards against which different kinds of tests were reviewed. A number of organizations reported that a rather unfavorable review of a test had been written by a psychologist who was in some way or other involved with a competitive test.

In an excellent summary of the criticisms of this portion of the *Yearbooks,* Melany E. Baehr (1967) of the Industrial Relations Center of the University of Chicago related how her attitude toward reviews changed when she published her own tests and read reviews of her tests. She felt the reviews were more negative than the tests justified. Further, Dr. Baehr cited a number of instances in which the reviews were contradictory in their interpretation and evaluation, which undoubtedly leaves the reader of the reviews more confused than before he started. She felt that the personal or professional biases of reviewers probably have more influence on the kind of review written than does the *APA Standards Manual* which is supposed to be the basis for the evaluation. We found no critics who stated that test reviews would mislead potential users into uses inappropriate for the test reviewed, however.

Another frequent criticism of the evaluative reviews is that they are beyond the comprehension level of those test users who most need them. It is unlikely, though, that any single reviewing document could meet the needs of

both the highly qualified professionals in the field and the marginally qualified users of many tests. Further, there is considerable doubt whether someone
who cannot understand the reviews should be engaged in test selection.

The third objective of the *Yearbook* is "to make readily available comprehensive and accurate bibliographies of references on the construction,
validation, use, and limitations of specific tests (Buros, 1965; p. xxviii)." We
heard no criticisms of the adequacy of this portion of the reviews. However,
some persons interviewed felt that the *Yearbook* would be more useful with
some things omitted; for example, bibliographies on testing technology could
appear less often, or separately.

The fourth objective is "to impel authors and publishers to place fewer
but better tests on the market, and to provide test users with detailed and accurate information on the construction, validation, uses and limitations of their
tests at the time they are first placed on the market (pp. xxviii–xxix)." Buros
feels that the *Yearbooks* have not done as good a job in this respect as he
would have liked. In fact, he states in the *Sixth Mental Measurements Yearbook*:

> When I initiated this test reviewing service in 1933, I was confident that
> frankly critical reviews by competent specialists representing a wide variety
> of viewpoints would make it unprofitable to publish tests of unknown or
> questionable validity. Now, twenty-seven years and five *Mental Measurements
> Yearbooks* later, I realize that I was too optimistic. Although many test users
> are undoubtedly selecting and using tests with a greater discrimination be-
> cause of the *Yearbooks*, there are many people who are not. Despite unfavor-
> able reviews, the publication and use of inadequately validated tests seems
> to be keeping pace with the population explosion (pp. xxiii–xxiv).

Of course it is not Buros' fault that the test-using public, provided with
considerable information and evaluation, has not responded by insisting on a
better product. That better product might come more quickly, however, if
more people were better able to understand the reviews.

Buros' last four objectives relate to making test users, publishers, and reviewers increasingly aware of the importance of test standards and of the importance of meeting the standards in order to provide a better service. Undoubtedly the test reviews in both Buros' and other publications have had
an impact in this area, although the *APA Standards Manual* (which Buros
helped to write) probably has been more effective, especially at the level of
test development.

Reviews of Tests in Journals

Test publishers reported that one of the more powerful sales tools available to them is a good journal review. Many professional journals and news-

letters attempt to perform a service by calling attention to selected new materials, with or without evaluative comments concerning the quality of such materials. For example, *Psychiatric Quarterly* regularly runs brief reports on some newly issued tests. This undoubtedly is a valuable information service for this journal's readers; however, the propriety of reproducing and circulating such brief and uncritical reviews and descriptive comments as an advertising tool may be questioned. Smaller test publishers frequently reproduce such quotable material and include it in packets sent to persons requesting information about a test.

Even more objectionable is the practice of journal or newsletter editors who ask a test author to obtain for publication descriptive or review materials on a test. Typically, the test author seeks an enthusiastic reviewer committed to the value of his test. If a review or description is then published, reproduction and distribution of the review as an additional unit of advertising is highly probable. The professional and ethical issue in this case involves the use of editorial judgment to establish fairness and balance in such reviews; responsibility clearly appears to rest on the shoulders of the editors of professional publications.

Research Reports on Testing

Journal publication of technical reports describing the use of a test often causes that test's sales to rise. Such reports alert buyers to tests that seem worthy of special notice. Journal articles also publicize tests for which some research application has been made; apparently, use in a research study "legitimizes" a test. But journal reports of test utilization range from highly technical articles in journals with high-quality editorial review to published research reports that are not reviewed at all.

Since the testing professional should know the research standards of established journals in his field, he should be able to distinguish levels of quality in research reports. On the other hand, a less sophisticated test buyer may be given a handful of research reprints, none of which need be based on any editorial or technical review. Undoubtedly, such reprints are quite influential in advertising and selling tests.

Inter-Association Council on Test Reviewing

One of the major problems frequently raised in connection with test reviewing is that some tests seem somewhat overreviewed, whereas a large number of tests are not reviewed at all or are reviewed several years after they are made available to the public. Organized, coordinated attention is being given to this problem by a group called the Inter-Association Council on Test Reviewing. Membership in the Council includes representatives of the American Psychological Association (APA), the American Educational Research Association, the American Personnel and Guidance Association, the divisions of those organizations which are concerned with testing, and editors of most of the journals which contain test reviews.

The Council's activity began in 1964 with the appointment of Warren T. Norman as chairman of a committee of the Division of Measurement and Evaluation of APA. The committee's function was to "determine whether there should be a regular program of review for psychological and educational tests and, if so, to recommend the procedures whereby such periodic reviewing could be implemented (IACTR, 1968; p. 1)."

Following the work of Dr. Norman's committee, representatives of interested organizations and journals met at the September 1966 annual meetings of the American Psychological Association and the February 1967 meetings of the American Educational Research Association. By the September 1967 APA meetings, sufficient progress had been made to hold a constitutional meeting for the creation of the Inter-Association Council. A steering committee was elected to draft bylaws for the Council and to further develop its structure and functions as a nonprofit professional council. Professor Jack Merwin of the University of Minnesota was elected chairman of the Steering Committee and, in the fall of 1968, was elected the first chairman of the Council.

The problems identified by the original test-review committee and later by the Steering Committee and Council are typical of the general problems relating to test reviewing. The Steering Committee's report to the first meeting of the Council in September 1968 (IACTR, 1968; pp. 2–4) lists the following seven problem areas:

1. There is no central coordinating agency to prevent duplication of reviews or to identify new and recent tests that should be reviewed.
2. There is a backlog of tests for which no current critical evaluations are available. Most journals, while they attempt to publish reviews, give priority to research articles rather than test reviews.
3. There is a need for reviews written for various levels of sophistication in measurement techniques. Unfortunately, most reviews assume a higher level of competence than exists among the majority of people reading test reviews.
4. Archival sources of test reviews (journals, *Mental Measurements Yearbooks, Tests in Print)* are not readily available to test users; in some cases, users may not even be aware of these sources.
5. There are not many non-archival sources of information concerning location of test reviews, information or bibliographies on tests that have been in print for some time, or information on who published which test.
6. There is no systematic method by which a test user can request a review

of a specific test; the user must either try to communicate with journal editors or wait until a review is published.

7. Editors and reviewers are frequently unable to obtain all relevant materials on a test.

At the September 2, 1968, meeting of the Council, a review of the Steering Committee's activities was presented along with a proposed set of bylaws which was accepted by the representatives present. Officers and an executive committee were elected, and some preliminary plans were made to open a central office which would implement the objectives of the organization. Representation in the Council is sufficiently broad to allow the expectation that the Council will be able to solve or cause to be solved most of the problems listed above.

The Council convened at the 1969 APA meetings in Washington, D.C. It was then reported that the Bureau of Research of the Office of Education (USOE), Department of Health, Education and Welfare, was asking for proposals for creation of an Educational Resources Information Center (ERIC) for test reviewing. The director of the ERIC Program in the USOE was present to report on that organization's concept of the requirements for such a Center. Finally, in 1970, Educational Testing Service contracted with USOE to establish an ERIC for test information. This development should further improve dissemination of test information to all who need it.

Advertising

Test reviews rather than test advertising probably are the major source of information for many test users who wish to learn about specific tests. Nevertheless, most test publishers use one or more means to advertise their products, especially new or revised tests. Means for advertising tests and testing services include direct-mail advertisements and catalogues, advertisements in technical and professional journals, and displays at professional meetings. A few publishers also use sales representatives and newspaper or nontechnical journals. Before looking at the advertising practices, let us review briefly the ethical standards which associations of testing professionals have developed as guidelines for advertising procedures.

Ethical Standards Covering Advertising and Claims for Tests

Both the American Psychological Association (APA) and the American Personnel and Guidance Association (APGA) include, as part of their code of ethics, principles dealing with the appropriateness of claims for test materials.

The APA *Ethical Standards Manual* (1963) states,

The psychologist associated with the development or promotion of psychological devices, books, or other products offered for commercial sale is responsible for ensuring that such devices, books, or products are presented in a professional and factual way.

1. Claims regarding performance, benefits or results are supported by scientifically acceptable evidence.
2. The psychologist does not use professional journals for the commercial exploitation of psychological products, and the psychologist-editor guards against such misuse.
3. The psychologist with a financial interest in the sale or use of a psychological product is sensitive to possible conflict of interest in his promotion of such products and avoids compromise of his professional responsibilities and objectives (p. 8).

Further, this manual states, "When information about the test is provided by the author or publisher in a separate publication, that publication should meet the same standards of accuracy and freedom from misleading impressions as apply to the manual (p. 7)." In the APGA *Ethical Standards Manual* (1961), Section C deals with testing practices; nine points are listed here. Paragraph C, Section C, applies directly to the question of advertising: "When making any statements to the public about tests and testing, care must be taken to give accurate information and to avoid any false claims or misconceptions (p. 208)."

These codes have been used consistently over the years to enforce standards of quality in advertising in cases involving association members who have permitted advertising materials to include overstatement of claims of the effectiveness of their tests. Occasional violations seem most often to have been made by test publishers without author concurrence; however, it is generally possible for test authors to obtain the cooperation of publishers in controlling the quality of advertising material for tests.

Direct-Mail Advertising

Direct-mail advertising in the form of test catalogues, flyers, brochures, reprints of journal articles or reviews is used extensively by both large and small test publishers. The purpose of such advertising is to arouse interest and to motivate a potential buyer to use certain testing materials. Descriptions of the power or utility of a test are usually more boldly presented in direct-mail ads than in journal or magazine advertisements.

Test authors occasionally have run into difficulty by entering into test- and book-distribution agreements with publishers who are not familiar with the ethical standards of psychologists and related professionals. These agreements between author and publisher often give the publisher extensive rights to advertise and merchandise materials without review or control by the author. Although most publishers try to utilize advertising materials that will be consistent with the standards of taste and ethics shared by most testing professionals, there is little that a test author can do about his publisher's occasional lapses of judgment or overstatements regarding the usefulness of tests. Fortunately, this is not a very frequent problem; most tests are published by persons acquainted with ethical standards, and the editors and readers of most media appropriate for test advertising are aware of these standards.

Presumably, professionals who buy tests are in a position to judge the adequacy of the products offered. Of greater concern is the fact that potential buyers who do not have a professional background therefore do not have the training and ability necessary to judge the value of a test or its appropriateness for a given purpose. They cannot properly evaluate advertising claims made about the tests.

Journal Advertisements

Many journals, magazines, and newsletters addressed to potential test buyers carry test publishers' ads describing the values of their merchandise. With rare exceptions, these are tasteful, reserved, and consistent with the ethical standards governing claims for tests.

Newspaper and Magazine Advertisements

There is, of course, one exception to this generally good picture: the newspaper and magazine advertisements for cut-rate mail-order testing. Originally these ads offered alleged intelligence tests at $1 to $5; more recently they have touted marital compatibility tests (at higher prices). These ads attract the unwary. Control of both such advertisements and such unprofessional service would be in the public interest.

Sales Representatives

Although the smaller test publishers almost never have sales representatives in the field, a considerable number of publishers employ one or more sales representatives. Several of the largest educational publishers employ more than one hundred professionals who regularly call on potential buyers. But selling tests is rarely the primary function of such personnel. Most frequently, sales representatives are primarily concerned with merchandising instructional materials; tests are a secondary concern. These representatives are backed up by test expertise, generally available from regional staffs as well as their home offices. Probably the best organizational arrangement among the large commercial publishers of educational materials and tests is that of Harcourt Brace Jovanovich, which employs a completely separate test-sales staff that reports to the head of the Test Division. This company's representatives are able to judge the competence of their customers to use properly the various tests available; they can also directly assist test users. We believe that standards of practice and efforts to seek qualified professionals to take different kinds of responsibilities as field representatives are in good order at the present time. Our impression has been that an effective representative of a test publisher must have certain competences in order to achieve his role as test salesman; this presents a quality control lever of considerable effectiveness.

Perspective

Obtainable information about tests may not meet all the standards, expectations, and needs for facts, but it is better than the information generally available for textbooks, programmed instruction materials, and other program material used in schools and industry. Continued vigilance of professional associations and improvements in test-information dissemination are needed.

REFERENCES

American Psychological Association. *Ethical Standards of Psychologists*. Washington, D.C.: APA, 1963.
American Personnel and Guidance Association. *Ethical Standards: American Personnel and Guidance Association*. Washington, D.C.: APGA, October 1961.
Baehr, Melany E. " 'A Frankly Critical Review' of the Mental Measurements Yearbooks." Industrial Relations Center, University of Chicago, 1967.
Buros, Oscar K. *The Sixth Mental Measurements Yearbook*. Highland Park, N.J.: Gryphon, 1965.
Inter-Association Council on Test Reviewing. 1968.

12

Testing in Relation to Employment Discrimination and the Invasion of Privacy

Some objections to the use of tests focus on the inadequacies of tests to meet their intended uses; for example, tests are used for selection though they lack adequate validation. Other objections center on undesirable by-products of testing, such as invasion of privacy. A third concern is the possibility that tests may be used to accomplish a nonlegitimate goal, such as racial discrimination in employment; or that they may be unintentionally used to thwart legitimate objectives of employees and applicants, of persons being tested, or of persons using tests. The role of testing in employment and education is discussed in this chapter in terms of these criticisms.

Testing and Discrimination in Employment

With the passage of the Civil Rights Act of 1964, attempts to ensure equal employment opportunities for all U.S. citizens were greatly intensified. Historically, the federal government has taken at least modest steps to guarantee fair-employment practices for employees working under government contracts. Government efforts did little to open up new opportunities for Negroes, Mexican-Americans, and others whose talents have been underutilized, however. In the last few years the Equal Employment Opportunity Commission (EEOC) and the Office of Federal Contract Compliance (OFCC) have re-examined the role of testing as a factor in employment-selection and promotion decisions and have evaluated other influences that have tended, at least in some cases, to permit or promote discrimination in employment.

EEOC has assembled an extensive file of complaints concerning testing. Dr. William Enneis, a personnel psychologist with EEOC, has estimated that some 15 to 20 percent of all complaints filed with the agency involve testing; for some years, this has represented as many as one thousand cases.

The real problem of testing and discriminatory employment practices lies in the enormous discrepancy between professional testing standards and the actual testing practices of many personnel departments. For example, Dr. Enneis (1969) stated that "most employers do not bother to determine whether test scores are systematically related to employee performance." He pointed out that the consequences of such practice are both potential denial of employment opportunities to minorities and waste of the employer's money. We do not know of any study that has documented the actual testing practices of a representative sample of personnel departments in the United States.

As cited earlier, Rushmore found considerable differences between test-administration practices in the field and standards which specify appropriate practices. But in a study of actual employment-testing practices in the San Francisco Bay area, Rushmore (1967) found serious discrepancies between the specified standards for test administration and the actual practices. Some employers relied on untrained personnel to administer tests; further, over half the companies in Rushmore's sample did not provide appropriate separate facilities for giving these tests. If this is typical of national practices, and we strongly suspect that it is, it is reasonable to conclude that a large percentage of test users are not applying proper testing procedures in a manner consistent with the directives of the publisher.

Spokesmen for test publishers, personnel directors in industry, and industrial psychologists agree overwhelmingly that unvalidated tests are commonly used in industry. The failure to use properly validated instruments indicates a break in the chain of procedures necessary for a sound assessment system. As emphasized throughout this report, it is not enough for good tests to be developed and published; tests and test batteries must be used by persons who are trained to understand both the advantages and limitations of these techniques and by persons capable of establishing test utility in different employment settings. Recent federally sponsored court decisions and regulations will very probably result in either the abandonment of certain testing activities or in the establishment of job-related validity data; this may improve the employment-testing situation. The new requirements are exactly what testing professionals have called for since the earliest days of testing.

Tests Used in Industry

Three major kinds of tests are used in employment selection: (1) tests of present abilities or knowledge, (2) specific and general aptitude measures, and (3) personality tests.

ABILITY AND KNOWLEDGE TESTS. Tests designed to assess specific abilities, such as typing or operation of a lathe, are important predictors of success on jobs. Therefore, various tests have been designed to appraise the knowledge that individuals have about different areas of vocational endeavor and to assess their ability to perform job tasks. Of all tests in the employment-selection and promotion field, these work-sample measures are generally considered by critics of testing to be least objectionable, probably because these measures have high face validity, i.e., the test items appear to require the skills demanded in the given job.

SPECIFIC APTITUDES. Tests of specific aptitudes have been developed to facilitate prediction of performance in certain classes of activity. For example, aptitude for success in a job requiring mechanical-assembly skills may be appraised by assessing eye-hand coordination and manual dexterity. There are dozens of tests offered as aids in estimating aptitude for vocational training.

INTELLIGENCE TESTS. Most intelligence tests used in industry are used to predict general learning ability. Because of the high cost of individual testing, the intelligence of job applicants is ordinarily assessed by use of group-administered tests rather than individually administered procedures. Typical intelligence testing in industry consists of a very brief written test which asks a person to demonstrate his knowledge of word meaning, his ability to deal with numbers, to use various logical and reasoning abilities, and to make deductions from problems presented visually.

From the perspective of minority-group members, the difficulty with this type of testing is that many of the intelligence tests in use have not been standardized appropriately for minority subjects. In addition, the content of these tests often relies heavily on the kinds of learning and social experiences typically available to white middle-class citizens. Further, job-related validity data are rarely available for intelligence tests. Without question, the brief, easily scored intelligence test has been found objectionable by a substantial number of job applicants.

PERSONALITY TESTS. Use of personality tests for purposes of employment-selection or promotion has been very limited. Considerable controversy regarding use of some personality measures within the federal government has resulted in virtual elimination of personality testing for employment in government agencies. Nevertheless, tests designed to reflect patterns of personal interests have been widely used, both in counseling and in personnel selection.

Major Elements in the Selection-Promotion Process

When tests are used in employment-selection work, they are but one step in a process. Other steps include acquiring a pool of applicants, evaluating application forms, checking references, and interviewing applicants. The relationship between discrimination and testing must be considered within the framework of all steps in the employment process. As we consider these elements, let us be aware of the implications of any weak link in this procedural chain. For, if any of the steps associated with personnel selection are tinged with discriminatory practices, intentional or otherwise, the fairness of the entire procedure will be jeopardized.

RECRUITMENT OF APPLICANTS. The first step in filling a job vacancy is obtaining a pool of applicants. Recruitment procedures play a decisive part in opening or closing off job opportunities for minority-group citizens. Unless an employer seeks applicants from all parts of society without any subtle or unintentional discriminatory limitations, the objectivity of the selection process will be compromised.

At the recruitment stage, many limitations may be introduced into specifications for applicants; these restrictions may unnecessarily preclude application by a sizable percentage of the available manpower pool. For example, it is common practice to require high school graduation for many kinds of employment, regardless of the significance of formal education as a predictor of job success. Many such specifications may be largely nonfunctional insofar as quality of selection is concerned. The establishment of unnecessary educational or experiential requirements has been a continuing impediment to equal-opportunity hiring. It is quite probable that more employment discrimination results from indefensible recruitment procedures than from any other part of the selection process.

FORMAL APPLICATION PROCEDURES. Most personnel departments use some kind of written application blank. This may range from a simple statement of name, address, phone number, and a brief listing of previous occupational experience, to an elaborate personal-history blank which encompasses interests, hobbies, occupation of parents, and other biographical data that may be highly personal.

The information on the application blank usually serves as a preliminary screening of applicants. Because the application-blank review is quite economical for an employer, it is typically used before testing; it usually eliminates more applicants than do tests. Some organizations use scorable application forms called Biographical Information Blanks or Biographical Data Blanks. These are used much like tests, with scores for one or more jobs derived from the answers on the forms. When such devices are used in the employment process in the same way that tests are used, they should obviously meet the validation standards applied to tests. Biographical data forms are typically validated on employees who are not representative of the applicant pool; thus the use of these forms may tend to institutionalize and re-enforce any discriminatory personnel practices that currently exist. Similarly, even on unscored application forms, automatic rejection criteria may result in discriminatory hiring practices. For example, minority-group leaders have been particularly concerned about questions relating to previous arrests, especially when the questions do not take into account what the alleged offense may have been or whether the person was acquitted.

JOB INTERVIEWS. The primary objective of job interviews may simply be to collect information or, more commonly, to evaluate an interviewee. While interviewing is probably the most commonly used technique for deciding who gets a job and who does not, it is also unquestionably one of the most unreliable and biased procedures applied in personnel work. All interviewers have built-in biases. Even educational films on preparation for job interviews leave little doubt that middle-class social and cultural standards often provide the yardstick against which behavior in an interview is evaluated.

Job interviews present a special problem in that an applicant is usually interviewed twice, once in the personnel department and again in the department where the vacancy exists. The applicant may thus be subjected not only to two sets of standards, but also to two sets of biases; either interviewer may disqualify an applicant.

TESTING PROCEDURES. Publishers of tests commonly used in employment situations almost invariably specify the exact conditions under which the tests should be used. These conditions often call for a quiet room or cubicle with adequate light and ventilation. Similarly, the instructions for administering tests are often described in considerable detail; so that validity can be maintained, verbatim instructions are usually essential, as is adherence to established time limits.

An attempt to reduce the irregularities of test administration is found in the Psychological Corporation's development of the Controlled Administration of Standardized Tests (CAST) which uses carefully timed tape-recorded instructions for administration of tests in the employment environment. It is too early to know whether this or similar techniques will become common enough to reduce significantly the test-administration irregularities.

Given the fact that the physical conditions surrounding testing are often inadequate in personnel departments, what about the psychological conditions associated with these procedures? Taking a test of any kind may be highly threatening, especially to an individual unfamiliar with testing procedures or one who has a history of failure or rejection following test taking. Good testing practices usually require introducing the subject to the task at hand, offering a word or two of reassurance, ascertaining that the instructions are properly understood, and so forth. On the basis of very limited experience, it would appear likely that much of what *should* be done in carrying out testing in many personnel departments is, in fact, not being done. However, a step in the right direction has been taken by some organizations which use minority-group members to carry out testing activities and other parts of the employment process.

Along a different line, some organizations which help minority citizens obtain employment have established employment-coaching clinics which include actual practice in test taking. Such coaching is by no means new. For many years, tests and other materials have been published and offered as aids for passing federal civil service tests and tests used for military classification and assignment. When properly used, this kind of preparation can serve the interests of both the employer and the potential employee. At times, however, test coaching has become highly controversial because of reports that job applicants are being given an opportunity to practice on tests actually used in some personnel departments. In itself, this practice could lead to a form of discrimination against those who have not been coached.

Question of Validity

We shall not be concerned here with a technical review of the multiple meanings, from a psychometric standpoint, of the term "validity." But it will be well to review the basic idea of predictive validity, for this is at the heart of the criticisms most frequently raised about employment testing. When we say that a test has high predictive validity, we mean that a score or a pattern of scores derived from that assessment instrument can be shown to correlate highly with an independent criterion measure of performance on a job or in a training program. The subsequent use of such a test for making predictions about success on the job or in training would, of course, apply only to populations that corresponded to the subjects on whom the tests were originally validated. Many other assumptions are essential, such as consistent procedures for applying the tests, stability of both the job or training requirements, and stable methods of appraising success or failure in such assignments.

Professor George Cooper, in an extensive review of certain legal implications of ability testing in employment and education, sees "widespread" but "inadvertent" use of tests which have the effect of acting as roadblocks to job opportunities for the disadvantaged (Cooper, 1968). With respect to low test validity, he charges, "The majority of employers using tests to screen applicants are doing so without empirical evidence that the test measures the ability sought—much less that it measures the abilities without regard to race (p. 696)." Cooper points out that at least three categories of invalid tests may be identified: (1) tests that are invalid for all races, (2) tests that are invalid for one race but not for another, and (3) tests that are valid for all races but which may require differential scoring patterns and interpretations (hence, the requirements for different norms according to race).

Cooper, who has had considerable legal experience representing clients alleged to have suffered discrimination with regard to equal employment issues, believes that ". . . the general standard of employment testing is abysmally low . . . (p. 710)." While the evidence for this generalization is not clear, there are disturbing examples of improper use of tests. For example, in the Hicks' case (Hicks, 1967) testimony developed in a federal court revealed that no trained test specialist was involved in the selection, administration, or use of personnel tests at one plant of a major corporation; that test scores were not recorded but instead were retained by memory alone; and that Negroes were almost never found to be suitable for promotion into certain jobs. In this one unusually well-documented case, there was clear evidence of unprofessional and improper use of tests, plus a total absence of any validity data to justify the use of locally established "cutting scores" to define a passing level.

Psychologists have also been outspoken in their criticism of poor testing practices and in their recognition that, too often, tests are not being used as intended by the test developer and publisher. Professor Ralph Berdie, serving as chairman of an APA committee on the social impact of psychological assessment, summarized the situation as follows: "Many tests are used today for selection, employment, and classification purposes in such a way that they actually lead to and encourage discriminatory practices. In many cases, tests are misused because psychologists have failed to take into account the differences in validity and perhaps reliability that tests have for different populations (1965; p. 146)."

Federal Agencies and Employment Testing

The two federal agencies most directly concerned with the rights of citizens in the employment area are the Equal Employment Opportunity Commission (EEOC) and the Office of Federal Contract Compliance (OFCC).

EQUAL EMPLOYMENT OPPORTUNITY COMMISSION. EEOC was established as a consequence of the 1964 Civil Rights Act. The Commission's federal authorization and mission statement are the most ambitious efforts on the part of our government to combat discrimination in employment. An independent federal entity, EEOC is empowered to initiate as well as to receive complaints of certain alleged civil rights violations. Section 703 (A) (1) under Title VII of the 1964 Civil Rights Act makes it an unlawful employment practice "to fail or refuse to hire . . . because of . . . race, color, religion, sex, or national origin." An amendment to Title VII, introduced by Senator Tower, was designed to assure employers the right to conduct competent testing programs in good faith. The Tower Amendment, which is now in Section 703 (8), reads in part ". . . nor shall it be an unlawful employment practice for an employer to give and to act upon the results of any professionally developed ability test, provided that such test is not designed, intended, or used to discriminate because of race, color, religion, sex, or national origin."

In an effort to clarify questions regarding what a "professionally developed" ability test might be, EEOC issued, on August 24, 1966, *Guidelines on Employment Testing Procedures*. These guidelines make clear the requirement of job-specific validity for tests used in employment situations. They take two additional steps which have important implications for test standards. First, they adopt as criteria for test development the *Standards for Educational and Psychological Tests and Manuals* compiled by the American Psychological Association, the American Educational Research Association, and the National Council on Measurement in Education. The *Guidelines* (1966) define a professionally developed ability test as ". . . a test which fairly measures the knowledge or skills required by the particular job or class of jobs which the applicant seeks, or which fairly affords the employer a chance to measure the applicant's ability to perform a particular job or class of jobs (p. 2)."

The staff of EEOC reports that approximately one thousand complaints per year involve questions relating to the use of tests in employment settings. The complaints, coupled with the hearings and court cases undertaken by the Commission or by complainants, are serving to make all users of tests aware that unjustifiable and unprofessional applications of tests are inconsistent with national policies and therefore intolerable.

OFFICE OF FEDERAL CONTRACT COMPLIANCE. OFCC, a division of the Department of Labor, conducts its activities through field workers assigned to different governmental departments. Responsibilities of OFCC involve monitoring federal contracts for compliance, especially in personnel and employment matters. Field representatives of OFCC are not required to await issuance of a complaint; they may call on employers and request an opportunity to review evidence of validation.

At the heart of OFCC's program for enforcing equal employment opportunity for personnel working under federal contracts, is Executive Order No. 11246, issued in September 1968. This Order is predicated on ". . . the belief that properly validated and standardized tests, by virtue of their relative objectivity and freedom from the biases that are apt to characterize more subjective evaluation techniques, can contribute substantially to the implementation of equitable and nondiscriminatory personnel policies (*Federal Register*, 1968; p. 14392)." The central thrust of the order is to place a very great responsibility for test validation upon an employer, for it requires that each contractor ". . . regularly using tests to select from among candidates for hire, transfer, or promotion to jobs other than professional and managerial occupations . . . have available for inspection . . . evidence that these tests are valid for their intended purposes (p. 14392)."

It is very likely that this order will have rapid impact upon questionable testing practices of the employers it covers; the result will probably be a reduction in testing. However, we can only wait and see what implications this order will have for enhancement of equal opportunities for minority-group job applicants. In any case, clear evidence exists that both EEOC and OFCC are now playing a major role in the enforcement of standards for test utilization.

Job Testing and the Disadvantaged

Recommendations regarding employment testing of the disadvantaged have been issued by an American Psychological Association task force (APA, 1969). The report of this group emphasizes the many hazards and difficulties that can contribute to unfair employment practices. More than anything else, the recommendations point up the discrepancy between high standards of professional practice applied to test development and use and the relatively low standards of practice believed to exist in the testing activities of personnel departments in many companies.

Testing and Invasion of Privacy

Whenever people collect information about other people, they raise the issue of invasion of privacy, whether the issue is apparently warranted or not. Can testing be done in a way that avoids invasion of privacy? If not, when do the needs of the testing program justify such invasion of privacy? What effect do school- and job-testing records have on a student or employee's opportunities many years later? How much of the total invasion of privacy problem is related to testing? What kinds of solutions are available for the general privacy problem and for that part specific to tests?

Widespread criticism of the use of personality tests, particularly the Minnesota Multiphasic Personality Inventory (MMPI), resulted in congressional hearings during 1965. Much of the background information and key testimony developed in these hearings was reported in a special issue of the *American Psychologist* (1965a).

Criticisms have concerned personality-test applications; however, there is a broader issue involved which relates to the right to privacy in a free society. The question of privacy and behavioral research, extensively discussed by Ruebhausen and Brim (1965), has many implications for invasion of privacy issues associated with personality testing and for the work of psychologists in clinical employment and other settings where the assessment of individuals is involved.

Let us examine the core issues raised in connection with invasion of privacy through personality testing. Congressman Cornelius E. Gallagher (D.-N.J.), one of the principal critics of such testing, delineated the problem as it related to federal employees and job applicants. A summary of his charges (Gallagher, 1965; pp. 881–882) follows:

1. Some federal job applicants were compelled to take personality tests as part of the employment screening process.
2. No effective appeal procedure was available.
3. Personality testing represented a form of "searching the minds of Federal employees and job applicants."
4. Tests improperly excluded desirable people from jobs they deserved to hold.
5. The reliability and validity of score patterns on personality tests used was an "unsettled controversy."
6. Personality test questions inquired into highly personal and intimate matters.
7. The tests were utilized by personnel workers who were not qualified for this activity.
8. Test reports were retained; they tended to follow a person through his career.
9. Test records were not kept confidential as promised.
10. Personality tests raised questions about applicants and, once questions were raised, personnel decisions were likely to be made against the applicant.
11. Personality testing was required of many federal job applicants in some agencies but was not required of top-level federal employees.

A similar set of criticisms was basic to charges raised by Senator Sam J. Ervin, Jr. (D.-N.C.), chairman of the Senate Subcommittee on Constitutional Rights. Senator Ervin (1965) noted, "We have received numerous complaints that some of the questions contained in the personality inventories relating to sex, religion, family relationships, and many personal aspects of the employee's life constitute an unjustified invasion of privacy. Furthermore, the charge has been made that aside from the invasion of privacy, the procedures surrounding the testing and the use made of the test results present serious due process questions (pp. 879–880)."

It is obvious that these criticisms and charges go far beyond the accusation that the tests are not sufficiently valid for the uses to which they have been put. Questions have been raised concerning the propriety of inquiring into a variety of personal matters, regardless of the usefulness of these factors as predictors of job success. Similarly, critics have expressed a need for caution in the use of test results for purposes other than originally intended.

Messick (1965) has approached the invasion of privacy issue through consideration of the way in which tests are used for different purposes. He provides a useful framework for examining the invasion of privacy question in relation to testing for diagnosis and guidance, academic and employment selection, and research on human behavior.

Assessment for Diagnosis and Guidance

Messick points out that when an individual applies for psychological or counseling assistance, he defines himself as a client seeking a *helping* relationship with a professional whom he presumably trusts. He thereby commits himself to follow certain clinical procedures that may be more fully understood by the professional than by him, and to trust the professional to represent his interests in a manner consistent with the welfare of the general public.

Ethical and moral issues concerned with invasion of privacy are by no means infrequently raised in connection with clinical work. For example, does the psychologist or counselor have license to circumvent the ego defenses that may have been erected by a client as an important part of his ability to function? Is it the obligation of the professional to seek the maximum information possible, regardless of a client's resistance? Questions of this kind involve a series of trade-offs and compromises which can only be resolved on the basis of individual judgments by professionals on a case by case basis. No general answers are going to take into account the many subtleties associated with competing values.

Although psychotherapists and counselors differ greatly in their theoretical orientation as well as their values and practices in client relationships, most practitioners today would probably take the position that self-discovery or insight is, at least in many cases, a desirable objective. They would feel that their professional efforts to understand as fully as possible the personality dynamics of a client should be viewed not as a one-sided "invasion of privacy," but as a collaborative effort designed to enhance the personal functioning of an individual who has asked for help.

Entry into helping relationships for the purpose of psychodiagnosis, psychotherapy, or counseling and guidance are usually, but not always, voluntary. Thus, a client who is not satisfied with the professional services' being rendered can withdraw from the relationship to protect his privacy rights. This, of course, is not the case when an individual is required to take personality tests as a condition of employment.

Assessment for Selection in Employment or Academic Settings

An individual who must take tests as part of a selection process for school admission or employment is usually tested by a person representing an institution. In the selection relationship, as contrasted with the helping relationship, the company, the business, the government agency, or the school is actually the client, not the individual being tested. Thus, the discovery process is much less likely to involve self-discovery than discovery by someone else. Nonetheless, a professional who administers tests also has ethical obligations to individuals. These obligations are clearly set forth in the codes of ethics of both the American Psychological Association and the American Personnel and Guidance Association. In addition, the professional is responsible for carrying out a competent assessment program in which the objectives of the organization he represents are met, at least as far as personnel selection is concerned. This sets up a pair of competing obligations in which the goals of an organization must be balanced against the professional's obligation to protect the dignity of an applicant and to shield him from improper, misleading, or professionally indefensible assessment practices.

It is considered unethical practice to fail to inform a client of the nature of the client relationship which exists when tests are administered or confidential information is obtained. However, no universally applicable guidelines help a professional to meet the competing obligations to an organization he is representing and to the individuals he is assessing. When professionals are unable to resolve this dilemma in a manner acceptable to those being tested, we may expect not only expressions of public concern about such practices but, more importantly, recommendations for the control or abolishment of testing procedures in general.

Where personality tests are concerned, extensive agreement exists among personnel psychologists that the inclusion of such tests in assessment batteries for job-selection purposes cannot be justified by existing evidence that personality measures enhance the predictive validity of test batteries commonly in use today.

The problems raised by file and record systems in schools have recently been described by Goslin and Bordier (1969) in a book edited by Stanton Wheeler. Often without the informed consent of either the pupil or his parents, many records of test scores and other data are accumulated on each student as he proceeds through school. Because of the division of authority with regard to school testing (school boards, administrations, principals, teachers, and counselors) and because of widespread testing in connection with daily classwork, much testing is done without appropriate safeguards. It is of utmost importance to consider the purpose of the testing, accuracy of the records and reports, and maintenance or destruction of the records after their original uses have been served.

Assessment in Research

The goal of research projects is to advance knowledge rather than to serve an individual client or organization. Since the behavioral scientist is ordinarily able to ensure the anonymity of subjects he is testing, some difficulties associated with assessment for selection purposes can be overcome. But some forms of self-revelation, especially as elicited by personality tests or experiments involving deception of the subject, may be highly offensive to individuals. This is especially true when tests such as the MMPI are applied to age groups for which they were never intended.

Ethical standards require that participation in psychological experiments be based on informed consent. However, the question must be raised: What is informed consent? Often the nature of a research project makes it impossible to give complete information regarding the objectives of the study without prejudicing the usefulness of the data to be collected.

Some very troublesome issues relevant to assessment in research have been raised, particularly by Ruebhausen and Brim (1965). But it may be said that there has been far less controversy about personality testing for research purposes than about the application of personality tests in selection situations.

Response of Professionals

In 1965, many psychologists appeared before congressional committees to give their opinions regarding the issue of testing and invasion of privacy. Some defended personality-testing procedures, pointing out that more individuals lose their jobs because of lack of skill or ability than because of personal factors. But even the defenders' endorsement of limited personality testing was far more qualified than had apparently been the practice in some government agencies. Other psychologists, who attacked the use of any tests for employment-selection purposes, pointed out the limitations of the predictive validity of even the best assessment programs.

The executive officer of the American Psychological Association, Arthur H. Brayfield, reviewed strategies and tactics associated with personnel selection, provided a series of action-steps that might be considered by congressional committees concerned with quality of practice involving testing, and reviewed many of the publications, standards, and technical recommendations issued by the American Psychological Association (1965b). When questioned by Senator Ervin regarding the amount of contribution personality testing made to employment selection, Mr. Brayfield responded as follows, ". . . personality measurements, appropriately used, . . . add some increment, maybe 5 percent . . . [to] 15 percent, to the accuracy of the unaided human judgment. It is a policymaker's decision as to whether or not that added increment is worthwhile (p. 898)."

Perspective

Concerning tests and the invasion of privacy, we recognize many moral questions and issues of value that are fundamental to a society. Professionals and public policy makers concerned with human assessment must continue to evaluate these questions and issues.

Although the causes of the original hue and cry about testing as an invasion of privacy seem to have been reduced, the long-term effect of testing and accumulating records of test scores and similar information should not be underestimated in an era when access to data is becoming less costly every year. As the ease of assembling, keeping, and transmitting data increases, increased attention must be paid to protecting the rights of persons on whom records are kept. Testing programs should not be administered unless they serve a useful purpose to the test taker or others for whom this method of assessment is justified. When the testing procedures have served their purpose, additional justification should be provided if records are to be maintained or released for other than the original purpose. Individual, informed consent of the test taker or his parent shoud be the rule rather than the exception for supplementary uses of tests and similar data.

The efforts of all persons and organizations involved in testing will be needed to ensure that tests do increasingly more of what they should do— provide valid information for decisions—and less of what they should not do —invade personal privacy and inappropriately limit opportunities.

REFERENCES

American Psychological Association. "Job Testing and the Disadvantaged," *American Psychologist*, 24 (1969), 637–650.

American Psychological Association. "Special Issue: Testing and Public Policy," *American Psychologist*, 20:11 (November 1965a), 855–1005.

American Psychological Association. "Testimony Before the Senate Subcommittee on Constitutional Rights of the Committee on the Judiciary," *American Psychologist*, 20:11 (November 1965b), 888–898.

Berdie, R. "The Ad Hoc Committee on Social Impact of Psychological Assessment," *American Psychologist*, 20:2 (February 1965), 143–146.

Cooper, G. "Legal Implications of the Use of Standardized Ability Tests in Employment and Education," *Columbia Law Review*, 68 (1968), 690–744.

Enneis, W. "Misuses of Tests." Unpublished report presented at the 1969 Annual Convention of the American Psychological Association.

Equal Employment Oportunity Commission. *Guidelines on Employment Testing Procedures*. Washington, D.C., Aug. 24, 1966.

Ervin, S. J. "Why Senate Hearings on Psychological Tests in Government," *American Psychologist*, 20:11 (November 1965), 879–880.

"Validation of Employment Tests by Contractors and Subcontractors Subject to the Provisions of Executive Order 11246," *Federal Register*, 33:186, Part II (Sept. 24, 1968).

Gallagher, C. E. "Why House Hearings on Invasion of Privacy," *American Psychologist*, 20:11 (November 1965), 881–882.

Goslin, D. A., and N. Bordier. "Record Keeping in Elementary and Secondary Schools," in Stanton Wheeler, ed., *On Record: Files and Dossiers in American Life*. New York: Russell Sage Foundation, 1969.

Hicks v. Crown Zellerbach Corporation, Civil Action No. 16638 E.D., LA, 1967.

Messick, S. "Personality Measurement and the Ethics of Assessment,"*American Psychologist*, 20:2 (February 1965), 136–142.

Ruebhausen, O. M., and O. G. Brim, "Privacy and Behavioral Research," *Columbia Law Review*, 65 (November 1965), 1185–1211.

Rushmore, J. E. "Psychological Tests and Fair Employment: A Study of Employment Testing in the San Francisco Bay Area." State of California Fair Employment Practice Commission, 1967. Mimeographed.

13

Summary and Recommendations

The formulation of requirements for competent assessment systems and their application to the activities of those involved in testing has shed some light on problems raised by critics of testing and has raised some new problems. These issues are summarized in this chapter in order of their importance, and recommendations are made for action by different groups.

Opportunities for Improvement

Competence of Complete Assessment Systems

The most serious testing problems generally occur when the persons in charge of testing programs do not monitor all aspects of the testing system. For example, this may result in the use of good tests for inappropriate purposes, or it may result in the continued use of poor tests rather than the development of better tests. Often, lack of quality control results in poor test administration and interpretation, even when adequate manuals, instructions, and interpretive materials are available. When these are not available, which occurs most frequently with locally developed tests, poor testing is almost certain to result.

Professional Qualifications of Testers

No amount of quality control in test selection, development, and preparation of feedback documents can overcome inadequacies brought to the system by the person who actually administers the test and interprets it to the user. We do not suggest that doctoral-level psychologists are needed for test administration; we recognize that most tests are administered by classroom teachers, personnel technicians, and others whose major occupation is not testing. Useful testing services can in all likelihood be carried out by personnel who do not have full professional qualifications in one of the areas primarily concerned with testing. However, influencing the activities of paraprofessionals then presents a major problem. Although professional associations are able to exert substantial quality control over testing practices of their members, the associations' ethics committees have no control over the practices of nonmembers. Thus, there is great need for improvement of quality-control measures in the paraprofessional area.

Unfortunately, the problem of setting standards for the training and experience expected of test users has not been resolved either through professional associations or through state legislation. We feel that groups attempting to improve testing practices in this country should give first priority to the definition of technical competences essential for various levels of involvement with testing procedures.

When these competence standards for different levels of testing work are adequately defined, the next priority should be given to improving existing training programs and establishing new ones that can help people meet the standards. Third, laws establishing licenses, certificates, and credentials for different levels and kinds of work in testing should be enacted.

Initiative for all these steps can be taken by the federal government, the state governments, and professional associations. An effort similar to the one which created the *Test Standards Manual* should be mounted, probably by the same organizations, to specify needed competences and to recommend training standards and laws relating to control of testing work.

The professional associations involved in testing should also take actions to strengthen the role of paraprofessionals in their own organizations, or should encourage the development of an organization of paraprofessionals concerned with administration of tests and feedback to test users. They should encourage and support legislation and other government activities to develop greater paraprofessional competence and responsibility.

Test Reviews

Since even trained test selectors, administrators, and interpreters depend on good test reviews for much of their work, the testing industry and testing professionals sponsor test reviewing. Thereby they serve as their own most frequent and often severest critics. The principal archival sources of information concerning tests and test reviews, the *Mental Measurements Year-*

books, unquestionably offer the most extensive compilation of information available on tests and related materials. The *Yearbooks* have received two major criticisms: (1) criteria used for the evaluation of tests have been far too variable, and the professional bias of a test reviewer has too often been the primary basis for an evaluation; and (2) test reviews are too technical for the level of understanding of many persons who regularly use tests.

Occasionally, clinically oriented journals publish test reviews that do not measure up to accepted standards of technical reviewing. This is regarded as a minor problem since it is unlikely that such reviews have a major impact on test sales. Current efforts to organize and coordinate test reviewing for publication in various journals will probably help to establish better standards for these activities.

The recently established Inter-Association Council on Test Reviewing has developed an ambitious and carefully prepared program to supplement and extend the test reviews provided by the *Mental Measurements Yearbook*. Though the Council is still relatively young, it has been influential in encouraging the federal government to establish an ERIC for test information; it appears to hold considerable promise for increasing the availability and quality of information required by test users.

The establishment of an Educational Resources Information Center (ERIC) for test reviews and related information is a valuable action by the federal government. Continued support of ERIC is, of course, essential. Further, the federal and state governments should assure that appropriate reviews and test information are available to persons selecting and using tests in government programs.

Test Standards and Ethical Codes

The Standards for Educational and Psychological Tests and Manuals has been developed over a long period of time by professionals working both in universities and in the testing industry. These standards, widely considered to be an important and effective technical foundation for test development, are well known by personnel working in the testing industry. Since the *Standards* provide criteria for test reviewing, test developers make a strenuous effort to comply with them. The importance of these standards has been greatly enhanced by the fact that both the Equal Employment Opportunity Commission and the Office of Federal Contract Compliance use the *Standards* as criteria for competently developed tests. The enforcement aspects of these laws unfortunately are weak. Stronger legislation is needed to give administrators of the existing laws the muscle needed to turn the intent of the laws into reality.

The ethical standards of both the American Psychological Association and the American Personnel and Guidance Association contain extensive material bearing directly on testing and, more specifically, on the rights of clients to whom tests are administered. These ethical codes and the committees that enforce them have made clear the multiple obligations of the test user relative to the rights of clients. Ethical codes, however, have virtually no direct influence on persons who are not members of the professional associations which have adopted such codes. Often, marginally trained persons who do not hold membership in professional associations are most in need of a stronger commitment to ethical practices and a concern for the rights of persons taking tests.

Pragmatically speaking, test publishers have not been able to control test distribution effectively. Though the publisher may make every effort to follow the procedures called for in the *Standards*, he cannot control test utilization once he has shipped the testing materials to a qualified purchaser. Practice indicates that it is relatively simple for a marginally qualified person to obtain most kinds of testing materials if he is determined to do so. Professional and industrial efforts to reduce poor testing practices by refusing test sales to unqualified or marginally qualified users are seriously hampered by restraints imposed on the industry by the Federal Trade Commission (FTC). The Commission should begin to protect the test "consumer" rather than limit its attention to restraint of trade actions. New legislation will probably be needed to give test producers the power to act together in the interest of good testing practice. The alternative is creation of a test distribution control agency through which government would exercise controls that it presently prevents test publishers from exercising.

Preparation of Feedback Documents

Perhaps the greatest help that can be given to test users is improved preparation of feedback documents. These materials should include scores, appropriate norms, and predictive or other interpretive statements tailored to the specific testee and purpose for which the test is given. Undoubtedly, if such material were better prepared, it could be given to the test user, whether a school administrator, personnel administrator, teacher, job applicant, or student. The material should obviously be in a form that a test user could readily understand and should almost always be supplemented by a personal interview with someone qualified to deal with any special questions or problems of the user.

New developments based on computer programs which interpret the results of tests or test batteries may be of considerable assistance in strengthening this testing service. Since most computer-based interpretation services have been developed to aid physicians and other clinical workers, however, the extent to which these procedures may be useful in school and personnel work remains to be explored. The various problems involved in such services should be the subject of research by the testing industry and government agencies.

Discrimination in Employment and Education

A major dimension of the quest for equal employment opportunities has involved severe criticism of the testing programs employed by many companies. There is considerable reason to believe that employment-selection tests are often used improperly, that far too many test users are inadequately trained for the responsibilities they have accepted, and that job-related validity data is typically not available at all. Not surprisingly, therefore, an estimated 20 percent of all complaints filed with the Equal Employment Opportunity Commission involve testing in some way. For some years, this has represented about one thousand cases annually.

We have concluded that the central problem of testing and discriminatory employment practices lies not in the use of "bad tests," but rather in the discrepancy between professional testing standards and the actual testing procedures of many personnel departments. Major changes are needed in the level of professional competence and training required of personnel responsible for the use of tests which contribute to employment decision-making.

Both the Equal Employment Opportunity Commission and the Office of Federal Contract Compliance have praised the use of objective assessment procedures where these procedures may be shown to contribute to the prediction of success in a job or in a training program. However, when tests contribute to hiring practices that have an adverse racial impact, both agencies now hold employers directly responsible for justifying the use of tests with job-related validity data. Many testing professionals from universities and from the testing industry have had an opportunity to contribute to development of the standards and guidelines adopted by these two federal agencies relative to the use of tests in employment selection. These guidelines and regulations are generally regarded by testing professionals as justifiable and in the public interest.

The testing industry and professional associations concerned with testing have shown considerable responsiveness to minority-group spokesmen's criticisms of testing practices in industry. The industry has been working to develop culture-fair tests and recommendations which bear on the proper use of tests in the evaluation of minority applicants. Further, increased communication through professional journals and national meetings has helped to spotlight a variety of problems concerned with testing and equal employment opportunities.

The short-term effect of equal opportunity programs has been less testing in industry; undoubtedly the long-term effect will be general improvement of industrial-personnel selection. That improvement, along with increased personnel specialization and costs, may lead to increased industrial testing in the future.

Invasion of Privacy

Through personality-testing procedures, it is possible to acquire highly personal and confidential information about individuals. This fact has raised many very serious ethical and professional policy issues and had led to congressional hearings concerned particularly with the use of personality tests as screening devices for federal employment. There has been a considerable history of professional concern with the ethical use of tests and the obligations of professionals to maintain confidentiality of test results and otherwise give proper attention to the rights of the clients tested. The code of ethics of both the American Psychological Association and the American Personnel and Guidance Association reflect these professional concerns. A 1969 publication of the Russell Sage Foundation, *Guidelines for the Collection, Maintenance, and Dissemination of Pupil Records*, expressed the report of a national conference on ethical and legal aspects of keeping test results as part of school records.

Despite the ethical standards, there is no question that personality tests have sometimes been used in ways which are offensive and objectionable not only to the public, but to professionals as well. For example, personality tests have occasionally been used as an employment-screening procedure by persons not properly qualified to use such tests; further, they have been used under circumstances in which their predictive value is highly uncertain. In addition, personality testing for research purposes has reportedly been carried out in some public schools. In one case, the test used in this research included items that were intended for adults and were phrased in ways considered most unsatisfactory by the parents of the school children. These and other incidents have received considerable attention both from the testing industry and from professionals concerned with testing. The public outrage regarding such testing practices appears to have had a considerable effect on increasing professionals' sensitivity and attentiveness to these issues.

Invasion-of-privacy issues related to testing probably are of greatest importance when tests are used for academic or employment-selection purposes. Testing for diagnosis and guidance is typically, but not always, a consequence of an individual's entering into a voluntary relationship wherein he is seeking some kind of help or information. Many invasion-of-privacy issues and rights of clients are associated with such a relationship. Nevertheless, it is comparatively simple for an individual to withdraw from a voluntary relationship, should he judge this to be in his best interests. In contrast, the individual who is asked to take tests as part of a selection procedure does not have the same options, unless he is willing to suffer whatever loss may be associated with withdrawing from testing. However, the personality tests most vociferously attacked as instruments that invade privacy have typically not been shown to contribute to the prediction of either academic or employment success. There is reason to believe that such measures are currently excluded from many selection-test batteries.

A problem that may be of considerable importance in the future relates to the increasing ease with which test scores and other confidential information may be retained and retrieved through computer applications. A considerable array of very important policy issues arises at the prospect of having new technical capabilities to retain test data and utilize it in ways that have historically been impractical or impossible. This opens important policy questions for all organizations and agencies that acquire confidential information. The problem, of course, is that information gained from testing may assist the individual, or it may prejudice his rights as a citizen. Some balance must be struck in the use, and control, of such confidential information.

Persons concerned with obtaining, organizing, and providing information about people should establish procedures to ensure that privacy is respected. Actions should include collecting data only for approved objectives and programs and only with the informed consent of the subjects. Information should be destroyed when the use for which it was collected has been served.

Copyrights and Answer Sheets

Publishers report that controlling reproduction of answer sheets is an important problem. From their point of view, the problem involves not only the possibility of significant alteration of test norms by use of a different answer-sheet format, but also the bread-and-butter problem of reduced opportunities to make a profit from a product in which an investment has been made. At this time, considerable legal uncertainty surrounds what attributes of an answer sheet may qualify for copyright protection. From the standpoint of quality control, however, it seems essential that the developer and publisher of a test be entitled to maintain necessary control of answer-sheet design if he is to back up his claims of normative data for a given test instrument.

The copyright problem has become especially difficult in one state as a consequence of an administrative ruling which specifies that answer sheets purchased with public funds must be bought from the lowest bidder, and that purchasers of answer sheets must not be concerned with copyright problems. This obviously opens the door for school districts or other government units to negotiate whatever arrangements they can to acquire answer sheets at the lowest possible cost.

A further complication of major importance is a consequence of the rapidly expanding development of test-scoring services. Some scoring services have developed answer sheets that serve as alternatives to publisher-developed forms. Other services have worked out cooperative agreements with test publishers whereby the test-publishing organization receives a rebate on the sale of answer sheets. Test-scoring services will probably continue to grow in importance; as a result, more and more test-answer forms will have to be designed in a format compatible with such services. This development alleviates the problem in several ways: it assures use of the same answer-sheet format for norm development and operational use; it assures the user of the low-cost, fast, high-quality scoring; and it assures the publisher's income from the sale of answer sheets.

Advertising

In general, advertising practices and merchandising techniques designed to sell test materials have conformed with ethical standards established by professional associations concerned with testing. One of the more powerful kinds of "advertising" for a test is use of the test in connection with research projects or other applications which result in description of tests in professional journals and textbooks. Such advertising is virtually free; it may be more effective than a paid advertisement in its influence on professional consumers.

Responsibilities of Change Agents

As we review the issues raised in this book, we find three principal groups of change agents that can implement actions on the public policy changes related to testing. These agents are the testing industry and professional associations, state governments, and the federal government.

Representatives of the industry are combined with representatives of the testing professions, because the leading organizations in industry are strongly influenced by their senior professionals. Often, the persons in top positions in the industry are also quite influential in the professional associations. For both government groups we include the legislatures and executive agencies.

These change agents can influence the solution of the testing industry's problems in four major ways: (1) formulation of new assessment system standards in response to technological developments which create new issues or problems, (2) formulation of new legislation for quality control and protection of the individual, in response to technological developments, (3) formation of new organizations which would help promote quality control to protect the individual, and serve as test review and information agencies, and (4) extension of research and development activities to improve quality of products and services and to investigate the relationship between testing and, for example, discriminatory practices.

Industry, Professionals, and Professional Associations

The major responsibility for change falls on members of the professions. They must take the initiative in many problem areas and communicate the urgency for action to the state and federal governments.

TEST ADMINISTRATION. These change agents should ensure that tests are administered by competent people and that results are fed back to the people who use the tests. Concurrently, the groups should ensure that the privacy and rights of testees are protected.

INFORMATION FLOW. These groups should improve the coordination of information flow to test users. This has been started through work of the Inter-Association Council on Test Reviews (IACTR); possibly the industry should consider financial support of IACTR through the industry associations. High priority should be given to test reviews keyed for paraprofessionals, since a high percentage of test decisions are made by the paraprofessionals. Existing journals should be examined to see if appropriate journals exist for the paraprofessional level; if not, a journal should be established for this group.

TEST USE AND INTERPRETATION. Professional and testing organizations should exert more effort to assure that tests are being appropriately used and interpreted to test users, particularly with respect to the impact of testing on discrimination in employment and education. Associations should maintain and expand such activities as those of the APA Assessment Committee and should offer services and support to such organizations as TACT (Technical Advisory Committee on Testing to the Fair Employment Practice Commission —State of California).

STANDARDS. The associations have done an excellent job of providing standards to their memberships and to the industry. They should continue to update standards and create new ones as technological changes create new issues. New standards should be considered for test interpretation and scoring activities and procedures.

DEVELOPMENT OF PARAPROFESSIONALS. Associations should either open a new class of membership or create new organizations that would encourage development of the paraprofessionals' skills. Associations should promote establishment of courses, training programs, and certification or licensing for paraprofessionals.

State Governments

PARAPROFESSIONALS. The primary efforts of the state governments should be directed toward the problems of the professional/paraprofessional level, with emphasis on the latter. States should develop licensing and certification laws that pertain to persons using tests. They should also develop training programs to prepare people for licensing and certification.

DISCRIMINATION. The states should provide additional legislation and services in the area of discrimination in employment and education. They should review their own personnel practices and should encourage development of organizations such as TACT, either as voluntary organizations or as state agencies.

PRIVACY. State governments should encourage state laws requiring written consent to be tested and to allow subsequent release of records. They should protect the privacy of the individual's test results and should require destruction of test records when the purpose of the testing is served.

COPYRIGHT. State attorneys general and state departments of education should not permit the purchase of answer sheets that do not conform to copyright laws. They should provide assurance that high-quality scoring is possible, and that the norms used in test interpretation match all aspects of the test-taking and test-validation situations.

FEEDBACK. Computerized interpretation services should be developed to improve feedback to test takers and users, especially in state-wide testing programs.

REVIEWS. State departments of education should make available reviews of tests used in the state's programs. Teachers and counselors should be able to understand these reviews, which may require both improvements in the reviews and in the training of persons who use them.

Federal Government

CONCERN WITH INDIVIDUAL RIGHTS. The federal government has been concerned with the rights of actual or potential federal employees and with the rights of minority members with respect to testing. The government should continue these efforts and should extend its concern to the rights of all persons taking tests. For example, written consent of persons to be tested for federal programs, except military programs, should be required. Further, the government should require written consent for release or use of test information for other than the original purpose.

QUALITY CONTROL. Rather than concern itself with the rights of business organizations to engage in testing activities under a federally protected *laissez faire* environment, the government should concern itself with the quality of the test as it affects the testee. In particular, the Federal Trade Commission and congressional committees concerned with consumer needs and rights should look at present laws and rulings and consider recommending new legislation that would encourage the professions and industry to help raise standards. It would be preferable to encourage the professions and organizations in this way rather than subject them to court proceedings when their attempts to raise standards could be considered in restraint of trade.

If this kind of action is not taken by the federal government, then the raising of standards may lead to the passing of laws that force the test industry to do what the government has been preventing them from doing.

COPYRIGHT. To continue to encourage good test development, the government should pass legislation to extend copyright laws to answer sheets.

FEEDBACK. Feedback to test users and takers should be improved. The focus of activity should probably be on research and development of computerized interpretation services which would assist both test takers and the persons providing the feedback.

INFORMATION FLOW. The testing component of ERIC should be continued, for information is a key element in sustaining the quality of a testing system.

Perspective

This study has found that over the more than fifty years that tests have been commercially available, testing companies, agencies, and professions have devoted considerable effort to improve the quality of their products and the manner in which they are used. Generally, improvement of the instruments has met with more success than improvement of processes at the user level. Both federal and state governments, as lawmakers, administrators, and managers of testing programs, have contributed significantly to test research and effective use. The good practices at the test-research and development level are not sufficient at this time to offset testing system inadequacies at the test user level.

The complexities of testing in education, government, and industry prevent the application of simple solutions. Nevertheless, many professional leaders and organization managers involved in testing are aware of ways to improve testing systems which the scope of their own activities precludes implementing. The federal government and some state governments provide examples of good practices which they discourage or prevent others from following. Greater education of persons interacting with test takers is needed, along with making their jobs easier by providing them with better feedback documents interpreting test results. Continued support of testing-system research and demonstration programs will continue to lead to system improvements.

All persons and organizations involved in the testing industry must continue to expand their efforts to assure that uses of their materials and programs will result in improved opportunities for all citizens. This may be accomplished through better evaluation of opportunities, qualifications for taking advantage of the opportunities, and improvement of our institutions to serve more effectively the changing needs of Americans.

Bibliography

American Personnel and Guidance Association. *Ethical Standards: American Personnel and Guidance Association.* Washington, D.C.: APGA, October 1961.

American Psychological Association. *Ethical Standards for the Distribution of Psychological Tests and Diagnostic Aids.* Washington, D.C.: APA, 1954.

American Psychological Association. *Ethical Standards of Psychologists.* Washington, D.C.: APA, 1963.

American Psychological Association. *Psychology As a Profession.* Washington, D.C.: APA, 1968.

American Psychological Association *et al. Standards for Educational and Psychological Tests and Manuals.* Prepared by a joint committee, John W. French, and William B. Michael, co-chairmen. Washington, D.C.: APA, 1966.

Anastasi, A. *Psychological Testing.* New York: Macmillan, 1968.

Baehr, Melany E. " 'A Frankly Critical Review' of the Mental Measurements Yearbooks," Industrial Relations Center, University of Chicago, 1967. Mimeographed.

Berdie, R. "The Ad Hoc Committee on Social Impact of Psychological Assessment," *American Psychologist,* 20:2 (February 1965), 146.

Black, H. *They Shall Not Pass.* New York: Morrow, 1963.

Buros, Oscar K. *The Sixth Mental Measurements Yearbook.* Highland Park, N.J.: Gryphon, 1965.

College Entrance Examination Board. *Report of the Commission on Tests: I. Righting the Balance.* New York, 1970.

College Entrance Examination Board. *Report of the Commission on Tests: II. Briefs.* New York, 1970.

Cooper, G. "Legal Implications of the Use of Standardized Ability Tests in Employment and Education," *Columbia Law Review,* 68 (1968), 690–744.

Donovan, J. J., ed. *Recruitment and Selection in the Public Service.* Chicago: Public Personnel Association, 1968.

Educational Testing Service. *Establishment of the Educational Testing Service: A Statement by the Board of Trustees.* New York: ETS, Dec. 27, 1947.

Enneis, W. "Misuses of Tests." Unpublished report presented at the 1969 Annual Convention of the American Psychological Association.

Equal Employment Opportunity Commission. *Guidelines on Employment Testing Procedures.* Washington, D.C., Aug. 24, 1966.

Ervin, S. J. "Why Senate Hearings on Psychological Tests in Government," *American Psychologist,* 20:11 (November 1965), 879–880.

"Validation of Employment Tests by Contractors and Subcontractors Subject to the Provisions of Executive Order 11246," *Federal Register*, 33:186, Part II (Sept. 24, 1968), 14392.

Fuess, C. M. *The College Board: Its First Fifty Years.* New York: College Entrance Examination Board, 1967.

Gallagher, C. E. "Why House Hearings on Invasion of Privacy," *American Psychologist*, 20:11 (November 1965), 881–882.

Goslin, D. A. "Criticisms of Standardized Tests and Testing." Unpublished report, CEEB, New York, May 20, 1967.

Goslin, D. A. *The Search for Ability.* New York: Russell Sage Foundation, 1963.

Goslin, D. A. *Teachers and Testing.* New York: Russell Sage Foundation, 1967.

Goslin, D. A., and N. Bordier. "Record Keeping in Elementary and Secondary Schools," in Stanton Wheeler, ed. *On Record: Files and Dossiers in American Life.* New York: Russell Sage Foundation, 1969.

Greenberg, H., and D. Mayer. "A New Approach to the Scientific Selection of Successful Salesmen," *Journal of Psychology*, 57 (1964), 113–123.

Gross, M. L. *The Brain Watchers.* New York: New American Library, 1963.

Messick, S. "Personality Measurement and the Ethics of Assessment," *American Psychologist*, 20:2 (February 1965), 136–142.

Pasanella, A. K., W. H. Manning, and N. Findikyan. "Criticisms of Testing I." Unpublished report, CEEB, New York, May 19, 1967.

Rosenthal, R., and L. Jacobson, *Pygmalion in the Classroom: Teacher Expectation and Pupil's Intellectual Ability.* New York: Holt, 1970.

Ruebhausen, O. M., and O. G. Brim. "Privacy and Behavioral Research," *Columbia Law Review*, 65 (November 1965), 1185–1211.

Rushmore, J. E. "Psychological Tests and Fair Employment: A Study of Employment Tests in the San Francisco Bay Area," State of California Fair Employment Practice Commission, 1967. Mimeographed.

Russell Sage Foundation. *Guidelines for the Collection, Maintenance, and Dissemination of Pupil Records.* New York: The Foundation, 1969.

Smith, K. U. Testimony, *American Psychologist*, 20:11 (November 1965), 907–915.

Uhlaner, J. E., ed. *Psychological Research in National Defense Today.* Washington, D.C.: U.S. Army Behavioral Science Research Laboratory, June 1967.

World Book Company. *Standardized Testing: An Adventure in Educational Publishing, 1905–1955.* New York: World, August 1954.

Appendix

This Appendix contains brief descriptions of the various testing and scoring companies and their activities. The individuals listed are those with whom we have had personal contact or correspondence.

Information about the companies and their tests or scoring services has been obtained by personal or telephone interview, by correspondence, or by searching Oscar K. Buros' *Mental Measurement Yearbooks*. For the most part, we have not attempted in these sketches to evaluate the information; there is no attempt in the selection to imply any evaluation. No information on government testing agencies is included.

American Association of Teachers of German
Box 43, Muhlenberg College
Allentown, Pennsylvania 18104

Adolphe Wegener: Treasurer

Test: AATG German Test

The American Association of Teachers of German (AATG) is not involved in psychological test production and related services. It does, however, sponsor cooperative tests which are made up by a committee of authorities in the field and printed by Educational Testing Service.

The AATG test is constructed to evaluate two levels of learning correct usage of German and achievement in reading comprehension in German. It is used for placement purposes.

American Association of Teachers of Spanish and Portuguese
1810 Chadbourne Avenue
Madison, Wisconsin 53705

Harry T. Charly: Chairman

Test: National Spanish Examination

The Association is not primarily engaged in test publication; rather, it is an organization for teachers of Spanish and Portuguese. The Association sponsors the annual National Spanish Contest for secondary school students.

The tests for these examinations are prepared by teachers of Spanish who are on the Test Development Committee of the Association. The tests, used primarily in the administration of scholarship programs for secondary students of Spanish, represent a national standard for all scholarship applicants. A summary of the results of any test administration is published in *Hispania* in the September following the administration of the tests.

American College Testing Program
Box 168
Iowa City, Iowa 52240

Dr. John L. Holland: Vice President (now at Johns Hopkins University)

Test: ACTP Battery, including English usage, mathematics usage, social studies reading, and natural sciences reading

The American College Testing Program (ACTP), a federation of state programs, was set up primarily to serve the admissions testing needs of state colleges and universities and private colleges whose needs were not met by the College Entrance Examination Board. ACTP serves as a central agency for the collection, analysis, processing, and reporting of information for use in educational planning by college-bound students.

Under contract, Science Research Associates provides test registration, printing and materials distribution services as well as test construction and development.

The Measurement Research Center provides electronic scoring of the ACTP battery, distribution of reports and other material, and data processing services for the research and development division of ACTP.

Approximately one thousand agencies and institutions comprise ACTP.

American Guidance Service, Inc.
Publisher's Building
Circle Pines, Minnesota 55014

Mr. John P. Yackel: Vice President

Types of tests: Achievement, aptitude, intelligence, maturity scales, school readiness, speech articulation

American Guidance Service (AGS) purchased most of the tests formerly published by the Educational Test Bureau; it has since developed considerable new material. The company now publishes tests and materials related to the instructional needs of education and industry; customers are predominantly schools, businesses, hospitals, government, and individuals.

A complete scoring and recording service is available for all AGS tests which are scored by hand on the test booklets. AGS recommends that teachers can obtain valuable information by scoring the tests they administer, especially diagnostic tests. Although the company does not interpret its tests, it does consult by mail with teachers and counselors on test uses and interpretation.

American Institutes for Research
P.O. Box 1113
Palo Alto, California 93402

Dr. John C. Flanagan: Chairman, Board of Directors

Test/Program: Airline Pilots Selection Battery, Project TALENT

The American Institutes for Research (AIR) conducts major test-research programs, including Project TALENT. This project was developed to assess the educational progress of students in the United States. The test battery developed for this program is in the public domain. It is AIR's hope that this battery may be used to describe and to some extent validate other tests.

AIR also has a program for selection of air-crew personnel for commercial airlines. This project, initiated under contract to United Airlines, has been extended to other airlines. A test battery for stewardesses will be added as soon as forward validation tests are completed.

The American Language Institute
Georgetown University
3605 O Street, N.W.
Washington, D.C. 20007

David P. Harris: Director

Test: English Usage Test

The primary purpose of the American Language Institute is to provide language training for foreign students brought to the United States by the Agency for International Development (AID) and the Bureau of Educational and Cultural Affairs of the Department of State.

In the late 1950's, AID asked the American Language Institute to prepare a simple English screening test for use in the overseas testing of applicants for grants and scholarships. Since then, the screening test has been supplemented by listening and vocabulary and reading tests; the latter are used by academic institutions only.

American Orthopsychiatric Association, Inc.
1790 Broadway
New York, New York 10019

Dr. Marion F. Langer: Executive Secretary

Test: Visual Motor Gestalt Test

The American Orthopsychiatric Association publishes and distributes only one test.

The Association's main interest is in research and publication related to a multi-disciplinary approach to the study and treatment of human growth and behavior.

Association Press
291 Broadway
New York, New York 10007

Roland E. Burdick: Assistant Director

Publication: Personal Adjustment Inventory

Association Press is a nonprofit educational publisher; it is not in the testing business. Since 1931, however, the press has published the Personal Adjustment Inventory developed by Dr. Carl Rogers. Dr. Rogers describes the inventory as an "exploratory instrument to help a psychologist come to know a child better." He emphasizes that this is not a test.

Association Press indicates that Rogers' instructions to the educator or counselor are carefully delineated; the company credits the user with the ability to follow these instructions.

Automata Corporation
1305 Mansfield Avenue
Richland, Washington 99352

Automata Corporation's principal product is a card reader intended for use in local school systems. The machine will provide visual feedback on the kinds of errors being made by students. There is no need to tie the machine to a computer; it operates independently.

The Bobbs-Merrill Company, Inc.
4330 East 62 Street
Indianapolis, Indiana 46206

Dr. Leo Gans: Director, Educational Division

Types of Tests: Academic achievement, aptitude, intelligence, and personality

The Bobbs-Merrill Company, a subsidiary of Howard W. Sams and Company, Inc., entered the testing business through its acquisition of two small publishing companies that owned some tests. At the time of our interview, this organization did not employ anyone to develop or revise tests, or did it offer scoring or interpretation services.

The company's primary commitment is to publication of educational textbooks and other instructional materials. The bulk of its test sales is made to educational institutions. No new tests were being developed.

Mrs. Barbara S. Boyle
337 Calcaterra Street
Palo Alto, California 94306

Mrs. Barbara S. Boyle: Distributor

Test: Shipley Institute of Living Scale for Measuring Intellectual Impairment

Mrs. Boyle is not strictly in the testing business. She distributes a test developed
in 1939 by her father, William C. Shipley, a test designed as a measure of intellectual impairment. Mrs. Boyle has distributed the instrument since her father's
death to old customers, largely Veterans Administration hospitals, consulting psychologists, school districts, and the like.

At the time of our interview, Mrs. Boyle was seeking professional assistance in
updating and revalidating the test prior to expanding its distribution.

Dr. Peter Briggs
University of Minnesota
School of Physical Medicine and Rehabilitation
Minneapolis, Minnesota 55455

Dr. Peter Briggs: Clinical Psychologist

Test: M-B History Record

Dr. Briggs, a clinical psychologist affiliated with the University of Minnesota
School of Physical Medicine and Rehabilitation, originally developed the History
Record as a questionnaire. One person filled out the Record by describing another,
e.g., a parent described a child's health history. The current questionnaire is self-
administering and self-descriptive; it evokes both personal and medical history.
Primary use of this new instrument is as a data base for other research work.

At the time of our interview, Briggs was working on two other instruments: the
Tellenauke Motor Battery, which is used to determine the status of a person's
motor coordination, and the VIZ test, which determines whether children can
organize forms and space. The latter test was to be published when Briggs felt he
had a useful and polished instrument with adequate norms.

The Bruce Publishing Company
400 N. Broadway
Milwaukee, Wisconsin 53201

Bruno B. Wolff, Jr.: Textbook Editor

Test: California Book Tests

Bruce Publishing Company publishes a small number of tests directly related to
some of the basic Catholic literary texts that the company also publishes. The
tests are usually developed by the authors themselves and are usually based on
actual classroom trials.

Martin M. Bruce, Ph.D., Publisher
340 Oxford Road
New Rochelle, New York 10804

Dr. Martin M. Bruce: Owner

Types of Tests: Ability, aptitude, achievement, judgment, insight, personality

Dr. Martin M. Bruce's test publishing activities are an adjunct to his clinical and consulting practice. He operates, not as a member of the industry, but as a professional person; he contracts the work done for him in handling the tests. The majority of his tests are for use in clinical, personnel, or industrial counseling. Tests are distributed in eight foreign countries as well as in the United States.

Test scoring may be done by the test administrator. Manuals include instructions on how to interpret profiles, scores, and data.

Bureau of Educational Research and Services
C-6 East Hall
University of Iowa
Iowa City, Iowa 52240

Dr. Darrell Sabers: Director

Types of Tests: Intelligence, achievement, language, mathematics, music, vocational, interest, and personality inventories

The Bureau of Educational Research and Services publishes its own tests and distributes tests published by others. The Bureau distributes over one hundred thousand test forms and an equal number of answer sheets each year; about 98 percent of them go to schools, primarily for measurement of academic aptitude or achievement.

Although the Bureau has nine employees, only the assistant director is principally concerned with testing. Tests were being updated at the time of our interview and new norms were being provided.

California Test Bureau
Del Monte Research Park
Monterey, California 93940

Dr. Joseph Dione: Director

Types of Tests: Intelligence, achievement batteries, reading, mathematics, language, science and social studies, aptitudes, adjustment, attitudes, and interests. Best-known tests: California Test of Mental Maturity, California Achievement Tests, Comprehensive Test of Basic Skills

The California Test Bureau, a division of McGraw-Hill, Inc., ranks third or fourth in test sales; 90 percent of its sales are made to primary and elementary schools.

CTB has approximately 125 full-time employees and, in addition, has temporary and part-time help for test scoring. Of these employees, about 25 are on the research and development and statistical staffs, and about 22 are on the field staff.

The company does not offer any automated test interpretation service, or does it provide individual interpretations as a regular service. CTB provides teachers and counselors with data feedback on all tests scored. Scoring service activities are changing and growing rapidly.

Program of Affiliation
The Catholic University of America
Washington, D.C. 20017

Miss Rita Watrin: Assistant to the Director

The Program of Affiliation was dissolved in 1969 on the recommendation of the Board of Trustees. This program had been established as a service to Catholic secondary schools and institutions of higher learning. It offered assistance in the areas of evaluation of educational programs and credentials for transfer of students between such schools.

Walter V. Clarke Associates, Inc.
1195 Southeast 17 Street
Fort Lauderdale, Florida 33316

Walter V. Clarke: President

Tests: Activity Vector Analysis. Measurement of Skill: a battery of placement tests

Walter V. Clarke Associates is a consulting company which publishes one private-personnel placement test. Clarke has developed training programs to teach senior personnel people and company executives how to use the AVA methods and materials for placement. The company also does individual assessment, using its own materials and personnel.

The total staff consists of about 20 people, of whom 5 are in the field. Clarke has about 200 client companies which range in size from 18 employees to several thousand.

John P. Cleaver Company, Inc.
1 Palmer Square
Princeton, New Jersey 08540

John P. Cleaver: President

Test: The Self-DISCription

The Cleaver company is a management consultant firm which publishes one private personnel test. Using the test, Cleaver helps managers to communicate human behaviors required for a job and helps corporate officers to evaluate the human criteria for jobs. The company offers a two-day executive training program.

There are 25 people employed in two offices. Of the 12 professionals on the staff, 3 are psychologists.

The College Entrance Examination Board
475 Riverside Drive
New York, New York 10027

Dr. Winton Manning: Director for the Commission on Tests (now ETS)
Dr. Sam A. McCandless: Assistant Director for the Commission on Tests
Dr. S. A. Kendrick: Executive Associate

Types of Tests: Aptitude, achievement, placement. Best-known test: Scholastic Aptitude

The College Entrance Examination Board, probably the oldest and best known of the testing organizations, is primarily concerned with developing an extensive program of examinations for guidance, college admissions, and placement. The organization also supervises numerous research projects in the area of guidance, testing, and educational progress and publishes a variety of informational and interpretive materials.

The staff consists of approximately 40 professional and administrative personnel in the central office in New York and 30 representatives in the Washington office and 5 regional offices. The bulk of the administration and scoring of the tests is carried out by Educational Testing Service.

Almost 1,000 member organizations comprise this nonprofit company. Approximately 700 of these organizations are colleges, 250 are secondary schools, and 50 are associations.

Committee on Diagnostic Reading Tests, Inc.
Mountain Home, North Carolina 28758

Dr. Frances O. Triggs: Chairman

Test: Diagnostic Reading Tests

The Committee on Diagnostic Reading Tests is a nonprofit educational service organization. Its work includes research and information exchange in the area of reading; its purpose is to contribute to the development of better reading practices. Thus this organization develops and distributes reading tests and teaching materials to aid agencies and persons interested in improvement of reading.

The Diagnostic Tests were constructed to help teachers recognize the reading level of each student so that students might be dealt with at their own level. The Committee revises its publications and tests materials, and it reports on those revisions in a newsletter sent to test users.

Consulting Psychologists Press
577 College Avenue
Palo Alto, California 94306

Dr. John Black: President

Types of Tests: Intelligence, aptitude and achievement, personality inventories, behavioral rating devices, interest tests, adjustment inventories. Best-known tests: California Psychological Inventory, Strong Vocational Interest Blanks

Consulting Psychologists Press started in 1956 as a one-test publisher. It now publishes and distributes a number of tests, counseling and clinical aids, and books. While some of their tests are widely used by schools, colleges, business and industry, clinics and hospitals, many instruments are specifically designed for behavioral scientists working in laboratories and assessment centers.

Consulting Psychologists Press does not score its own tests; however, it lists approved scoring services in its catalogue.

Creativity Research Institute
The Richardson Foundation
P. O. Box 3265
Greensboro, North Carolina 27402

Dr. Robert J. Lacklen: Director

Tests: Alpha Biographical Inventory, Beta Biographical Inventory (research edition)

The Creativity Research Institute began work a number of years ago on biographical data blanks and the use of these blanks for selection and placement. The Institute for Behavioral Research in Creativity, also in Greensboro, and Prediction Press, which is the publisher of some new biographical inventories, are now responsible for the work on the data blank.

The Diebold Group, Inc.
430 Park Avenue
New York, New York 10022

A. J. Walsh: Director of Personnel

Test: The Diebold Personnel Tests

The Diebold Group is a management consulting firm which has, from time to time, made efforts to develop a battery of tests for specialized occupations. The company published the Diebold Personnel Tests in 1959, but at the time of our interview it did not publish or distribute tests of any kind.

Arthur A. Dole
Graduate School of Education
University of Pennsylvania
Philadelphia, Pennsylvania 19104

Arthur A. Dole: Professor of Education

Test: Vocational Sentence Completion Blank (experimental edition)

Arthur Dole, a professor of education at the University of Pennsylvania, published the first form of his test in 1951. From 1958 to 1966, while Dole was a professor at the University of Hawaii, sale of the test was handled by the University of Hawaii Bookstore. Requests for copies of the manual were referred to Dole, who responded only to qualified psychologists. He forwarded the manual without charge along with a personal letter explaining the experimental nature of the instrument. In a few instances foreign psychologists were given permission to translate or modify the blank to fit their circumstances.

The Dow Chemical Company
Midland, Michigan 48640

L. J. Bollinger: Manager, Psychology Department

Test: Chemical Operators Selection Test (revised edition)

Dow Chemical Company's Psychology, Education, and Personnel departments have developed an aptitude test to assist in Dow's own personnel placement and selection. At the time of our interview, Dr. L. J. Bollinger was developing norms for present chemical operators and was validating test performance against supervisory assessment of job performance. There was no plan to modify the test.

Three other companies in the chemical field, plus ETS and the University of California, have been using the test on an experimental basis. Dow sells the test to other, similar companies.

Educational and Industrial Testing Service
Box 7234
San Diego, California 92107

Mr. Robert K. Knapp: Owner

Types of Tests: Personality, interest, ability and aptitude, special purpose

Educational and Industrial Testing Service (EITS) publishes and distributes a number of books and tests; test sales account for 60 percent of the company's business. The majority of the tests are used for personality assessment or for counseling or guidance primarily by schools, government, and individuals engaged in research.

Mr. Knapp and independent test authors are responsible for design and development of the company's tests. EITS will score all its tests; however, this scoring service is not often requested. No interpretation services are provided, but consulting services are available to purchasers who request them.

Educational Records Bureau
21 Audubon Avenue
New York, New York 10032

Dr. William S. Litterick: President

Types of Tests: Aptitude, achievement, special purpose

The Educational Records Bureau (ERB) is a nonprofit membership organization engaged in testing, consultation, and research. The organization recommends and supplies to member schools aptitude and achievement and special-purpose tests selected from all available sources; scores and reports tests; computes and reports independent school, public school, regional and local norms, and statistical analyses; offers professional consultation services in fields of guidance, testing, curriculum development, and administration; and maintains educational research programs. ERB prefers to buy tests rather than build them.

About 50 full-time employees plus 100 to 200 temporary and part-time employees operate the company. ERB has 1,200 member organizations and some affiliates.

Educational Testing Service
Princeton, New Jersey 08540

William W. Turnbull: President
John S. Helmick: Vice President
Samuel J. Messick: Vice President
Robert J. Solomon: Vice President

Types of Tests: Admissions tests, ability, achievement, language, examination programs for professional groups. Best-known tests: College Board Admissions Tests, College Placement Tests, Graduate Record Examination

Educational Testing Services (ETS) is primarily engaged in testing, research, and advisory activities directed toward the major university and private-college market. The services offered by ETS include test development, evaluation, information and professional counseling to educators regarding the construction, use, and interpretation of tests. The company is developing instructional programs in a wide variety of areas.

The present staff of regular employees is about 1,200; almost 1,000 temporary workers augment the staff during the winter peak activity.

ETS tests are scored by the College Entrance Examination Board.

Educators'/Employers' Tests and Services Associates
120 Drexel Place
Cincinnati, Ohio 45219

Mrs. Sarah M. Drake: President

Types of Tests: Personality rating, reading, mental ability, intelligence, aptitude and ability, entrance examination for schools of practical nursing

This company publishes only some of the tests it sells; it distributes tests for Personnel Press, Columbia University Press, and Iowa State University. The tests sold by Educators'/Employers' Tests and Services Associates are designed and adapted for industrial use by Psychological Services Bureau, Indiana, Pennsylvania.

The majority of tests are designed to be administered and scored by persons with no extensive training or psychological knowledge; nonetheless, Mrs. Drake keeps an extremely strict check on her clients, selling only to qualified psychologists. Some of the tests, including the PBS Examination for Schools of Practical Nursing, are scored and reported on by Psychological Services Bureau.

The English Language Institute
The University of Michigan
North University Building
Ann Arbor, Michigan 48104

Dr. John Upsher: Research Associate

Tests: Michigan Test of English Language Proficiency; ELI English Achievement Series; Test of Aural Comprehension

The English Language Institute (ELI) has been concerned for many years with research on the teaching of English and with development of programs and program materials for use in teaching and understanding English.

ELI has about three hundred examiners around the world who, in addition to their other duties, administer the language tests. The tests are scored at the University of Michigan.

Essay Press
P. O. Box 5
Planetarium Station
New York, New York 10012

Florence G. Roswell: Professor

Tests: Roswell-Chall Auditory Blending Test, Roswell-Chall Diagnostic Reading Test of Word Analysis Skills

The Auditory Blending Test was developed by its authors at the Educational Clinic of the City College of New York in 1955. The test was part of a longitudinal study of factors in success in beginning reading. The authors published the test without accomplishing the developmental work which would make the test acceptable according to the *APA Standards Manual*. It is not clear, however, that the authors intended the test to be used as a standardized instrument.

Family Life Publications, Inc.
Box 6725, College Station
Durham, North Carolina 27708

Dr. Gelolo McHugh: Director

Types of Tests: Courtship analysis, dating-problems check list, marriage-adjustment form, prediction schedule, role-expectation inventory, sex-knowledge inventory

Family Life Publications is a publisher of books and teaching and counseling aids. Some of the latter are inventories, check lists, and schedules; they are not tests. These instruments are for use in schools and in counseling agencies.

Ginn and Company
Statler Building
Boston, Massachusetts 02117

Robert N. Walker: Head, Test Department; Editor, Personnel Press

Test: McCullough Word-Analysis Tests (experimental edition)

Ginn and Company is primarily a book publisher; however, it does produce a test. In 1962, the company acquired Personnel Press (see listing), a publisher of several tests; Ginn distributes these tests through its national sales organization. The Xerox Corporation has recently purchased Ginn and Company.

The company operates a scoring service known as the Personnel Press Scoring Service. Scoring is done at the Educational Records Bureau and at Kent State University.

Great Eastern Lumber Company
2315 Broadway
New York, New York 10024

Mr. N. Nash: Vice President

Test: The Potter-Nash Aptitude Test for Lumber Inspectors and Other General Personnel Who Handle Lumber

Great Eastern Lumber Company is strictly in the lumber business. Nevertheless, Mr. N. Nash, the vice president, has developed and published a test with the assistance of Mr. Floyd Potter, chief grader of the National Lumber Graders Association. The test, essentially an algebra test, is designed to help the company determine whether to send employees to a lumber-graders' school.

The test has been sold in small quantities to other lumber companies. Each company determines its own standards, although the publisher does recommend standards based on the experience of the Great Eastern Lumber Company.

Grune & Stratton, Inc.
381 Park Avenue South
New York, New York 10016

Mr. Duncan MacIntosh: Editor in Chief

Tests: Developmental Potential of Pre-School Children; Freeman Anxiety Neurosis and Psychosomatic Tests; Bender Gestalt Tests, Rorschach, and Szondi

This company, primarily a publisher of medical and scientific books, is involved only in a very minor way in the publication and distribution of test materials. It provides no testing services of any kind. Nor does this organization contract for the development of new tests.

The primary users of most of the testing materials are personnel in clinical settings, such as clinical psychologists and psychiatrists. Test sales are promoted through direct mail, advertising in professional journals, and exhibiting materials at professional meetings. It is clear from the limited number of test offerings that the distribution of psychological test materials is a very small part of the publishing activity of this organization.

Guidance Testing Associates
6516 Shirley Avenue
Austin, Texas 78752

Mr. Herschel T. Manuel: President

Tests: Inter-American Tests (new series), Cooperative Inter-American Tests (1950 edition)

Guidance Testing Associates is a small nonprofit corporation organized primarily for the publication and distribution of the Inter-American series of tests. The tests are published in parallel English and Spanish editions for use in the Western Hemisphere wherever these languages are spoken or used in schools.

The Inter-American Tests were originally developed by the Committee on Modern Languages of the American Council on Education for use in a study of the teaching of English in Puerto Rico. After some revision, the tests were published by the Educational Testing Service for general use under the title, Cooperative Inter-American Tests. In 1959, publication was transferred to Guidance Testing Associates.

The New Series of Inter-American tests, resulting from research projects directed by Dr. Manuel, has been prepared with the assistance of U.S. Office of Education funds. The company invites the cooperation of educators in the preparation of its tests. Scoring may be done by the test administrator.

Harcourt Brace Jovanovich
757 Third Avenue
New York, New York 10017

Dr. Roger Lennon: Vice President

Types of Tests: Intelligence, achievement, aptitude, ability, reading. Best-known tests: Stanford Achievement Tests

Harcourt Brace Jovanovich is primarily engaged in educational publishing for the primary grades through college. Although it is one of the largest merchandisers of tests and test services, these account for only 10 percent of the company's total sales.

The Test Department handles all testing activity; its staff exceeds 100 people, including professionals involved in test development, a field staff in 5 separate locations, and 35 field representatives, consultants, and foreign representatives. This is the only major educational publisher with a separate test sales and consulting staff.

The company offers scoring service; through an arrangement with Measurement Research Center, MRC performs the mechanical and computational tasks to Harcourt Brace's specifications.

Harvard University Press
79 Garden Street
Cambridge, Massachusetts 02138

L. B. Lincoln: Sales Manager

Test: Thematic Apperception Test

Harvard University Press publishes the Thematic Apperception Test which is published in two versions, the original Murray version and the Thompson modification which was designed for use with minority-group populations. There is no indication that the publisher takes responsibility for the tests; the authors are responsible for meeting test standards.

Hayes Educational Test Laboratory
7040 N. Portsmouth Avenue
Portland, Oregon 97203

Dr. Ernest Hayes: Director

Tests: Minimum Essentials for Modern Mathematics, Portland Prognostic Tests for Mathematics

Activity in the testing field is primarily an avocation for Dr. Ernest Hayes who is Dean of the School of Education at the University of Portland. His chief effort in the testing area is as a consultant for the Portland Metropolitan area and as a researcher. He has developed and supplied some prognostic tests in mathematics to schools. Most of his customers are located in the three Pacific Coast states; California provides only a small market, however.

Dr. Elisabeth F. Hellersberg
P. O. Box 104
Harvard, Massachusetts 01451

Dr. Elisabeth Hellersberg: Retired Writer

Test: Horn-Hellersberg Test

Dr. Elisabeth Hellersberg is a psychologist who has been making cross-cultural studies of personality for a number of years. She adapted the Horn Art Aptitude Inventory, developed in 1938 by Mr. Charles A. Horn of the Rochester Atheneum and Mechanical Institute, so that she might use the test for studying personality, particularly as it relates to reality. She has used the adapted test in her studies for the past twenty years.

The test is now published and distributed by Dr. Hellersberg who sells it and gives it away to persons interested in research. She is a part of the testing industry only insofar as she sells tests to those who request them. When she is no longer involved with the test, its publication will probably cease unless someone interested in her research on personality chooses to carry it on.

Hoeber Medical Division
Harper & Row, Publishers
49 East 33 Street
New York, New York 10016

Test: Myokinetic Psychodiagnosis Test

This company is not in the test publishing or development business. The Myokinetic Diagnosis Test was actually a book which set forth an approach to psychodiagnosis and offered some record forms. The book is no longer in print; the company does not intend to issue any subsequent edition.

Houghton Mifflin Company
110 Tremont Street
Boston, Massachusetts 02107

John Sommer: Editor in Chief

Types of Tests: Achievement, arithmetic and mathematics, English, intelligence, reading, social studies, vocational and guidance. Best-known tests: Stanford-Binet Intelligence Scale, Iowa Tests of Basic Skills

Houghton Mifflin is primarily an educational publisher. About 10 percent of the company's income comes from test sales and services; most of the remainder comes from the sale of books and similar printed educational material.

The staff of the Test Department includes 15 people who work in the editorial office and 5 field coordinators who assist the 150 textbook and test salesmen with test-related activities. This company does not write its own tests, but seeks competent authors from whom tests can be bought and edited.

The company provides a scoring service under contract with Measurement Research Center. Houghton Mifflin administers the activity, writing scoring programs specifications and so on; MRC does the actual scoring and preparation of feedback documents.

Humm Personnel Consultants
P. O. Box 15433
Del Valle Station
Los Angeles, California 90015

Catherine Humm: Owner

Test: Humm-Wadsworth Temperament Scale

This company, founded in 1929, has specialized in offering consulting services to industry. It has relied almost exclusively on a single product, the Humm-Wadsworth Temperament Scale. This organization is clearly not a test publisher. Rather, it offers direct services, including limited educational and vocational guidance services, to business organizations.

In 1955, additional normative data were offered to support a revised version of the test. This instrument is distributed in a way remarkably different from that used for most test materials in the United States. The company maintains virtually complete control of the test booklets, offering them for rent to client organizations; only the answer sheets for the booklets are sold. Further, personnel utilizing the Humm-Wadsworth Temperament Scale are required to complete a specialized training program which prepares them to use this instrument.

University of Illinois Press
Urbana, Illinois 61801

Mrs. Isabel Slater: Assistant Sales Manager

Test: Illinois Test of Psycholinguistic Abilities

The University of Illinois Press publishes one test which appears to be the result of considerable research by the principal authors and others at the University of Illinois. A book, *The Development and Psychometric Characteristics of the Revised Illinois Test*, is available to the general public.

Industrial Psychology, Inc.
515 Madison Avenue
New York, New York 10018

Mrs. Joseph King: Owner

Types of Tests: Factored aptitude, personality

Industrial Psychology, Inc. (IPI) was formed by the late Joseph King to develop factored aptitude tests for use by laymen. His goal was to establish a good basic program for all types of business, especially at the lower levels. The program would be a mail-order operation with consultants who could give assistance on special cases and problems.

The staff consists of three or four people and a consultant, Dr. Peter Dubnow, a psychologist and professor of management at New York University. The company assists its clients, predominantly industrial firms, in tailoring testing programs. Should such support prove beyond IPI's capability, the company recommends consultants who can give guidance. At the time of our interview, IPI was not developing or modifying its tests.

In addition to its own programs, IPI handles programs for Gray-Cattell, including the 16PF, the CPF, and the NPF. IPI tests may be scored and interpreted by the test administrator. Instructions for these purposes are included with the test package.

Industrial Relations Center: University of Chicago
1225 East 60 Street
Chicago, Illinois 60637

Dr. Melany Baehr: Division Director

Types of Tests: Personnel, public employment

The primary goal of the Industrial Relations Center is to carry out research and training services and to prepare and apply personnel tests on a consulting basis on behalf of industries or organizations which contract with the Center. Tests are not developed and published for sale.

The Center's activities begin with systematic job and worker analyses; only after completion of these analyses are tests developed or tried out. Results of testing and assessment procedures in contracting organizations are followed up over a couple of years.

Institute for Behavioral Research, Inc.
2426 Linden Lane
Silver Spring, Maryland 20910

Thomas E. Baker: Director, Administrative Services

The Institute for Behavioral Research provides automated scoring service for the

Holtzman Inkblot Technique. The computer output is a printout which gives scores for each of the 17 Holtzman Inkblot scales; it includes a table of means, standard deviations, and percentiles for each subsample of 100 records.

Institute for Personality and Ability Testing
1602 Coronado Drive
Champaign, Illinois 61822

Dr. Raymond Cattell: Chief Consultant, Research and Development

Types of Tests: Intelligence, personality, psycholinguistic ability

The Institute for Personality and Ability Testing offers nine tests, principally for use in schools, business, and government. The tests are primarily used for personality assessment, intellectual assessment, personnel selection, and vocational or educational counseling and guidance.

Although the Institute is independent of the University of Illinois, many of the personnel connected with test development are affiliated with the university. All professional personnel are APA or APGA members.

Clients are referred to National Computer Systems for scoring and interpretation services.

Institute of Psychological Research
Columbia University Teachers College
New York, New York 10027

Dr. Robert L. Thorndike: Head

Test: Vocabulary Test—GT

The Institute of Psychological Research is not primarily a publisher of tests. However, it does publish a vocabulary test that was an incidental by-product of a study that Dr. Thorndike carried out with Dr. George Gallup before World War II. Dr. Irving Lorge, who was then director of the Institute, thought the test was of sufficient merit to make it available to others; so the Institute became involved in test publication.

Other test development is for specific testing programs in Teachers College itself or for some of the local school systems. For example, a screening program for doctoral candidates has been developed, and an entrance examination for the science high schools in New York City has been designed.

Intercontinental Medical Book Corporation
381 Park Avenue South
New York, New York 10016

Oscar R. Hirshfield: Vice President

This company is not in the business of developing tests of any kind. Rather, it imports and distributes medical books from around the world. Coincidentally, it occasionally became involved in selling psychological test materials; however, test sales represent a very minor part of the company's annual income. The Rorschach test is the best-known material the corporation offers.

As an importer of books and related materials, the company does not evaluate the technical competence of test content.

Iowa State University Press
Press Building
Ames, Iowa 50010

Merritt E. Bailey: Director

Types of Tests: Interest inventories

The Iowa State University Press publishes several interest inventories. At one time, the Press published the Owens Test for Machine Design; this test has recently gone out of print because of problems of developing norms and validity data.

No expansion in the test field is under consideration.

Johnson O'Connor Research Foundation
Human Engineering Laboratory, Inc.
347 Beacon Street
Boston, Massachusetts 02116

Dr. Johnson O'Connor: Director

Tests: Johnson O'Connor English Vocabulary Worksamples, Johnson O'Connor Vocabulary Tests

The Human Engineering Laboratory administers tests that it has developed over a period of more than forty years. The company has no catalogue.

The step-by-step development of the tests is recorded in a series of over six hundred technical reports; these reports are available to persons interested in them.

Life Insurance Agency Management Association
170 Sigourney Street
Hartford, Connecticut 06105

Dr. Paul W. Thayer: Vice President

Tests: Aptitude Index Battery, Life Insurance Sales Selection Battery

The Life Insurance Agency Management Association (LIAMA) is basically a research agency. The test scoring and publishing done by LIAMA is primarily for convenience and is subsidiary to its major role in the research area.

A test group from LIAMA advises member companies with respect to tests and selection programs. Member companies may use the test in any manner they wish.

LIAMA has approximately 350 full members in the United States and Canada and over 100 associate members overseas.

Lyons and Carnahan, Educational Publishers
407 East 25 Street
Chicago, Illinois 60616

Mr. Norman J. York, II: Administrative Assistant, Reading Department

Tests: The Pribble-Dallmen Diagnostic Tests in Elementary Language Skills, The Pribble-McCrory Diagnostic Tests in Practical English Grammar Developmental Reading Tests. Silent Reading Diagnostic Tests: The Developmental Reading Tests

Lyons and Carnahan, an affiliate of Meredith Publishing Company, is primarily concerned with publication and sale of elementary school texts and with the Developmental Reading Series. The company does not publish psychological or any other forms of tests, except that in conjunction with the Reading Series, the company develops and publishes reading tests. The tests and texts have interlocking authorship; vocabulary for the tests was selected from the same word list used in writing the developmental reading series.

Schools are the market for these tests, the purpose of which is evaluation of reading skills.

Marketing Survey and Research Corporation
175 West 13 Street
New York, New York 10011

Dr. Herbert Greenberg: Founder and President

Test: Multiple Personal Inventory

The major activity of Marketing Survey and Research Corporation is assessment of job applicants, particularly for sales and sales-related jobs. The company has developed and published a proprietary test for use in its assessment programs.

The staff consists of 20 people in New York and 30 others around the world in offices concerned with sales rather than with evaluation. About 800 client companies in the United States and elsewhere use the corporation's materials, which are printed in seven languages.

McCann Associates
2755 Philmont Avenue
Huntingdon Valley, Pennsylvania 19006

Forbes E. McCann: President

Types of Tests: Personnel tests for policemen, firemen, clerical workers, carpenters, electricians, plumbers, public employees, etc.

McCann Associates is a privately owned organization that develops and distributes public-personnel tests to government agencies throughout the nation. Where special needs or secure tests are essential, the company undertakes a program of custom test development which ranges from job analysis through development of new questions, scoring, item analysis, and interpretation and reporting of results. The company does not supplement its testing programs with materials produced elsewhere, or does it produce personality tests.

Measurement Research Center
P. O. Box 30
Iowa City, Iowa 52240

Dr. E. F. Lindquist: President and Founder

The Measurement Research Center (MRC) is involved in test scoring in two ways. It does a high volume of test scoring, and it sells test-development services to publishers and test-consulting services to schools and other organizations.

MRC scores material on either its own separate answer sheets or on disposable booklets. The organization's equipment and processes are specifically designed to deal with large testing programs where the "get-ready" cost is high, but the unit processing cost is very low.

The Merrill-Palmer Institute of Human Development and Family Life
71 East Ferry Avenue
Detroit, Michigan 48202

Dr. Aaron L. Rutledge: Head, Psychotherapy Program

Test: Individual and Marriage Counseling Inventory

The Merrill-Palmer Institute is not in the testing business; its primary concern is with interpersonal behavior and family counseling. Dr. Rutledge, head of the Psychotherapy Program at the Institute, is the author of an inventory and record form which is published by the Institute. This inventory is not a test in any sense of the word; rather, it is a combination information blank and record system which is used widely by individual practitioners and by some smaller clinics. The Inventory has been revised and retitled the Psychotherapy Inventory.

University of Minnesota
Center for Interest Measurement Research
Minneapolis, Minnesota 55455

Dr. David Campbell: Director

The primary concern of the Center for Interest Measurement Research is the study of interests and their relationship to occupations. The Strong Vocational Interest Blank (SVIB) is the major test used in the study.

The Center is not involved with test sales, but rather with research and development of the SVIB.

National Assessment of Educational Progress
2222 Fuller Road
Room 201 A
North Campus
University of Michigan
Ann Arbor, Michigan 48103

Dr. Frank Womer: Staff Director

Type of Tests: Assessment

The goal of the National Assessment of Educational Progress (NAEP) is the collection, analysis, and distribution of comprehensive, dependable data that can be used as a basis for public understanding of educational progress. Test items in each of ten subject-matter areas have been developed by Educational Testing Service, Science Research Associates, the American Institutes for Research, and the Psychological Corporation.

The North Carolina Triangle Research Center and the National Opinion Research Center are also involved in the development of this program.

NAEP's testing of the nation's school children and young adults has begun, and its findings are being studied with interest by educators and others.

National Association of Independent Schools
4 Liberty Square
Boston, Massachusetts 02109

Wellington V. Grimes: Director of Academic Services

Test: Junior Scholastic Aptitude Test

This test was originally developed by the Bureau of Research of the Secondary Education Board (SEB). SEB merged with another organization in 1962 to form the National Association of Independent Schools (NAIS). The Educational Records Bureau (ERB) distributes and scores the test. The initiative to revise or study the test may come from either ERB or NAIS; the actual work would be done by ERB.

National Computer Systems
1015 South Sixth Street
Minneapolis, Minnesota 55415

Harlan Ward: President

Test scoring and the sale of test-scoring machines constitutes 70 percent of the business of the National Computer Systems (NCS); surveys account for the other 30 percent. The company has three divisions: the Test Scoring Division; the Forms Division, which produces the forms which are run through the machines; and the Equipment Division, which sells equipment produced by NCS.

The company prepares computerized interpretations of the MMPI, using the interpretations developed by Pierson and Swenson of the Mayo Clinic. Development of answer sheets in connection with new tests is an important concern of the company.

C. H. Nevins Printing Company
311 Bryn Mawr Island
Bayshore Gardens
Bradenton, Florida 33505

Mr. Wilson Barker: Manager

Test: Group Diagnostic Reading Aptitude and Achievement Tests

C. H. Nevins is a printing company which publishes a test authored in 1939 by Dr. Marion Monroe, who was a specialist at the Reading Institute of the Pittsburgh Public Schools, and Eva Edith Sherman. The test was evaluated in Pittsburgh and California in 1939. Dr. Monroe then asked C. H. Nevins to publish and distribute it.

The test is used in all states of the United States and in New Zealand, Japan, and several provinces of Canada. At the time of our correspondence, the printing company intended to continue publishing the test as long as there is any demand for it.

Newsweek Educational Division
444 Madison Avenue
New York, New York 10022

Richard N. Burch: Manager, Circulation Department

Tests: Newsweek Current News Test, Newsweek NewsQuiz

The Newsweek Educational Division publishes the monthly NewsQuiz and semester-review Current News Test as part of the Newsweek Educational Program. The tests are prepared on a free-lance basis by a former high school social studies instructor; they are edited by Mr. Burch and other members of the Newsweek staff. Along with other teaching aids, the tests are distributed at no cost to instructors enrolled in the Newsweek Educational Program; individual copies of the test are provided for each student subscriber to the program. The tests serve as a review or grading tool for the instructor.

OAIS Testing Program
Box 388
Ann Arbor, Michigan 48107

Dr. Benno G. Fricke: Chief, Evaluation Examinations Division, University of Michigan

Test: Opinion, Attitude, and Interest Survey (OAIS), Verbal-Math Aptitude Test

The OAIS Testing Program was set up by Dr. Benno Fricke to publish and handle sales and information on his OAIS Survey. About seventeen years ago, Dr. Fricke began a research project with the goal of creating a single test that would give multiple measures. The result of his work is the OAIS test and testing program used for screening candidates for college admission, scholarships, etc.

A new test offered in 1968 by OAIS was developed primarily to meet a need at the University of Michigan for a brief ability test to obtain better descriptions of the quality and characteristics of various groups of incoming students.

The OAIS test is scored exclusively by Measurement Research Center in Iowa.

Personnel Institute, Inc.
1832 Franklin Blvd.
Santa Monica, California 90406

Morris Pickus: President

The Personnel Institute is in the management consulting field. The company's president has gradually developed a program of personnel selection which includes tests developed by psychologists who served as consultants to his organization. At the time of our interview, the company was not publishing a test nor was it developing, revising, or offering psychological tests for sale.

Personnel Press
20 Nassau Street
Princeton, New Jersey 08540

Dr. B. E. Bergesen, Jr.: President

Tests: Kuhlmann-Anderson Intelligence Test (seventh edition), Clymer-Barrett Prereading Battery, Wisconsin Contemporary Test of Elementary Mathematics, Torrance Tests of Creative Thinking

Personnel Press is affiliated with Ginn and Company, which purchased Personnel in 1962. Ginn has recently been purchased by Xerox Corporation. During the last five years, Personnel Press has developed and released several new tests which are distributed through the national sales organization of Ginn.

New tests, especially textbook-related tests, were being developed at the time of our interview.

Personnel Press offers scoring services; the actual scoring is done by either the Educational Test Bureau in New York or Kent State University in Ohio.

Personnel Research Associates, Inc.
814 Gibraltar Life Building
P. O. Box 2994
Dallas, Texas 75221

Mr. J. H. Norman: President

Types of Tests: Academic alertness, performance alertness, reading adequacy, survey of clerical skills, typing, shorthand, survey of personal attitude, and occupational interest survey

Personnel Research Associates publishes the Individual Placement Series, a group of eight tests designed to assist business and personnel executives and industrial psychologists in their efforts to upgrade the professional level of their testing programs. Testing services are offered to companies desiring assistance in establishing or evaluating their testing programs. The major service offered is establishment of test standards, validation, and other statistical evaluation.

Scoring and interpretation may be done by the test administrator; instructions are presented in the Series manual.

Personnel Research Institute
Case Western Reserve University
11105 Euclid Avenue
Cleveland, Ohio 44106

Dr. Jay Otis: Director

Types of Tests: Alphabetizing, arithmetic reasoning, filing, name comparison, number comparison, spelling, tabulation, classification, shorthand skills, factory series

Personnel Research Institute, a division of the Psychology Department at Case Western Reserve University, is primarily concerned with training graduate students in research methods in personnel psychology. Publication of tests for sale is strictly a sideline.

This organization employs three well-qualified test-development persons in supervisory positions. Test consulting and custom development work are carried out on a limited scale under the guidance of the director or assistant director.

Professional Examination Service
American Public Health Association
1740 Broadway
New York, New York 10019

Mrs. Ruth S. Shaper: Associate Director

Types of Tests: Laboratory science, medicine, pharmacy, physical therapy, psychology, sanitation, veterinary medicine, nursing home administration

The Professional Examination Service (PES) has developed testing procedures for evaluating professionals in twenty-five professional fields. For a single fee, state agencies may make unlimited use of over seven hundred examinations. Consultation and scoring services are included.

New materials are produced annually. PES assists the states and the Medicare program in carrying out licensing programs and in establishing the qualifications and standards of practitioners in science fields. PES is working with appropriate federal agencies to develop nationwide examination programs.

The Psychological Corporation
304 East 45th Street
New York, New York 10017

Dr. George K. Bennett: President
Alexander G. Wesman: Vice President and Treasurer
Wimburn L. Wallace: Vice President

Types of Tests: Ability, aptitude, intelligence, personality, language; testing programs for medical college, veterinary medicine, dental hygiene. Best-known tests: Wechsler Adult Intelligence Scale, Differential Aptitude Test Series, MMPI

Psychological Corporation is composed of the Test Division, which develops and sells tests and related services; the Professional Examinations Division, which contracts examination services to schools, licensing boards, etc.; and the Industrial Services Division, which uses psychological assessment programs in various industries. This company probably sells more products and services to industry, both in dollar volume and in percentage of total sales, than any of the other large publishers. Harcourt Brace Jovanovich has purchased Psychological Corporation. Dr. Roger Lennon, vice president of Harcourt Brace, is the new president of the Psychological Corporation.

The company has been experimenting for a number of years with various techniques and equipment for mechanical scoring, standardized group-test administration, and related problems.

Psychological Services, Inc.
4311 Wilshire Blvd.
Los Angeles, California 90057

Dr. Floyd Ruch and Mr. William Ruch: Owners and Managers

Tests: Employee Aptitude Survey, Leadership Evaluation and Development Scale, Crissey Dexterity Test, Harris Inspection Test

Psychological Services develops and publishes tests primarily used by businesses for personnel selection, classification, and promotion. The company also makes validity studies on a contract or consulting basis. It sets up employee-selection programs which can be administered by the client; the company also evaluates existing programs.

Dr. Ruch and Mr. Ruch, both APA members, are responsible for test development within the company. Sometimes they develop tests; at other times, they arrange with a test author to standardize and publish his test. The author is reimbursed by royalty arrangements. Many of the tests submitted for publication come from the author's dissertation.

A scoring service is offered, but there are almost no users of this service.

Psychological Test Specialists
Box 1441
Missoula, Montana 59801

Dr. Carol Ammons: Editor

Types of Tests: Intelligence, personality, memory for designs, picture vocabulary

Many of the tests made available through this company are intended for individual administration in a clinical or educational setting. The company sells its tests to schools, hospitals, and government agencies.

Psychological Test Specialists relies primarily on test development by personnel not connected with the organization. About four employees run the entire operation. Most of the tests offered by this company do not lend themselves to machine scoring; scoring services are not offered.

Psychometric Techniques Associates
444 Amberson Avenue
Pittsburgh, Pennsylvania 15232

Dr. John C. Flanagan: Director

Tests: Tapping Test: A Predictor of Typing and Other Tapping Operations, Clinical Observation Record

Psychometric Techniques Associates was set up by John Flanagan to publish and market the Flanagan Aptitude Classification Test and the Flanagan Industrial Tests. These tests are now published by Science Research Associates. Flanagan's company currently publishes the Tapping Test and the Clinical Observation Record for student nurses. Customers include businesses, schools, government, and hospitals.

Public Personnel Association
1313 East 60 Street
Chicago, Illinois 60637

Steve Byerly: former Senior Examiner, PPA

Types of Tests: Subject matter tests for many areas of civil service employment

The Public Personnel Association (PPA) is a membership organization which provides to member government agencies an extensive testing program geared to public-employment selection and promotion. Virtually every occupation is covered by one or more of the job-knowledge tests available from this organization.

Approximately fifty employees are concerned with PPA's test-development activity.

School and College Service
New York Times
Times Square
New York, New York 10036

Tests: New York Times *Current Affairs Test,* New York Times *Current Affairs Test for College*

Personnel of the *New York Times* School and College Service Department prepare these tests which are issued monthly. Distribution is restricted to schools subscribing to the publisher's School Service Program, which includes a daily copy of the *New York Times,* a monthly copy of the test, and other teaching aids.

Educational Division, Reader's Digest Services, Inc.
Pleasantville, New York 10570

Test: New Standard Vocabulary Test

The Educational Division first published this test in 1955; the test has been reprinted from the educational edition of the *Reader's Digest.* The purpose of the test is to provide a means for discovering the extent of vocabulary growth of pupils during a school year. An individual's class standing may be determined and may be compared with the group on which the test was standardized.

Roche Psychiatric Service Institute
Roche Laboratories
Division of Hoffman-LaRoche, Inc.
Nutley, New Jersey 07110

Marvin L. Miller: Director

The Roche Psychiatric Service Institute provides computer scoring and interpretation of the MMPI, using a computer program developed by Dr. Raymond D. Fowler, Jr., at the University of Alabama. The program is designed to simulate the decision making functions of the skilled MMPI interpreter. It is marketed to psychologists and physicians.

Dr. Saul Rosenzweig
8029 Washington Street
St. Louis, Missouri 63114

Dr. Saul Rosenzweig: Professor of Psychology

Test: Rosenzweig Picture-Frustration Study

Dr. Saul Rosenzweig, a professor of psychology at Washington University, is the author of a projective test designed to enable investigators to study typical reaction patterns in potentially frustrating situations. The test is used as a research tool for testing theories on frustration tolerance and for individual diagnostic assessment of frustration related behavior tendencies. The instrument is widely used internationally; there is much reference material on it.

Rosenzweig has never distributed his test to anyone who is not a qualified psychologist with either a Ph.D. or an Ed.D. degree; however, he has given it to students working under qualified people. The reason for this restriction is that Rosenzweig believes special skills are required for adequate use of his test and similar instruments.

Scholastic Testing Service
480 Meyer Road
Bensenville, Illinois 60106

Mr. Herbert Greig: Founder and President

Types of Tests: Academic achievement and ability, academic placement, reading and interest inventories

This company primarily sells its tests to schools; it has given considerable effort to developing the parochial school market. An extensive test-development program has been sponsored under the direction of Dr. Oliver N. Anderhalter in St. Louis, Missouri. A large part of this effort is directed toward modification of existing instruments, as this organization offers secure tests with new forms annually.

Machine and hand scoring services are available. Optional services include extensive breakdown of scores from various test batteries.

Science Research Associates
259 East Erie Street
Chicago, Illinois 60611

Dr. William Clemons: Head, Division of Testing and Guidance

Types of Tests: Ability, aptitudes and skills, achievement, interest, personality and attitude inventories. Best-known tests: Iowa Tests of Educational Development, Army General Classification Test, Kuder tests

Science Research Associates (SRA), recently purchased by IBM Corporation, is primarily involved in the development and publication of instructional materials. Between one-third and one-fourth of the company's total business is test sales.

SRA has 1,500 employees, of whom 100 are currently involved in test development and revision. The sales organization consists of 250 staff associates. All of the company's products are distributed by direct sales through this sales force.

The company offers very extensive scoring services in cooperation with the Measurement Research Center; it handles well over a million tests each year. Considerable information is provided with the test scores.

Science Service, Inc.
1719 N Street, N.W.
Washington, D.C. 20036

Mr. E. G. Sherburne, Jr.: Director

Test: Science Aptitude Examination

Since 1942, Science Service, Inc., has published annually the Science Aptitude Examination for use in the selection process in the Westinghouse Talent Search. Dr. Harold A. Edgerton, President of Performance Research, Inc., of Washington, D.C., is the person responsible for preparation of test material and use of test scores.

The test, basically an academic aptitude test which uses science materials, is designed for the very bright and academically superior high school senior. A new form of the test is produced each year; no test questions are used more than once. After the tests have been given, copies of the questions are released to give succeeding groups of contestants an idea of the type of material to expect.

Slosson Educational Publications
140 Pine Street
East Aurora, New York 14052

Mr. Richard Slosson, M.A.: President

Tests: Slosson Intelligence Test (SIT), Slosson Oral Reading Test (SORT), Slosson Drawing Coordination Test (SDCT)

Slosson Educational Publications, in addition to publishing educational and mental health materials, publishes three tests. Slosson's purpose in constructing the SIT was to set up an abbreviated form of the Stanford-Binet Intelligence Scale which could be readily and easily used by the clinical worker. The drawing coordination test, published in 1967, was designed to identify individuals with various forms of brain dysfunction or perceptual disorders where eye-hand coordination is involved.

Spastic Aid Council, Inc.
1850 Boyer Avenue
Seattle, Washington 98102

Dr. Kate Kogan: Research Project Director

Test: Children's Picture Information Test

The Spastic Aid Council publishes this test for children aged two to six who have motor handicaps. The test was devised for the relatively rapid assessment of young children who lack corporal and manipulative skills.

Stanford University Press
Stanford, California 94305

James W. Torrence, Jr.: Sales Manager

Test: Strong Vocational Interest Blank

The Stanford University Press publishes one test, the Strong Vocational Interest Blank. This test is distributed by Consulting Psychologists Press and the Psychological Corporation. Stanford University Press owns the copyrights on several tests which are distributed by Consulting Psychologists Press.

C. H. Stoelting Company
424 North Homan Avenue
Chicago, Illinois 60624

Mr. B. Wessell: Purchasing Manager

Types of Tests: Concept formation, intelligence, performance, dexterity

C. H. Stoelting Company is primarily in the laboratory instrumentation field; it manufactures and sells lie detection apparatus and graphic recording equipment for physiological and behavioral research.

The company does not develop or sponsor psychological tests. Its role in the testing industry is limited to arranging for printing and distribution of tests submitted by test authors.

Dr. Murray A. Strauss
University of Minnesota
Sociology Department
Minneapolis, Minnesota 55455

Dr. Murray Strauss: Professor of Sociology

Test: Rural Attitudes Profile

Dr. Murray Strauss developed this test in 1956 when he was in the rural sociology department at Washington State University. The test must be reproduced locally. Originally, the manual, norms, and scoring keys were free to users who would agree to make the results available to the author; at the present time, there are no such restrictions. Though the manual is now out of print, xeroxed copies may be obtained from libraries that have copies of the Washington Agricultural Experiments Station Bulletin ("A Technique for Measuring Values in Rural Life"), in which the manual was first published. At the time of our interview, Strauss had dropped further work on this test.

Testscor
2309 Snelling Avenue
Minneapolis, Minnesota 55404

Elmer J. Hankes: Owner

Testscor does some scoring of the Strong Vocational Interest Blanks and the MMPI. The company uses a machine developed by Elmer J. Hankes.

Hankes does not score for unidentified practitioners; he returns answer sheets and scores to psychologists and counselors unless requested by them to send this material to test takers. He does score for company personnel departments. Individuals who request scoring services are referred to professionals in the area.

Dr. H. C. Tien
S-215 Medical Center West
701 North Logan Street
Lansing, Michigan 48915

Dr. H. C. Tien: Psychiatrist

Test: Organic Integrity Test

Dr. Tien developed the Organic Integrity Test as a part of his research on brain disorders. The test is marketed by Psychodiagnostic Test Company, also in Lansing. At least 90 percent of the purchasers of this test are Ph.D.'s or M.D.'s.

Dr. Tien is continuing research on the relationship between the OIT and EEG's.

Dr. Edwin E. Wagner
Department of Psychology
University of Akron
Akron, Ohio 44304

Dr. Edwin E. Wagner: Professor of Psychology

Test: The Hand Test

Dr. Wagner, the author of a projective test, first marketed the test himself through the Mark James Company. When the test became established, he transferred publication rights to Western Psychological Services.

The Hand Test is believed to reveal significant perceptual or motor tendencies readily expressed in an individual's interaction with others and the environment.

J. Weston Walch, Publisher
919 Congress Street
Portland, Maine 04104

Mr. J. Weston Walch: Owner

Tests: Novelty Grammar Tests (second revision), Outside Reading Tests for Freshmen and Sophomores, Outside Reading Tests for Juniors and Seniors (third edition), Outside Reading Tests for Junior High Schools

J. Weston Walch is a publisher of educational materials: supplementary texts, workbooks, teacher manuals, and enrichment materials. He also publishes four tests. Test users are allowed to reproduce the tests without permission. Because of this, Walch is unconcerned with copyright violations; further, he does not expect repeat sales from the same customer.

Dr. Henry Weitz
Counseling Center
Duke University
309 Flowers
Durham, North Carolina 27706

Dr. Henry Weitz: Director, Co-Author

Test: Duke University Political Science Information Test (American government)

Robert H. Connery, Richard H. Leach, and Henry Weitz, professors at Duke University, are the authors of this political science test which is distributed by Mr. Leach. The test was developed as an instrument for evaluating some experimental teaching procedures at the university; it was standardized at seven institutions.

At one time, the test was available for free distribution to political science teachers who were authorized to reproduce copies as needed locally. It is no longer available for use as a test, although the authors might make some items available.

Western Psychological Services
Box 775
Beverly Hills, California 90213

Mr. Ira Manson: Assistant Director

Types of Tests: Spatial relations, projective, marriage inventories, interest inventories, and a variety of clinical schedules and interview aids

Dr. Morse P. Manson founded Western Psychological Services (WPS) in 1948 for the purpose of publishing and distributing his own psychological test materials. In the ensuing years, the company has become a distribution facility for tests and professional supplies, books, and a limited amount of apparatus. The bulk of test sales is directed toward psychologists working in schools and hospitals.

This company has not sponsored new test development; further, it assigns to the test author the entire responsibility for updating and revising tests. Prior to adding test items to its inventory, WPS seeks professional advice.

Winter Haven Lions Research Foundation
P. O. Box 1045
Winter Haven, Florida 33880

Mr. H. R. Summerville: President

Test: Perceptual Forms Test

The Foundation is not strictly in the test publishing business. However, this test resulted from the Foundation's search for a simple test that might be used to detect the child with reading problems; the test is predictive rather than diagnostic. Using geometrical forms developed by Dr. Arnold Gesell of Yale University, the test measures visual maturation of children under nine years old. Because the test uses universal symbols, it may be used internationally without any problems.

Over two thousand schools have requested Lions' testing and training materials. Profits derived from sale of the material can only be used for research, such as grants in aid for postgraduate studies. Research continues on this material.

Dr. Herman A. Witkin
Psychology Clinic
University of California
Berkeley, California 94720

Dr. Herman A. Witkin: Professor of Psychology

Test: Embedded Figures Test

Dr. Witkin is not in the testing business. The author of this test, he arranged for its publication by the Downstate Medical Center of New York as a service to the field. The rationale and format of the test were the product of research on cognitive styles carried out by Witkin when he was at the State University of New York School of Medicine.

Witkin has recently completed a manual which includes extensive information on validity and reliability as well as normative data. He is turning the test over to a commercial publisher.

E. F. Wonderlic and Associates, Inc.
P. O. Box 7
Northfield, Illinois

Mr. Charles F. Wonderlic: Vice President

Test: Wonderlic Personnel Test

In addition to operating twenty small loan companies in Florida, Wonderlic Associates publishes a test that has enjoyed extensive sales over the past several decades. In recent years, additional forms of the test have been added, and two books concerned with the review of the literature and with additional normative data have been published. The test is most widely purchased by personnel departments in various business organizations, in government and, less frequently, in educational institutions. Employment agencies also use the test as a screening and brief assessment device.

This organization does not retain personnel who are primarily concerned with test development, revision, or studies of validation.

Index